HIDDEN PATTERNS

HIDDEN PATTERNS

Studies in Psychoanalytic

Literary Criticism

EDITED AND WITH INTRODUCTION BY

Leonard *and* Eleanor Manheim

THE MACMILLAN COMPANY, NEW YORK

COLLIER-MACMILLAN LIMITED, LONDON

DEDICATED TO THE MEMORY OF

Merrill Moore, M.D. (1903-1957)

POET AND PSYCHIATRIST

Library of Congress Catalog Card Number: 66-24052

FIRST PRINTING

The Macmillan Company, New York
Collier-Macmillan Canada Ltd., Toronto, Ontario
Printed in the United States of America

"Hawthorne's Symbolism and Psychoanalysis" by Leon Edel, copyright © 1966 by Leon Edel, printed by permission of the author. "Ulysses: A Monologue" by C. G. Jung, from the forthcoming Vol. XV of The Collected Works of C. G. Jung, Bollingen Series XX, by permission of the Bollingen Foundation and Routledge and Kegan Paul, Ltd. Copyright © 1966 by Bollingen Foundation.

ACKNOWLEDGMENTS

The editors wish to make grateful acknowledgments to the following for permitting articles to be reprinted:

"The Use and Abuse of Psychoanalysis in the Study of Literature" by William J. Griffin, by permission of the author and of Literature and Psychology.

"The Language of the Pundits" by Alfred Kazin from Contemporaries, by permission of Little, Brown and Company, copyright © 1961 by Alfred Kazin.

"Literary Form and Psychic Tension" by Frederick J. Hoffman, by permission of the author, Kenyon Review, and Louisiana State University Press.

"The Oedipus Trilogy" by Mark Kanzer, from Psychoanalytic Quarterly, XIX, 1950, pp. 561–572, by permission of the author and Psychoanalytic Quarterly.

"The Theme of the Three Caskets" by Sigmund Freud, from Chapter XV, Vol. IV, *Collected Papers of Sigmund Freud*, Basic Books, Inc., Publishers, New York, 1959, James Strachey, translator. By permission of Basic Books, Inc., Sigmund Freud Copyrights, Ltd., and The Hogarth Press, Ltd., London.

"Thanatos: The Death Instinct in Dickens' Later Novels" by Leonard Manheim. Reprinted from *Psychoanalysis* and *The Psychoanalytic Review*, Vol. 47, No. 4, Winter 1960–61, through the courtesy of the editors of *The Psychoanalytic Review* and the publishers, the National Psychological Association for Psychoanalysis, Inc., New York.

"Saint and Sinner—Dostoevsky's *Idiot*" by Simon O. Lesser. Reprinted from *Modern Fiction Studies*, Vol. IV, by permission of the author and Purdue Research Foundation.

"Freud and the Poet's Eye" by Norman N. Holland, by permission of *Literature and Psychology*, the author, and McGraw-Hill, Inc.

"Thomas Mann and Psychoanalysis: The Turning Point" by Joyce Crick, by permission of *Literature and Psychology* and the author.

"Kafka's *A Country Doctor*—Microcosm of Symbolism" by Stanley Cooperman, first published in *The University Review*, Vol. XXIV, No. 1, Autumn 1957. By permission of *The University Review*, The University of Missouri, and the author.

"Psychiatrist and Saint in *The Cocktail Party*" by Richard B. Hovey, by permission of *Literature and Psychology* and the author.

"The Grotesque-Comic in the Snopes Trilogy" by Lewis Lawson, by permission of *Literature and Psychology* and the author.

"A Psychological Analysis of William Golding's *Lord of the Flies*" by Claire Rosenfield, by permission of *Literature and Psychology* and the author.

"In Gertrude's Closet: Incest-Patterns in Recent Literature" by William Wasserstrom, first published in *The Yale Review*, copyright Yale University Press, by permission of *The Yale Review* and the author.

Acknowledgment is also made to the following for permission to quote from copyrighted material:

To Harcourt, Brace & World, Inc., for permission to quote from *The Cocktail Party* by T. S. Eliot in Richard B. Hovey's essay. To Putnam's and Coward-McCann for permission to quote from *Lord of the Flies* by William Golding in Claire Rosenfield's essay. To Basic Books, Inc., and The Hogarth Press, Ltd., for permission to quote from *Collected Papers of Sigmund Freud*, edited by Ernest Jones, in Norman N. Holland's essay.

Contents

But often, in the world's most crowded streets,
But often, in the din of strife,
There rises an unspeakable desire
After the knowledge of our buried life;
A thirst to spend our fire and restless force
In tracking out our true, original course;
A longing to inquire
Into the mystery of this heart which beats
So wild, so deep in us—to know
Whence our lives come and where they go.
And many a man in his own breast then delves,
But deep enough, alas! none ever mines.
And we have been on many thousand lines,
And we have shown, on each, spirit and power;
But hardly have we, for one little hour,
Been on our own line, have we been ourselves—
Hardly had skill to utter one of all
The nameless feelings that course through our breast,
But they course on for ever unexpress'd.
And long we try in vain to speak and act
Our hidden self, and what we say and do
Is eloquent, is well—but 'tis not true!
    —Matthew Arnold, from "The Buried Life" (1852)

INTRODUCTION

In *The Nation* for April 22, 1961, Norman Holland, one of the contributors to this present collection of essays, wrote, in an article entitled "The Next New Criticism":

Some day, when the intellectual history of this century is written (by what amoebas or opossums?), one of the great puzzles will be, Why did two disciplines so closely related in methods and interests as New Criticism and psychoanalysis stand so long apart? A few critics, among them Edmund Wilson, William Empson, and Kenneth Burke brought psychoanalysis proper into their criticism early and well. There are more now, Leon Edel, Leslie Fiedler, Lionel Trilling, Gordon Smith, Simon Lesser, Louis and Selma Fraiberg, and others writing for the important, but still little, little magazine *Literature and Psychology*. Nevertheless, most New Critics have ignored psychoanalytic criticism, so that New Criticism and psychoanalytic criticism rest uneasily like two momentarily divided but potentially dangerous chunks of plutonium.

The editors of that "little, little magazine" are also the editors of the present collection, and their hope is that the essays here presented will bring the type of criticism which that journal represents to a larger and less specialized audience than it now reaches. The journal was founded in order to be a "clearinghouse for materials germane to the approach to literature through psychology, particularly depth psychology." (For convenience—if not with strict accuracy—"depth psychology" will hereafter be referred to as "psychoanalysis.") On the one hand, literary criticism and analysis written from such a viewpoint is much older than psychoanalysis considered as a formal discipline. Henry James wrote such criticism, at times at least; so did Matthew Arnold (also at times); Coleridge wrote it almost all the time; it might well be argued that Aristotle wrote it, and Plato, at least in the *Ion*, certainly did. On the other hand, responsible literary criticism which is informed by the specific data of psychoanalysis is a recent discipline; younger, perhaps, than many people think. Certainly it is younger than the use of such data by twentieth-century novelists, poets, and playwrights—and there is little doubt that their use of the data has not always been productive of the best in art. Certainly it is younger than the use of literary materials by psychoanalysts, medical and psychological, for purposes which we can best call "clinical"—and here too the results have not always been fortunate, as Mr. Griffin's opening essay amply demonstrates. As a result, and despite the pioneer efforts of critics like Maud Bodkin and, perhaps most important of all, Thomas Mann, the academic fraternity of scholar-critics has been slow to accept studies like ours as valid contributions; young and less influential scholars were understandably timid in venturing into a field that was generally considered suspect.

That aura of suspicion has been disappearing, especially within the past dozen years or so, the period of the existence of our "little, little magazine." In 1962, for example, Wilbur Scott edited a collection devoted to *Five Approaches to Literary Criticism,* and of those five approaches one was psychological and another "archetypal." Walter Sutton, in his *Modern American Criticism* (1963), devotes one of his nine chapters to "Early Psychological Criticism" and another to "Psychological and Myth Criticism." And the most telling straw in the wind is the publication in 1966 by the Modern Language Association of a monograph entitled *Relations of Literary Study: Essays on Interdisciplinary Contributions,* in which the chapter on psychoanalytic criticism, specifically written for the graduate student and the younger professor, is the work of Frederick C. Crews, who demonstrated in *The Pooh Perplex* that he knew a great deal about the abuse of psychoanalysis in criticism and who has now demonstrated equally well that he knows even more about its legitimate use. We cannot mention here more than a few of the special works in the field which have been successfully published during these years: works like William Phillips' collection of essays, *Art and Psychoanalysis* (1957, recently reprinted in paperback), Simon O. Lesser's *Fiction and the Unconscious* (1957, also now in paperback), and Louis Fraiberg's *Psychoanalysis and American Literary Criticism* (1960). We should like to think that some part of this revolution has been accomplished by those who, like our contributors, demonstrate by precept and example what we "mean by good psychoanalytical criticism." [1]

The criteria which have been used in the selection of papers for our journal and for this collection, although they may be subtle and difficult to apply, are comparatively easy to state. We have systematically rejected all examples of the "here-a-phallic-symbol-there-a-phallic-symbol" school of criticism, believing that lists of undigested symbol patterns are both bad criticism and bad psychoanalysis. We have insisted that contributors exhibit basic familiarity with psychoanalytic theory, but that they use that knowledge with a deftness and subtlety in applying it to the study of literature that will arouse confidence, not antagonism. We have found no place for the critic who thinks he is pronouncing new and great findings when he has merely discovered that the grass is green. On the other hand, we have found acceptable even speculative investigations when they tended to cast light into some hidden corners of a literary work and which did so without using a farfetched theory when a simple one would apply. If there is any single principle that can be said to have guided us, it is expressed in the words of Arthur Symons in his introduction to Coleridge's *Biographia Literaria:*

The aim of criticism is to distinguish what is essential in the work of the writer. It is the delight of the critic to praise; but praise is scarcely part of his duty. . . . *What we ask of him is that he should find out for us more than we can find out for ourselves.* [Our italics.]

None of the above statements—and none of those which follow—constitutes any sort of creed or program to which adherence is required on the part of contributors. However, on the basis of observation of papers submitted, published, and discussed, formally and informally, in public and in private, we believe that there are a few general principles which may be profitably set forth here.

I

The literary critic who uses psychoanalysis is primarily and at all times a student of literature as an art form, only secondarily an investigator in the craft or science of psychology in any of its branches. It is entirely understandable that the practicing or theorizing psychologist should view a piece of literature as a document for the study of human behavior, should consider literature as "an original record of the results of an experiment or investigation . . . made during or immediately following the event." [2] Nietzsche declared that man is *das kranke Tier.* There is no reason, then, why those whose task it is to examine the nature, causes, and progress of his *Krankheit* (as a man rather than as a mere animal) should not make use of any evidence, including the evidence offered by that special form of human behavior which man calls *art.* But, as Thomas Mann pointed out in 1936, the artist (and the critic) must not be content with the mere identification or classification or even cure of man as "ailing animal"; their interest goes far beyond the direct scientific concern of the psychologist and psychoanalyst:

There is no deeper knowledge [of the human psyche] without the experience of disease . . . all heightened healthiness must be achieved by the route of illness. This attitude . . . is bound up with the nature of the intellectual man in general, of the creative artist in particular, yes, with the nature of humanity and the

human being, of which last of course the creative artist is an
extreme expression. "L'humanité," says Victor Hugo, "s'affirme
par l'infirmité." . . . Man has been called *"das kranke Tier"*
because of the burden of strain and explicit difficulties laid upon
him by his position between nature and spirit, between angel
and brute. What wonder, then, that by the approach through
abnormality we have succeeded in penetrating more deeply into
the darkness of human nature . . . ? [3]

II

There is a necessary corollary to this principle: in dealing
with a work of art the critic must understand that he is not
dealing with a pathological abnormality called a neurosis,
but with an even more astounding anomaly of human behavior: the *avoidance* of neurosis through another kind of
"abnormality" which is not pathological—artistic creation.
The distinction was stated succinctly both by an eminent
psychoanalyst and by a well-known popular novelist and
biographer. The British psychoanalyst Edward Glover put
it this way:

There is . . . one essential difference between the pure work of
art and the neurosis. The neurosis is the result of a *regression*
of libido leading to a breakdown of a repression system which is
already faulty, hence the emergence of compromise between the
repressed and repressing forces. It is also an unconscious instrument of self-punishment. Whatever its original unconscious aim,
the work of art represents a *forward* urge of the libido seeking
to maintain its hold on the world of objects. Its instinctual compromises are not the result of a pathological breakdown of the
repression system. It is in the truest sense a sublimation, and
consequently obviates the need for self-punishment. [4]

André Maurois expressed what is roughly the same idea in
a conversation in one of his novels:

"Then according to you, Doctor, all novelists, men and
women, are neurotic?"
"More exactly, they all would be neurotic if they weren't

novelists. The neurosis makes the novelist, and the art cures the neurosis."

"Why that's ridiculous! . . . There were great artists who were sane: Tolstoi, Victor Hugo, Dickens—"

"Couldn't be worse-chosen examples! . . . Tolstoi, Victor Hugo and Dickens all three certainly owed part of their genius to pronounced neurosis; some day I'll show you—" [5]

If this distinction is clearly in the forefront of our thinking, there will be no need for the suggestion of some of the earlier apologists (notably, of course, Lionel Trilling in "Art and Neurosis" [6]) that, since modern men are all more or less neurotic, the artist is *no more* neurotic than his fellow-men. For the truth would seem to be that, *as* artist, he is essentially *less* neurotic. Not that it is always possible, or ever easy, to distinguish between the products of what we call, for want of a better name, the "art impulse" from the patterns and symptoms which might be called specifically neurotic. We find the two always present in varying quantities, but we also find that the non-neurotic art impulse predominates in what the critic (at his best an artist in his own right) will intuitively recognize as an author's major literary achievements.

III

Is there any way to account for the phenomenon that instinctual drives produce conflict and the retreat called neurosis in one man, and a forward urge, which creates a work of art, in another? The older psychoanalysis could not even begin to answer this question, and Freud could only protest that in the face of the problem of the artist psychoanalysis must "lay down its arms." [7] More recently, theoretical analysts have formulated the principles of ego psychology, firmly rooted in classic Freudian principles but developing some of its later concepts along revolutionary lines. These theories go a long way toward increasing the ability of psychoanalysis "to cope with certain social aspects of human life on terms which approach more closely than ever before the assumptions of non-psychoanalytic thinkers —philosophers, critics, artists." [8] So far these formulations have been highly theoretical; they are probably less subject to experimental validation than even the older of psychoanalytic theory. But they bid fair to be so important in bringing about a *rapprochement* between literary and psychoanalytic theory that they should be made available, even in most rudimentary form, to readers who are interested in the general theory of literature and artistic creativity.

The reader may remember the classic metaphoric representation of the psyche, first offered by Freud in *The Ego and the Id* (1923). It is roughly like an egg standing on its small end. The upper surface represents the region of contact with the outer world, and the upper part of the area of the psyche is uncolored, representing the area of consciousness. Below that there is a lightly shaded area which may be taken to represent the preconscious, and below that the large dark area (the underside of the iceberg in another metaphor) representing the unconscious. In 1923, in refining his older theory of the unconscious, Freud placed the ego in the area of the consciousness, extending downward *toward* (but no one knows how far *into*) the unconscious, which is the habitat of the id. The superego is like a wedge driven along the side of the egg, through the area of consciousness and deep into the unconscious.[9]

The id is, of course, the primitive, original portion of the psyche, from which the other parts develop. It is the source of what has been called "instinctual energy." It has no contact with external reality; its workings can be perceived, or rather postulated, only by indirect means. It is an "amoral idealist," for it recognizes no moral sanctions and knows nothing of the interference by reality, not even the interference of time relationships, with the gratification of its drives. The ego, in contact with external reality, mediates between it and the id; in this sense it is an "amoral realist." Its compromises are achieved not through its recognition of moral sanctions but by its awareness of what is externally, socially, acceptable. The "moral" sanctions are inherent in the superego, which strives to impose them on the ego (consciously) and on the id (unconsciously). It is therefore a "moral idealist." The result is a constant three-way struggle.[10]

Let us, for the moment, alter the analogy from biology to geopolitics. Now the ego is a tiny country with a long sea-coast giving it access to the outer world. The id is a land-locked power which must use the ego as its only way of access to the sea, which must endure the political compromises imposed by the ego—in form at least—but which is powerful enough to dictate the terms of these compromises, to dominate in spite of them, and even at times to break them, invade the ego, and threaten its very existence (its "sanity"). But the trials of ego-land do not end here. Not only must it struggle to impose its compromises on the id; not only must it run the dangers of dealing with the sea ("reality," the outer world); it must also contend with another great power which has a small foothold on the sea of reality but which is, like the id, really a great power of the hinterland. The superego finds itself in constant battle with the id, a battle which is, for strategic reasons, waged over the territory of the ego!

What wonder, then, that the older psychoanalysis thought of the ego as nothing more than a puppet, a battleground, a buffer state, without any real autonomy even in its own territory, and constantly engaged in efforts to achieve what could never be more than temporary compromises, constantly threatened and constantly renewed. Hence early psychoanalysts in their study of literature were intent on revealing the hidden nature of these compromises, "seeing through" the work of art, as Philip Rieff puts it, explaining it "by something other than—even contradicting—itself," viewing it as "a museum piece of the unconscious, an occasion to contemplate the unconscious frozen into one of its possible gestures." [11]

We wonder, however, whether the geopolitical metaphor

might not be pushed a bit further. Is it not true that history tells us of at least one tiny country with "access to the sea" which did succeed in contributing certain "spiritual" traditions to the world in spite of the threats of great world powers and the hazards of the sea? Can we not see in the gift of the Judeo-Christian tradition to the world by tiny Judea a parallel to what we call "autonomy of the ego"? There was no historical reason to suspect the possibility of such a gift; yet it was given. There was no reason to believe that an autonomous ego could be, under special circumstances, said to exist; yet it has been postulated, and it seems that the postulation is a valid way of understanding what could not otherwise be adequately explained.

But let us return from biological and geopolitical metaphors to a restatement of the conclusions of ego psychology expressed in somewhat more technical terms. For the oversimplifications just used ignore the fact that the contending drives in the power struggle have never been simple; there is always the ubiquitous phenomenon of bipolarity (ambivalence) to be taken into account.[12] The motive power in both id and superego (or in a combination, what the physicist might call a "resultant" of the two forces) is both libidinal (erotic) *and* aggressive—both *pro*gressive (leading toward maturity, later life, and ultimately, of course, death) and *re*gressive (returning to childhood, immaturity, and ultimately, of course, death in the guise of "prelife")—both Eros and Thanatos. It has been a large enough assignment for the psychoanalytic critic to account for the interplay of these complex motive-forces to give him a far more elaborate function than is suggested by Mr. Rieff. But now, to quote Mr. Fraiberg again and, if you will permit us, a bit more fully:

Recent ego psychology sees creativity as a natural expression of the psyche with its basic dual and reciprocating motive forces, but it has now reached a stage of sophistication in the formulation of theory which is no longer satisfied with merely accounting for the polar interaction of libidinal and aggressive drives.

. . . The newer view begins by accepting the work on its own terms as an artistic entity and not merely as the sum of its tendencies.[13]

It is now possible to find in psychoanalytic theory a justification for the judgment of the critic that there is such a thing as an "art impulse." It is possible to see the creative ego as one which is not limited to juggling with the motive forces of the unconscious and presenting them in socially acceptable, palatable forms; which does not deal solely with sublimations which are, after all, merely attenuated forms of crude drives. Nor, on the other hand, need we go along with those who insist that the artist is at his best only when he is completely under the domination of the unconscious—an impossibility, of course, but a theory which has produced some rather horrendous results, from the era of surrealism to the present day. Instead we see the artist as one who is endowed with the ability to permit material from the unconscious to enter into consciousness and to use it for the production of universal, humanly attractive products called works of art, without being dominated or destroyed by that material; one who can play with the forces that lead to neurosis and worse and tame them, without loss to himself and for the benefit of mankind. The word "play" is used advisedly here, for Norman Holland has cogently argued the case for viewing literature as a species of "play" in the psychoanalytic sense of play as a "means of hallucinating ego mastery."

Play (and literature) can be understood in this sense as first, letting a disturbing influence happen to us, then, second, mastering that disturbance. The classic example is the "doctor game." Little Beowulf is frightened by his visit to the doctor. His parents, having read their Spock, buy him a toy doctor's kit, and (typically) within a few days the little lad is enthusiastically acting out the part of the doctor. The "doctor game" satisfies him because he re-creates the disturbing influence but, instead of being overwhelmed by it, masters it by identifying with the aggressor. The "doctor game," for many children in our culture, is a satisfying form of play—it is "good" in the sense I am defining.

Saying a literary work is "good," then, from the psychoanalytic point of view, predicts the work will pass the test of time; that it "can please many and please long"; that it is a widely satisfying form of play; or, more formally, that it has the power to disturb many readers over a long period of time and, built in, as it were, a defensive maneuver that will enable its readers to master the poem's disturbance.[14]

This, then, suggests the process by which the theories of ego psychology may be translated into a comprehensive theory of literature. The reader, like the child, "plays" with a threat from without and, with the aid of the artist, whose ego is vested with the peculiar power to do so, "plays" with the threat from within. But the ego mastery that the reader merely "hallucinates" has been *actually achieved* by the artist. And the result of such a formulation is to restore to the artist that special eminence which, the traditional critic has feared, the psychoanalyst sought to take from him.

IV

Not all of the essays in the present collection make use of ego psychology directly, although most of them imply at least intuitive awareness of its tenets. Each essay has something to say about psychoanalytic theory even when its main concern is with literature in general or with individual authors or individual works. The essays which may be said to stress theory are the first three, but the theory is rather that of psychoanalytic criticism than of psychoanalysis itself. Mr. Griffin's 1951 paper constitutes, as much as anything can, a sort of manifesto on good and bad psychoanalytic criticism; it has always been a system of guidelines for our journal and of the group which sponsors it. Mr. Kazin's 1961 essay gives evidence of the passing of ten years; it also seeks to evaluate the psychoanalyst as critic, having unreserved praise for none but Freud, an extravagant position perhaps, but one with which we shall not quarrel here. Mr. Hoffman's 1956 study marks a halfway point; it was the first of several to deal with the function of form in resolving intrapsychic tension. (At least one other such study merits more than passing notice here; it is Simon Lesser's 1957 *Fiction and the Unconscious,* particularly chapter V, "The Functions of Form.")

From this point on the essays deal with books and authors. Most of these books and authors represent the nineteenth and twentieth centuries; yet it would have been injudicious for a symposium on psychoanalytic criticism to ignore the two giants of literature, Sophocles and Shakespeare, who were also, by the same token, the greatest precursors of psychoanalytic theory. It is an interesting, albeit fortuitous, result of this grouping that these essays should be the work of psychoanalysts-as-critics. Dr. Kanzer is outstanding among contemporary American psychoanalysts who write about literature. Of his several studies of the Oedipus plays, the one here presented is least technical and is unusual in offering a broad view of the Sophoclean trilogy as a whole. Dr. Kanzer has also written on Shakespeare, but here we could do no better than to return to Freud for a study which analyzes *The Merchant of Venice,* to be sure, but which casts a great deal of light on *King Lear.* The "Three Caskets" essay is Freud at his best, "a little gem," one commentator has said.

The papers which follow deal with three nineteenth-century American, British, and Russian authors (Hawthorne, Dickens, and Dostoevsky) whose works seem to be singularly appropriate for this kind of analysis if the evidence of psychoanalytic indexes means anything. The critics represented are Leon Edel, who here departs from his customary concern with Henry James; one of the editors; and Mr. Lesser.

The bridge to the twentieth century is embodied in Norman Holland's ingenious application of the methods of pschoanalytic criticism to a writer whose literary fame is attested by his having been awarded the Goethe Prize in literature, to wit, Sigmund Freud. Six major twentieth-century authors are then treated, mainly through analysis of a single work rather than the entire body of the author's productions—the only feasible approach in a collection of this size. Thus Stanley Cooperman deals with Kafka's "A Country Doctor"; Joyce Crick with those works of Thomas Mann which reflect his changing attitude toward psychoanalysis; Richard Hovey with T. S. Eliot's *The Cocktail Party* (it is regrettable that space limitations made it impossible for us to add Maud Bodkin's comparative analysis of Eliot's *The Family Reunion* and the *Eumenides* of Aeschylus); C. G. Jung approaches Joyce's *Ulysses* with remarkable naiveté; Claire Rosenfield analyzes Golding's *Lord of the Flies;* and Lewis Lawson brings some unusual insights to the Snopes trilogy of William Faulkner. The collection concludes with William Wasserstrom's investigation of the theme of sexual "initiation," an omnibus essay which deals with a number of figures in recent American, British, and continental literature. Further information and comment may be found in the notes at the beginning of each essay.

If the function of all good criticism is to send the reader back to the work itself, then we think that the selections made (out of a wealth of material, much of which we have, for various reasons, regretfully passed by) constitute very good criticism by any standard. We wish that we were still deep enough in the nineteenth century to be comfortable in addressing you by your proper title—gentle reader. Perhaps, though, you will not be so gentle when you have read these studies. You will be aroused, possibly fighting mad, possibly bemused with unsuspected possibilities and frightening depths. But we do not think you will be bored or indifferent. And in that spirit we present our book to you.

LEONARD F. MANHEIM
ELEANOR B. MANHEIM

NOTES

1. The conclusion of William J. Griffin's essay in the present collection (p. 32) ; originally in *Literature and Psychology* (hereafter referred to as *L & P*), I, 5 (November 1951), 20.

2. This is the psychologists' definition of the word "protocol"; see English and English, *Dictionary of Psychological and Psychoanalytic Terms* (New York, 1958).

3. "Freud and the Future" (Lowe-Porter translation) in *Essays of Three Decades* (New York, 1947), p. 414. For an account of the development of Mann's attitude toward psychoanalysis see Joyce Crick, "Thomas Mann and Psychoanalysis: The Turning Point," pp. 171–190 in the present collection; originally in *L & P*, X, 2 (Spring 1960), 45–55.

4. Edward Glover, *Freud or Jung* (New York, 1950), p. 185.

5. André Maurois, *Women Without Love,* trans. Joan Charles (New York, 1945), p. 141.

6. In *The Liberal Imagination* (New York, 1953, paperback), pp. 159–178.

7. "Dostoevsky and Parricide" (1928) in *Collected Papers,* trans. and ed. Joan Riviere, 5 vols. (London, 1924–1950), V, 222. See also Norman N. Holland, "Freud and the Poet's Eye," in this collection, p. 168 n; originally in *L & P*, XI, 2 (Spring 1961), 36 n.

8. Louis Fraiberg, "New Views of Art and the Creative Process in Psychoanalytic Ego Psychology" (hereafter cited as "New Views"), *L & P*, XI, 2 (Spring 1961), 46. For much of what we have to say on ego psychology and creativity we are indebted to Mr. Fraiberg, both in this essay and in the opening chapters of his *Psychoanalysis and American Literary Criticism* (Detroit, 1960).

9. In *Standard Edition* of the *Works of Freud,* trans. James Strachey, Anna Freud, Alix Strachey, and Alan Tyson, 24 vol. (London, 1953–   ), XIX (1961), 3–66. Freud's diagram in *The Ego and the Id* is substantially different from the one given here. Freud offered still other variants of the diagram in *The New Introductory Lectures, The Interpretation of Dreams,* and even as far back as a letter to Fliess in 1896. The present version is from an adapta-

tion in Healy, Bronner, and Bowers, *The Structure and Meaning of Psychoanalysis* (New York, 1930), p. 56.

We are not directly concerned with the preconscious here, but because of the increasing importance of this postulation for the understanding of creativity, especially in the work of Dr. Lawrence S. Kubie, we may note here Mr. Fraiberg's brief description:

> Preconscious thoughts are those which are repressed; i.e., kept unconscious, not out of psychic necessity but simply for mental convenience. There is no particular objection to their becoming conscious; there is just not enough room on the stage of conscious-ness for all of them at once. Consequently, they remain uncon-scious until attention is directed to them, thus providing them with the energy necessary for emergence. "New Views," pp. 47–48).

10. Freud's analogy of the ego, "like a man on horseback, who has to hold in check the superior strength of the horse" (*The Ego and the Id,* p. 24), has an interesting parallel in the description of the charioteer with one well-behaved and one unruly horse in Plato's *Phaedrus.* The parallel was developed by James Robert Wilson in a note in *L & P,* X, 1 (Winter 1960), 2.

11. *Freud: The Mind of the Moralist* (Garden City, N.Y., 1961), p. 134.

12. "Ambivalence [bipolarity] denotes contradictory emotional attitudes toward the same object arising alternately, or existing side by side without either one interfering neces-sarily with or inhibiting the expression of the other. . . . The most obvious example of ambivalence is found in the love-hate relationship." The term "ambivalence" was originated by the Swiss psychiatrist Eugen Bleuler (*The Structure and Meaning of Psychoanalysis,* pp. 20–21). Statements which deal with, or at least imply, ambivalence and bipolarity are to be found in almost every essay in the present collection.

13. Fraiberg, "New Views," pp. 45, 46. An amplification of this brief quotation may impel the reader to search out and read thoroughly Professor Fraiberg's illuminating presen-tation of this somewhat difficult but highly important subject:

> Creativity . . . may be regarded as a special form of sublima-tion in which natural endowment facilitates the development of the ego towards mastery of its psychic environment and towards

an increasing ability to devote itself to activities which are relatively independent of conflict. The part played by sexuality in
this process has long been an object of study; currently, increased
attention is being paid to the role of aggression. As basic forces
in the psyche, they must both be involved significantly in creativity. According to the newer conceptions, there are actually three
sources of psychic energy. Besides the sexual and aggressive instincts, there is . . . a stock of neutral energy helping to activate
the ego.

Not only is this available for higher psychic functions, but
exchanges and enhancements also are possible between it and the
other two. This neutral energy "may stem from and may be re-
transformed into either libido or aggression." A tremendous reservoir of energy is therefore available for creative thought, some
of it neutral and some of it tinged with sexual or aggressive characteristics. The artist, with his strong ego—i.e., one that can
neutralize large quantities of energy from instinctual sources—is
most fortunately equipped to bring maximum psychic resources
to bear upon his artistic work. He also has a great deal to "invest"
in the product, permitting it to attain a high degree of independence (secondary autonomy in ego functions), since he can tap
the instinctual reservoir for replacements at need. ("New Views,"
p. 49, citing Hartmann, Kris, and Loewenstein, "Comments on
the Formation of Psychic Structure.")

14. "Literary Value: A Psychoanalytic Approach," *L & P*, XIV,
     2 (Spring 1964), 43–55.

HIDDEN PATTERNS

The Use and Abuse of Psychoanalysis in the Study of Literature [1]

by WILLIAM J. GRIFFIN

William James Griffin, after completing his undergraduate studies at Park College in Missouri, earned advanced degrees in English literature at the University of Iowa. After teaching in Kansas and Minnesota and serving as an officer in the Navy during World War II, Mr. Griffin was for two years visiting professor of American literature at the University of Brazil, and in 1957 he held a similar professorship in Portugal. Since 1948 he has been a professor of English at George Peabody College for Teachers in Nashville, Tennessee, where he was, for many years, also editor of the *Tennessee Folklore Bulletin.*

The present essay was the first of the annual papers read at the Conference (later Discussion Group) on Literature and Psychology of the Modern Language Association and was published in *Literature and Psychology* (I, 5, 3–20). Along with Leon Edel's "Notes on the Use of Psychological Tools in Literary Scholarship," also published in the same journal (I, 4, 1–3), it has constituted a working basis for the later development of that group and as a standard for its journal.

THE alliance between literature and the study of human psychology is ancient and honorable. It is also inevitable, for the writer perforce makes a report on the nature of his own psyche, while at the same time he may, with varying degrees of accuracy, set down reports on manifestations of that of his fellowman. And what he writes has meaning in the mind of a reader.

It follows that the study of literature is centrally concerned with the understanding of psychology.[2] Surely, any new evidence about the nature of the psyche or any new insights into its modes of activity should be welcomed and put to use by students of literature.

Such new evidence and insights have been offered in our own day by Freud and his successors. Numerous scholars and critics have indeed welcomed and exploited them. Further, the impact of ideas traceable in part at least to psychoanalysis has been registered even by those who have been skeptical of the new science, or who have not been consciously interested in it.[3]

Certain areas of literary study, it is true, appear to have especially benefited from the suggestions of psychoanalysis. Aesthetic theory and the understanding of the creative act, for example, have been partially rescued from the realm of cloud and chaos. As Richard Chase has remarked, "Aside from Freudian psychology, we do not have in our current literary criticism any working idea of the imagination." [4] If Freudians have had more to say of the wound than of the marvelous bow, and if they have been more willing to explore the likenesses between dreams and the work of art than to take account of the differences, their contributions have yet been substantial. They have widely commanded respect, and as long as the discussions have remained on the level of general theory the issues raised have been debated with goodwill. A fair statement of the situation is made by Lionel Trilling, who, while he points out some of the shortcomings to which the Freudian view may seem predisposed, also emphasizes the immense advantages in the fact that "of all mental systems, the Freudian psychology is the one which makes poetry indigenous to the very constitution of the mind." [5]

Increased knowledge of the constitution of the mind has had the specific effect of opening up new explorations of the functions of imagery and symbols, and the significance of myths and folklore. I shall later have something to say about abuses of symbols, and there may be reason to suspect some investigators of confusing the mythic with the mystic, but the point to be made here is that impressive studies using the suggestions of psychoanalysis have been made under the most respectable auspices.

Again, as one might expect, modern psychology figures prominently in the discussions of modern literature. No consideration of Faulkner's *As I Lay Dying* would be complete without some attention to Freudian ideas; no analysis of O'Neill's *Lazarus Laughed* could afford to neglect those of Jung. In the study of such writers as Joyce, D. H. Lawrence, Kafka, and Thomas Mann, some use of a knowledge of psychoanalytic theory and practice is naturally expected and highly valued.[6]

It is evident that in a sense it is true that "to clamor for critical recognition of psychoanalysis . . . is to knock at an open door." [7] Yet it is equally true that the critic is regarded with suspicion when he attempts to apply psychoanalysis to the works of writers who knew not Freud. Particularly in the academic world, auspicious to studies of contemporary use of the new concepts in psychology, the application of those concepts to the pre-Freudian writer is usually regarded with a dropping eye. And the distrust appears to increase as the study becomes less general and more specific and detailed.

To identify the ideas an author consciously made use of, to judge the accuracy of his understanding of those ideas, and to gauge the literary effect of his employment of them are, however, traditional tasks of the critic. Much more exciting are the possibilities offered by the new psychology in the pursuit of things unattempted yet in criticism. Perhaps it is the adventure of such pursuit that has attracted so many, both literary men and professional psychologists, to undertake it.[8] I cannot claim to have had the opportunity to assess more than a sampling of the results, but even a limited acquaintance with the published accounts has suggested some reasons for the reservations with which they have often been received.

Some frequently heard explanations for dissatisfaction ought, I think, to be discounted. Least significant of all is the supposition that it is illogical to apply Freudian psychology to, let us say, the work of Shakespeare because Shakespeare predated Freud by three hundred years. The implication would be that Freud created men instead of studying them, or that Shakespeare was not a man as other men are, or that he was incapable of registering his own impressions of his fellowmen. An almost equally absurd notion is reflected in the suggestion that the psychological patterns in Shakespeare's writings are wholly explained by Timothy Bright but are not dealt with by Freud. These allegations cannot be taken seriously, surely, even by those who give voice to them.

A more reasonable objection is sometimes raised against the "jargon" of psychoanalysis in literary studies.[9] Annoyance is understandable when a reader finds that he has only been told in unfamiliar terms what he already knew. Exercises in verbalization, of course, will not command respect. The offense is compounded by the critic whose knowledge is little and whose desire for display is great.[10]

The barrier of a specialized vocabulary may, of course, be raised by the writer who has a genuine desire to make a contribution.[11] It is reasonable to expect a new science to develop terminology indispensable to the application of its concepts. Students of literature, fond of digging into the linguistic debris of alchemy and astronomy, seem unlikely to be put off by mere words if the referents have interest for them. If they protest the vocabulary of psychoanalytic critics, they probably have more crucial objections. At any rate, it seems to me there are more important reasons for the distrust we set out to explain.

An easy way to account for rejection of psychoanalytic criticism is to say it meets the irrational "resistance" of readers. It is comforting to think of those you do not convince as weak or narrow-minded people fond of their illusions. But the same comfort is available to all true believers, including advocates of the "science" of Velikovsky's *Worlds in Collision* and the theosophy of Mme. Blavatsky. It is instructive to note that Galileo and Darwin found resistance to their ideas, but if we are tempted to take rejection as a mark of merit, let us observe that men resist falsehood as well as truth. We may also note with profit that imperfections in the ideas of Galileo and Darwin merited a degree of resistance, and ask what progress in science would have accrued had they commanded uncritical acceptance.

It would, of course, be impossible to say how much of the coldness toward psychoanalytic approaches to literary study is founded on emotional unwillingness to accept the evidence modern psychology has accumulated on the nature of man, or specifically on an aversion to the frank discussion of sex. It has been more than sixty years, however, since the publication of Freud's *The Interpretation of Dreams,* and it is my impression that in that time there has developed a sufficiently large body of the sympathetic and (at least partially) informed to provide a gratifying audience to the critic who can apply his understanding of psychoanalysis with discrimination. I am convinced, at least, that in the academic world the significant reasons for disapproval are usually neither ignorance nor affective prejudice against the science itself.

Prejudice *has* been generated by widely publicized travesties that have passed for representatives of what the science could be used for. We have had, for example, a spate of biographies whose misdirected exploitation of ideas and methods associated with psychoanalysis should certainly inspire an attitude of extreme wariness. One thinks of Lewis Mumford's speculations on the night life of Mrs. Melville. Or one recalls the "parlor psychoanalysis" of the earlier Van Wyck Brooks, who combined it in *The Ordeal of Mark Twain* with just enough insight to assure its being taken

seriously and enough misunderstanding and misrepresenta-
tion to discredit it. Even the useful, relatively restrained and
wholly honest study of Poe by Joseph Wood Krutch has not
been entirely reassuring, for near the end of his book Krutch
announces, "We have, then, traced Poe's art to an abnormal
condition of the nerves. . . ." [12] In that sentence he epitomizes the fallacious thinking that has quite properly annoyed
the student of literature in many a psychological analysis of
writers.

The purpose of these remarks is not to introduce a discussion of the shortcomings of biographies written in the
light of psychoanalysis.[13] It is rather to emphasize the associations that have from the first encouraged misgivings about
the nature of that light. With the same end in view, attention should also be called to the effect produced by such a
prodigy as Ludwig Lewisohn's *Expression in America*.
Judged by some of its best advertised fruits, psychoanalysis
has appeared unpromising.

To call the roll of literary men who have misapplied psychoanalytic theory out of half-knowledge, or a desire to be
sensational, or an eagerness to make out a case, would not be
enough to explain the situation. Professional psychoanalysts
themselves have also frequently been undiscriminating when
they have made excursions into the field of literary study. I
do not here have in mind the errors into which they may fall
through some lack of purely literary training. Those may be
charitably passed over. I refer to the failure to make reasonable distinctions, to a lack of caution and a susceptibility to
what are vaguely spoken of as "excesses." [14] In these respects
the honors seem to be about even between literary men and
professional psychoanalysts.

Let us ask what one does or can do when he attempts to
apply psychoanalytic theories and methods to a piece of literature or to the whole body of an author's work. The
purposes and problems are obviously different from those of
a clinician consulted by a patient.

We may say that both critic and clinician engage themselves to unravel meanings that are knit up with unconscious motivations. But who or what does the critic analyze? [15] Certainly not the piece of literature itself, for ink and paper have no psyche to be explored.

It may be suggested that the characters presented in literature have a kind of life of their own. This is a type of pleasant illusion that authors like to foster and critics often applaud. Developed to pathological proportions, it leads to such monstrosities as Mrs. Clarke's *Girlhood of Shakespeare's Heroines.* Surely, a concern with non-rational psychology need not have the effect of encouraging hallucinations, yet the tenor of some psychoanalytic disquisitions suggests that more than one analyst may have in the works a volume on *The Infancy of Shakespeare's Heroes.* James Clark Moloney and Laurence Rockelein in "A New Interpretation of Hamlet" show that they have known the temptation. Having asserted that psychoanalytic experience proves the unconscious guilt-feelings with which Ernest Jones had invested Hamlet would in fact have spurred the Prince on to kill Claudius, they explain that actually Hamlet did not want to kill his uncle because Claudius was a "protective figure shielding Hamlet from growing up," and under no circumstances did he *"want* the responsibility of becoming an adult." They then remark that "His primary fear of killing Claudius . . . was also magnified by certain traumatic experiences which can be read into his antecedent biography from the foregoing insights." [16]

To read into the interpretation of a character the experiences, traumatic or otherwise, in an imagined antecedent biography is a beguiling possibility. Traditional critics have often been lured by it, but it is particularly seductive to those who apply psychoanalysis to character study. The reasons for its attraction are obvious. The uneasy suspicion that they allow themselves limitless liberty in supplying a context for characters beyond that provided by the author is, however, an important factor in the widespread reluctance to take their studies seriously.

The fact is that characters in a play, poem, or novel are of a different order of creation from those who may in the flesh consult the psychoanalyst. Presumably, we ought to distinguish bushes from bears.[17]

Frederic Wertham has observed that "practically every functional mental disorder has been adduced at one period or another by psychiatrists as the solution of Hamlet." He elaborated the statement by listing twenty-two separate diagnoses that have been solemnly offered as if the unfortunate Dane had been under the direct observation of so many clinicians.[18] In passing we may note the attractiveness of the reductive fallacy, and remark divergence of opinion that raises doubts about medical competence. I wish to propose, though, a question on the legitimacy of the whole proceeding. Is it rational to allege, for example, that Hamlet had an Oedipus complex? I believe it is not a mere quibble to insist that the most we can sensibly support is the statement that he acts, under the given circumstances, as a young man tormented by such a complex might well have acted. It seems to me that it is the maintaining of such an approach that makes Wertham's own comments on Hamlet in *Dark Legend* [19] so much more impressive than those of more pretentious explanations of the play.

I believe that the "psychological awareness that our own age has conferred upon us" [20] can be effectively brought to bear on the discussion of characters whose creators were mortal, but the moment we imply that we can "psychoanalyze" them or explain their motivations as if they were living beings we confront the irrefutable logic of Professor Stoll.[21] For if we ask why Hamlet delayed his revenge, we must be prepared to include among our answers the admission that Shakespeare arranged matters so.

Perhaps, then, we may hope to psychoanalyze the author. As a matter of fact, most of the writers who have applied depth psychology to literary characters have clearly had other subjects in mind. Freud's seminal remarks about Hamlet left no doubt that behind the creature he saw the creator. Ernest

Jones [22] and Ella Sharpe [23] have with equal explicitness made it plain that their ultimate concern was with Shakespeare. And Arthur Wormhoudt, inspired by Edmund Bergler, assures us that Hamlet's behavior toward Ophelia and Gertrude, which looks like a manifestation of the Oedipus complex, is simply Shakespeare's personal defense "for his more deeply rooted oral conflict with the mother." [24] Similarly, we are told that Posdnischew reflects Tolstoy's "paraphiliac trend," [25] and that Alton Locke reveals Kingsley's particular neuroses,[26] while Macbeth is an objectification of Shakespeare's fantasies of guilt relating to his son's death.[27]

Now, if the author under analysis has created more than one character, it seems reasonable to ask on what grounds it may be supposed that in one rather than another he has expressed "the core of his psychical personality." [28] When answers to this question are attempted, they are usually vague and subjective.

But after all, we are not confined in the analysis of an author to a study of his projection into one or many characters whom he may have given shape to. We may learn that Lucretius had a mother fixation,[29] or that the writer of the Book of *Ecclesiastes* was impotent.[30] If the author, not a figment of fiction, is on the couch, why is he there, and what are the relations between him and the analyst?

The purpose of analysis cannot be therapy. Coleridge cannot now be retrieved from his addiction to opium nor Poe from his dipsomania; nor can the analyst help Shakespeare to resolve his "deeply rooted oral conflict with the mother." Yet it is apparently difficult not to adopt the tone of a diagnostician with an eye to improvement of the patient's behavior. Readers of psychoanalytic criticism are frequently irritated by what Charles Baudouin speaks of as an "air of medical superiority." [31]

If the purpose is not control, it is just as clearly not prediction. Presumably, the intention is simply to arrive at understanding of the author's motivations and meanings.

Even conscious motivations are complex; it is unlikely that

hidden ones are less so. Yet a common characteristic in psychoanalytic criticism appears to be schematic simplification. It is the besetting sin in such criticism to make over-much of the kind of causation that might be centrally important if the end in view were therapy, overlooking the fact that when the purpose which would give certain determinants significance is altered, the significance is automatically altered. We may say that in an author's work we have a set of symptoms, but as Rudolf Ekstein has pointed out, "the symptom really is determined through an unlimited series of causes." [32] The traditional scholar, whatever his own shortcomings, cannot fail to be annoyed by a reading that finds *the* answer to the "riddle" of *Macbeth* in Shakespeare's fantasies of guilt about the death of his son—even if they were reactivated by the death of the barren Elizabeth.[33]

Perhaps, however, those who apply psychoanalysis to the study of an author recognize the relativity of importance of various kinds of motivation and do not intend the impression they often give. We may still ask, what practicing psychoanalyst would presume to behave with an actual patient as many seem anxious to behave with Wordsworth, or Poe, or Tolstoy?

If on the basis of a given amount of writing by and about a man a dependable psychoanalytic diagnosis could be arrived at, we might initiate psychoanalysis by mail-order and merchandise it through Sears Roebuck and Company. But how can such a diagnosis be achieved? The writer who is not present in the flesh will not develop his free associations; if he has dreamed dreams, he will reveal no more of them than he has already seen fit to set down on paper; he will not give himself away in the quality of his voice or a muscle twitch or the hesitation that might mark inhibition. I do not mean to imply that we can learn nothing about an author by following out the hints which psychoanalysis gives us. On the contrary, we may discover much and conjecture a great deal more. But when mere conjecture is presented in the same tone of conviction as verifiable fact, as it often is, we need not wonder if the judicious reader receives the report with some suspicion. It seems to me that in psychoanalytic criticism there has not been sufficiently clear and consistent distinction maintained between what is only possibly true and what would pass the reasonable tests for credibility.

Deprived of the advantages of the kind of evidence a living patient provides, lacking particularly the crucial test of success or failure in therapy, the psychoanalyst (whether professional or literary) who studies an author through his writing is at a great disadvantage. If the author will not speak, the analyst must speak for him. The analyst must supply the associations that an image suggests; he must dream the dreams; he must see the "possible puns"; he must make the identifications. Who, actually, is being psychoanalyzed? Perhaps it is the critic who occupies the couch.

I cannot help feeling that it is often the recognition that the psychoanalytic critic, while he professes to be bringing science to bear on a piece of literature, is really talking about himself that accounts for a lack of sympathy in many readers. In Marie Bonaparte's analysis of Poe,[34] for example, we have a great deal of evidence about Mme. Bonaparte that we can accept as dependable, while much of what she tells us about Poe is questionable in the extreme. We may be interested to learn, for instance, that for her "The Purloined Letter" symbolizes a stolen penis, but what significance it may have had in Poe's unconscious we probably will never be sure about.

A symbol, by its very nature, *can* carry any of an indefinite number of meanings. Surface contexts provide manageable limits of potentialities for traditional interpretation. But suppose we exploit our understanding of repression, displacement, condensation, inversion, and transference; suppose we insist that the opposite of what is said is unconsciously meant, and that psychic defenses may be several layers deep. May we not find grounds for any interpretation that pleases *us?*

This argument should not be misconstrued. There is obviously a possibility of uncovering in a piece of literature

meanings that were present in the author's mind though he
may have been unaware of them. Edwin A. Armstrong, in
*Shakespeare's Imagination: A Study of the Psychology of
Association and Inspiration,* has shown how Miss Spurgeon's
more mechanical study of imagery may be extended with
profit.[35] It is possible to find tests, such as those of recurrence
and associations in clusters, that prevent an investigation of
an author's imagery from being mainly subjective speculation. Surely it would be possible to find reasonable checks on
subjectivity in other types of inquiry that attempt to take
us beneath the surface of a writer's mind.

Still more important, however, it should not be supposed
that if the critic is on the couch his position is necessarily
awkward. It is only if he pretends he is not there that objection may justly be raised. After all, what the author meant
when he wrote may be less important to us than the meanings we do or may attach to what he wrote. That is to say,
meaning has residence in the minds of readers.[36] The meanings a piece of literature may have for the critic informed
in depth psychology can be useful to all of us, though their
relative value will depend on the quality of his mind. Only,
let him be clear about what he is doing, and not misrepre-
sent his activity.

There is still another answer possible when we ask who
is analyzed in psychoanalytic criticism. Recalling that once
the author is dead the meaning of what he wrote can exist
only in the minds of readers, we can say that psychoanalysis
has a great deal to contribute through examination of those
minds in their relations to the piece of literature. In other
words, you and I may be the subjects of analysis. As a matter
of fact, is it not true that the most impressive (and useful)
criticism is that which reveals ourselves to ourselves? Again,
however, the critic ought to be clear about what he is saying. For what a work of art may mean to the generality of
readers may be different from what it suggests to a particular
critic and from what it meant to its creator. When decent

distinctions are respected, when discriminate interpretations are made, and when judicious caution controls the critic, his applications of psychoanalysis to literature can yield fruit that will be valued.

Note what happens when the critic admits that he is exploring his own mind or marking out paths of exploration for the reader. If Arthur Wormhoudt tells us that *he* identifies Geraldine with the phallic mother, and that *his* identification is reinforced by his recollection that her name means " 'spearwielder' according to its Teutonic origin," [37] we can credit the report as a statement of fact about Wormhoudt. Or if he suggests that in the phrase "gossamer sails" *we* can "perhaps" see a pun on " 'gossemere' (French *gosse,* boy; *mere,* mother)," [38] we are free to consider the suggestion. The question then is whether we find, for ourselves, some significance in the possibility. We are not forced to draw conclusions about Coleridge—or Wormhoudt.

The immense advantage of the psychoanalytical critic who has regard for the distinctions that have been recommended is illustrated in the work of Maud Bodkin.[39] Though her readers will, perhaps, not wish to accept all that she has had to say, they will find it readily possible to separate the useful from what they may question, for she has not intertwined fact with fantasy nor dogma with the demonstrable, and she has respected the reasonable limitations under which she has worked. Though her own scope of interest and understanding is broad, she is disarmingly modest, avoiding "insistent judgments of the 'nothing but' type."

Too frequently, however, it has seemed that critics have attempted to stretch their subject on the procrustean bed of preconceived theory, to represent possibility for fact, to mistake the subject of their inquiry, and to make out a case by means of what Kenneth Burke calls the "heads I win, tails you lose mechanism." [40] Nobody who wishes to explain his doubts about the use of psychoanalysis in literary study is at a loss for some ridiculous piece of speculation or some fine piece of unreason in action to point to as he says, "See, that is what I mean by psychoanalytic criticism."

Yet there have also been a respectable number of excellent studies that have contributed to our resources for understanding and appreciation. They have indicated what can be accomplished when we make reasonable use of "the psychological awareness that our own age has conferred on us." Some such studies are buried in the files of special journals, along with many others that could well remain interred there; others are in books that have had little general circulation; very few are widely known. In addition to the work of Armstrong and Bodkin, some that have come to my attention are Hanns Sachs's admirable essay on "The Measure in *Measure for Measure*," [41] Freud's "Dostoevsky and Parricide," [42] Roy P. Basler's interpretation of Tennyson's *Maud*,[43] certain sections of Leonard Manheim's "The Dickens Pattern," [44] a chapter in Kenneth Burke's *The Philosophy of Literary Form*,[45] and Ernst Kris's "Prince Hal's Conflict." [46]

It is regrettable that no attempt has been made to rescue the useful essays from obscurity. It would be gratifying to have easily accessible a collection representative of the best that has been done, to which we could point and say, "See, that is what I mean by good psychoanalytical criticism."

NOTES

1. The terms "psychoanalysis" and "psychoanalytic," the reader should be warned, will be used rather loosely in this article to refer to any of various sets of theories and methods relating to the study of the psyche that grew out of Freud's researches into the unconscious.

2. These preliminary statements are so obvious that there would seem no point in them had not René Wellek and

Austin Warren in their influential compendium, *The Theory of Literature* (New York, 1949), pp. 75–88, argued the case for an extremely narrow conception both of "psychology" and what "belongs to literary study."

3. John Livingston Lowes and Caroline Spurgeon come readily to mind as examples.

4. Richard Chase, "Myth Revisited," *Partisan Review*, XVII (1950), 891.

5. Lionel Trilling, *The Liberal Imagination* (New York, 1951), p. 52.

6. Frederick J. Hoffman, in *Freudianism and the Literary Mind* (Baton Rouge, 1945), has discussed at length the effects of psychoanalysis on modern literature and, as a consequence, the critic's necessary concern with them.

7. Harry Levin, "Clinical Demonstrations on Four Poets," *Saturday Review of Literature*, XXXII (January 1, 1949), 15.

8. So far as I know, there exists no comprehensive bibliography of this subject, though the running bibliographies in *Literature and Psychology* may provide a basis for such a compilation. *Psychological Abstracts* reports a steadily increasing number of studies of literature.

9. See, for example, Leo A. Spiegel, "The New Jargon: Psychology in Literature," *Sewanee Review*, XL (1932), 476–491.

10. Leonard Manheim has discussed this subject in "The Dickens Pattern" (unpublished Columbia Ph.D. dissertation, 1948), pp. 3–7.

11. Excellent advice on the matter is given to "psychocritics" by Leon Edel in "Notes on the Use of Psychological Tools in Literary Scholarship," *L & P*, I, 4 (September, 1951), 3.

12. Joseph Wood Krutch, *Edgar Allan Poe, A Study in Genius* (New York, 1926), p. 234.

13. Leon Edel (*op. cit.*) has also some sensible advice for biographers. It is likely that some biographers, operating on principles such as those recommended by Mr. Edel, have profited by psychoanalytic investigations that do not obtrude themselves on the reader's attention in the finished biography. As a *genre*, however, the "psychoanalytic biography" has a deservedly bad reputation. Stefan Zweig's *Mental Healers* (New York, 1932) and Jack Lindsay's *Charles Dickens* (London, 1949) illustrate that such biog-

raphy need not be narrowly conceived or injudicious. Edward Hitschmann in "Boswell: the Biographer's Character . . . ," *Psychoanalytic Quarterly*, XVII (April, 1948), 212–225, also shows what can be done.

14. Stanley Edgar Hyman, for instance, alludes to "the familiar excesses of psychoanalytic criticism." *The Armèd Vision* (New York, 1948), p. 142.

15. It should be clear that the word "analyze" is here used in the technical sense given to it when a psychoanalyst speaks of analyzing a patient. A traditional function of the literary critic, of course, is that of analyzing (in the ordinary sense of the word) the texts he studies.

16. James Clark Moloney and Laurence Rockelein, "A New Interpretation of Hamlet," *International Journal of Psychoanalysis*, XXX, Part II (1949), 94. In more hypothetical terms, of course, Ernest Jones had already supplied Hamlet with an antecedent biography. See his study in *Hamlet* (London, 1947).

17. E. E. Stoll has argued this matter out in *Art and Artifice in Shakespeare* (Cambridge, 1933).

18. Frederic Wertham, "The Matricidal Impulse," *Journal of Criminal Psychopathology*, II (April, 1941), 4.

19. Frederic Wertham, *Dark Legend* (New York, 1941).

20. Maud Bodkin, *Archetypal Patterns in Poetry* (London, 1934), p. 334.

21. E. E. Stoll, *op. cit.* I do not wish to imply general agreement with Professor Stoll's arguments on other points.

22. Ernest Jones, *op. cit.*, p. 9.

23. Ella Sharpe, "An Unfinished Paper on Hamlet, Prince of Denmark," *International Journal of Psychoanalysis*, XXIX (1948), 98–109.

24. Arthur Wormhoudt, *The Demon Lover* (New York, 1950), pp. 7–8.

25. B. Karpman, "The Kreutzer Sonata, A Problem in Latent Homosexuality and Castration," *Psychoanalytic Review*, XXV (1938), 20.

26. Felix Deutsch, "Respiratory Neuroses in Charles Kingsley," *American Imago*, IV (December, 1947), 88–97.

27. Ludwig Jekels, "The Riddle of Shakespeare's Macbeth," *Psychoanalytic Review*, XXX (1943), 361–385.

28. The phrase is adapted from Ernest Jones, *op. cit.*, p. 9.

29. B. J. Logre, "The Anxiety of Lucretius," *Psyché*, IV (1949), 50.

30. Frank Zimmerman, "The Book of Ecclesiastes in the Light of Some Psychoanalytic Observations," *American Imago,* V (1948), 301–305.

31. Charles Baudouin, *Psychoanalysis and Aesthetics,* trans. by Eden and Cedar Paul (London, 1924), p. 33. But not Baudouin's protest that such an air need not be adopted.

32. Rudolf Ekstein, "The Tower of Babel in Psychology and Psychiatry . . . ," *American Imago,* VII (July, 1950), 115.

33. Ludwig Jekels, *op. cit.* It further seems clear that the present state of development in the science of psychology does not justify dogmatism in theoretical explanations. The sectarianism among psychoanalysts suggests that there are numerous areas of uncertainty. Freud, to the end of his life, continued to revise his own doctrines, and his reference to "our mythology" implies his recognition that he and his associates dealt in useful constructs that may be altered or discarded. See his *New Introductory Lectures in Psychoanalysis* (New York, 1933), p. 131.

34. Marie Bonaparte, *The Life and Works of Edgar Allan Poe* (New York, 1949).

35. Edwin A. Armstrong, *Shakespeare's Imagination . . .* (London, 1946).

36. I do not wish to be misunderstood as deprecating inquiry into what the author intended. That is one approach to finding what meaning it may have for us. Nor do I agree with Arthur Wormhoudt (*op. cit.,* p. 14) that "any full and coherent interpretation of a work of art has value regardless of the truth or falsity of the scientific data on which it rests," unless a special definition is given to "value" or the statement is extended to show to whom the value accrues. What value has Diana Pittman's full and coherent interpretation of the works of Poe as a "coded allegory . . . of propagandist efforts in connection with British Reform?" (See Philip Young, "The Earlier Psychologists and Poe," *American Literature,* XXII [1951], 443–444.)

37. Arthur Wormhoudt, *op. cit.,* p. 27.

38. *Ibid.,* p. 34.

39. Maud Bodkin, *op. cit.*

40. Kenneth Burke, *Counter-statement* (New York, 1931), p. 93 n.: "Having defined the nature of a man's psychosis, they can fit any act into the scheme. For if the act follows the same pattern as the psychosis, they can explain it as

consistent—but if it does not follow the pattern, they can account for it as 'sublimated' or 'compensatory.' "

41. In *The Creative Unconscious* (Cambridge, Mass., 1942).

42. In *Collected Papers*, Vol. 5 (London, 1950).

43. In *Sex, Symbolism and Psychology* (New Brunswick, N. J., 1948).

44. Unpublished Columbia Ph.D. dissertation, 1948.

45. Kenneth Burke, *The Philosophy of Literary Form* (Baton Rouge, 1941).

46. *The Psychoanalytic Quarterly*, XVII (1948), 487–506.

The Language of the Pundits

by ALFRED KAZIN

Alfred Kazin's broad range of interests takes in many fields other than literature. His literary studies have included essays about psychoanalytic criticism like the present study, but he has not published psychoanalytic criticism as such. He lectures and teaches in this country and abroad, his most recent academic affiliation being with the State University of New York at Stony Brook, Long Island. Probably his best-remembered book is his study of American literature, *On Native Grounds*. The present essay appeared in a collection, *Contemporaries* (1962), in a section entitled "Freud and His Consequences."

I T is curious that Freud, the founder of psychoanalysis, remains the only first-class writer identified with the psychoanalytic movement. It was, of course, Freud's remarkable literary ability that gave currency to his once difficult and even "bestial" ideas; it was the insight he showed into concrete human problems, the discoveries whose force is revealed to us in a language supple, dramatic, and charged with the excitement of Freud's mission as a "conquistador" into realms hitherto closed to scientific inquiry, that excited and persuaded so many readers of his books. Even the reader who does not accept all of Freud's reasoning is aware, as he reads his interpretation of dreams, of the horror associated with incest, of the Egyptian origins of Moses, that this is a writer who is bent on making the most mysterious and unmentionable matters entirely clear to himself, and that this fundamental concern to get at the truth makes dramatis personae out of his symbols and dramatic episodes out of the archetypal human struggles he has described. It is certainly possible to read Freud, even to enjoy his books, without being convinced by him, but anyone sensitive to the nuances and playfulness of literary style, to the shaping power of a great intellectual conception, is not likely to miss in Freud the peculiar urgency of the great writer; for myself, I can never read him without carrying away a deeply engraved, an unforgettable sense of the force of human desire.

By contrast, many of the analysts who turn to writing seem to me not so much writers as people clutching at a few ideas. Whenever I immerse myself, very briefly, in the magisterial clumsiness of Dr. Gregory Zilboorg, or the slovenly looseness of Dr. Theodore Reik, or the tensely inarticulate essays of Dr. Harry Stack Sullivan, or the purringly complacent formulas of Dr. Edmund Bergler, or even the smoothly professional pages of Dr. Erich Fromm, I have a mental picture of a man leaping up from his chair, crying with exultation, "I have it! The reason for frigidity in the middle-aged female is the claustrophobic constitution!," and straightway rushing to his publisher. Where Freud really tried to give an explanation to himself of one specific human difficulty after another, and then in his old-fashioned way tried to show the determination of one new fact by another, it is enough these days for Dr. Bergler to assert why all writers are blocked, or for Dr. Theodore Reik, in his long-winded and inconsequential trek into love and lust, to announce that male and female are so different as to be virtually of different species. The vital difference between a writer and someone who merely is published is that the writer seems always to be saying to himself, as Stendhal actually did, "If I am not clear, the world around me collapses." In a very real sense, the writer writes in order to teach himself, to understand himself, to satisfy himself; the publishing of his ideas, though it brings gratifications, is a curious anticlimax.

Of course, there are psychoanalyst-writers who aim at understanding for themselves, but don't succeed. Even in Freud's immediate circle, several of the original disciples, having obtained their system from the master, devoted themselves to specialties and obsessions that, even if they were more than private *idées fixes,* like Otto Rank's belief in the "birth-trauma," were simply not given the hard and lucid expression necessary to convince the world of their objectivity. Lacking Freud's striking combination of intellectual zeal and common sense, his balanced and often rueful sense of the total image presented by the human person, these disciples wrote as if they could draw upon Freud's system while expanding one or two favorite notions out of keeping with the rest. But so strongly is Freud's general conception the product of his literary ability, so much is it held together only in Freud's own books, by the force of his own mind, that it is extraordinary how, apart from Freud, Freudianism loses its general interest and often becomes merely an excuse for wild-goose chases.

Obviously these private concerns were far more important to certain people in Freud's own circle than was the validity of Freudianism itself. When it came to a conflict between Freudianism and their own causes (Otto Rank) or their desire to be uninhibited in mystical indefiniteness (C. G. Jung), the body of ideas which they had inherited, not earned, no longer existed for them. Quite apart from his personal disposition to remain in control of the movement which he had founded, Freud was objectively right in warning disciples like Ferenczi, Rank, Adler, and Stekel not to break away from his authority. For the analyst's interest in psychoanalysis is likely to have its origin in some personal anxiety, and some particularly unstable people (of whom there were several in Freud's circle), lacking Freud's unusual ability not only to work through his own neuroses but to sublimate everything into the grand creative exultation of founding a movement, committed themselves fruitlessly to the development of their unsystematic ideas, found it impos-

sible to heal themselves by the *ad hoc* doctrines they had
advanced for this purpose, and even relapsed into serious
mental illness and suicide.

Until fairly recently, it was perfectly possible for anyone
with a Ph.D. (in literature or Zen or philology) to be a
"psychotherapist" in New York State. I have known several
such therapists among the intellectuals of New York, and
I distinguish them very sharply from the many skillful and
devoted lay analysts, with a direct training in psychoanalysis,
who are likely to have an objective concern with the malady
of their patients. The intellectuals with Ph.D.'s who transferred from other professions to the practice of psychoanalysis still seem to me an extreme and sinister example of
the tendency of psychoanalysis to throw up the pundit as a
type. Like modern intellectuals everywhere, intellectuals as
self-made analysts are likely to have one or two ruling ideas
which bear obvious relation to their private history, but
which, unlike intellectuals generally, they have been able to
impose upon people who came to them desperately eager
for orientation in their difficulties. In short, the ruling
weakness of intellectuals, which is to flit from idea to idea
in the hope of finding some instrument of personal or world
salvation, has often become a method of indoctrination. All
the great figures in psychoanalysis have been egotists of the
most extreme sort; all the creative ones, from Freud himself
to the late unfortunate Dr. Wilhelm Reich, were openly
exasperated with the necessity of having to deal with patients
at all. They were interested only in high thinking, though
Freud at least tempered his impatience enough to learn from
his patients; the objective power, the need to examine
symptoms in others, never left him.

By contrast, the intellectual who is looking for an audience or a disciple has often, as a psychotherapist, found one
in his patient. And the obvious danger of exploiting the
credulous, the submissive, the troubled (as someone said, it
is the analyst's love that cures the patient, and certain intellectuals love no one so much as a good listener), which

starts from a doctrine held by the analyst in good faith but which may be no less narrow-minded or fanatical for all that, seems to me only an extension of the passion for explaining everything by psychoanalysis which literary intellectuals have indulged in so long. When I think of some of the intellectuals who have offered their services as therapists, I cannot but believe that to them the patient is irrelevant to their own passion for intellectual indoctrination. My proof of this is the way they write. Ever since Freud gave the word to so many people less talented than himself, it has become increasingly clear that, whatever psychoanalysis may have done for many troubled people, it has encouraged nonwriters to become bad writers and mediocre writers to affect the style of pundits. For the root of all bad writing is to be distracted, to be self-conscious, not to have your eye on the ball, not to confront a subject with entire directness, with entire humility, and with concentrated passion. The root of all bad writing is to compose what you have not worked out, *de haut en bas,* for yourself. Unless words come into the writer's mind as fresh coinages for what the writer himself knows that he knows, knows to be true, it is impossible for him to give back in words that direct quality of experience which is the essence of literature.

Now, behind the immense power and authority of psycho-analytical doctrines over contemporary literature—which expresses itself in the motivation of characters, the images of poetry, the symbol hunting of critics, the immense congregation of psychiatric situations and of psychiatrists in contemporary plays and novels—lies the urgent conviction, born with modern literature in the romantic period, the seedbed of Freudian ideas, that literature can give us knowledge. The Romantic poets believed in the supremacy of imagination over logic exactly as we now believe that the unconscious has stories to tell which ordinary consciousness knows nothing of. And just as the analyst looks to free association on the part of the patient to reveal conflicts buried too deep in the psyche to be revealed to the ordinarily conscious mind, so the Romantic poets believed that what has been buried in us, far from the prying disapprovals of culture, stands for "nature," our true human nature. A new world had been revealed to the Romantics, a world accessible through the imagination that creates art. And Freud, who also felt that he had come upon a new world, said that his insights had been anticipated by literary men in particular; he felt that he had confirmed, as scientific doctrine, profound discoveries about our buried, our archetypal, our passionate human nature that philosophers and poets had made as artists.

Had made as artists. Nietzsche, who also anticipated many of Freud's psychological insights, said that Dostoevsky was the only psychologist who had ever taught him anything. No doubt he meant that the characters Dostoevsky had created, the freshness of Dostoevsky's perceptions, the powerful but ironic rationality of Dostoevsky's style had created new facts for him to think of in comparison with the stale medical formulas of psychiatry in his time. Similarly, Freud said of Dostoevsky that "before genius, analysis lays down its arms," indicating that with the shaping power of the artist who can create characters like old Karamazov and Prince Myshkin, with the genius that in its gift of creation actually parallels life instead of merely commenting on it, analysis cannot compete. And in point of fact we do learn more about the human heart from a stupendous creation like the Karamazov family than we ever do from all the formulary "motivations" of human nature. Just as each human being, in his uniqueness, escapes all the dry formulas and explanations about human nature, so a great new creation in imaginative literature, a direct vision of the eternal like William Blake's or an unprecedented and unassimilable human being like old Karamazov, automatically upsets and rearranges our hardened conceptions of human nature.

There is no substitute for life, for the direct impression of life; there is no deep truth about life, such as writers bring home to us, that does not come in the form of more life.

To anyone who really knows how rare and precious imaginative creation is—how small, after all, is that procession which includes Dante's Paolo and Francesca, Shakespeare's Othello, and Tolstoy's Natasha—how infinitely real in suggestion is the character that has been created in and through imagination, there is something finally unbearable, the very opposite of what literature is for, in the kind of metallic writing which now so often serves in a novel to "motivate" a character.

Maybe the only tenable literary role which novelists and poets, as well as critics and psychologists, now want to play is that of the expert—the explainer, the commentator, the analyst. Just as so many psychoanalysts want to be writers, so many writers now want to be analysts. And whenever I rise up at intervals from my dutiful immersion in certain specimens of contemporary literature, I find it hard to say who has less to contribute to literature, the psychiatrist who wants to push a few small ideas into a book or the novelist who in the course of a story breaks down into writing like a psychoanalyst.

The deterioration of language in contemporary fiction into the language of pundits is not often noticed by critics —perhaps because the novelists have taken to writing like critics. But it is by no means the highbrow or intellectual novelist—like Mary McCarthy, who in a single story for *Partisan Review* is likely to produce so many deliberate symbols—who is the only offender against art. John O'Hara in *From the Terrace* wrote, of the mother of his hero, that "What had happened to her was that she unconsciously abandoned the public virginity and, again unconsciously, began to function as a woman." Of the Eaton brothers, O'Hara made it clear that "If William slapped Alfred or otherwise punished him, the difference in ages was always mentioned while William himself was being punished; and each time that that occurred the age separation contributed to a strengthening of the separation that was already there

because of, among other considerations, the two distinct
personalities." This is a novelist? Frankly, I have the impression that many of the younger novelists have learned to
write fiction from reading the New Critics, the anthropologists and psychologists. I cannot begin to enumerate
all the novels of recent years, from Ralph Ellison's *Invisible
Man* to Vance Bourjaily's *Confessions of a Spent Youth,*
which describe American social customs, from college up,
as fulfilling the prescription of tribal rites laid down by the
anthropologists. But whereas an angry and powerful novelist, as Ellison is in *Invisible Man,* whatever helpful hints he
may get from psychiatrically oriented literary critics, will
aim at the strongest possible image of Negro suffering and
confusion in a hostile society, Vance Bourjaily, in his novel,
has his hero preface his description of a business smoker by
apologizing that "it would take the calm mind of an anthro-
pologist to describe objectively the rites with which the
advertising tribe sent its bachelor to meet his bride."

I don't know what repels me more in such writing, the
low spirits behind such prosiness or the attempted irony
that is meant to disguise the fact that the writer is simply
not facing his subject directly but is looking for something
to say about it. No wonder that a passage like this sounds
not like fiction but a case history: "I had a good time with
Vicky during those two or three months; at the same time,
I was learning about the social structure of the town and
that of the school which, with certain exceptions for unusual individuals, reflected it; Vicky was more or less middle
middle. As a friend of hers, since my own status was ambiguous, it seemed to me that I must acquire hers by association." And Mr. Bourjaily's book *is* a case history, though
so meanderingly self-absorbed, for the most part, that it
comes splendidly alive when the hero describes a visit to his
relatives in the Near East; for a few pages we are onto
people whom Mr. Bourjaily has to describe for us, since they
are new types, and then we get free of the motivational
analysis that is the novelist's desperate response to people

who he thinks are too familiar to be conveyed directly. This is a curious idea of a novel—as if it were the subject, rather than the point of view, which made it boring.

The true writer starts from autobiography, but he does not end there; and it is not himself he is interested in, but the use he can make of self as a literary creation. Of course, it is not the autobiographical subject that makes such books as Mr. Bourjaily's flat; it is the relatively shallow level from which the author regards his own experience. The mark of this is that the writer does not even bother to turn his hero into a character; he is just a focus for the usual "ironic" psychological comment. If the writer nowadays sees himself as a pundit, he sees his hero as a patient. What, in fact, one sees in many contemporary American novelists today is the author as analyst confronting his alter ego as analysand. The novel, in short, becomes simply an instrument of self-analysis, which may be privately good for the writer (I doubt it) but is certainly boring to his readers.

The deterioration of language in contemporary "imaginative" literature—this reduction of experience to flat, vaguely orphic loose statements—seems to me most serious whenever, in our psychiatrically centered culture, spontaneity becomes an arbitrary gesture which people can simulate. Among the Beat writers, spontaneity becomes a necessary convention of mental health, a way of simulating vitality, directness, rough informality, when in fact the literary works produced for this pose have no vitality, are not about anything very significant, and are about as rough as men ever are using dirty words when they cut themselves shaving. The critic Harold Rosenberg once referred scathingly to the "herd of independent minds"; when I read the Beat and spontaneous poets en bloc, as I have just done in Donald Allen's anthology of the "new" American poetry, I feel that I am watching a bunch of lonely Pagliaccis making themselves up to look gay. To be spontaneous on purpose, spontaneous all the time, spontaneous on demand is bad enough;

you are obeying not yourself but some psychiatric commandment. But to convert this artificial, constant, unreal spontaneity into poetry as a way of avoiding the risks and obligations of an objective literary work is first to make a howling clown out of yourself and then deliberately to cry up your bad literature as the only good literature.

The idea of the Beat poets is to write so quickly that they will not have to stand up for the poem itself; it is enough to be caught in the act of writing. The emphasis is not on the poem but on themselves being glimpsed in the act of creation. In short, they are functioning, they are getting out of the prison house of neurosis, they are positive and free. "Look, Ma, no hands!" More than this, they are shown in the act of writing poems which describe them in the act of living, just about to write poems.

Elsewhere, the hysterical demand for spontaneity as an absolute value means that everything in the normal social world becomes an enemy of your freedom. You want to destroy it so as to find an image of the ecstasy that has become the only image of reality the isolated mind will settle for. It is a wish for the apocalypse that lies behind the continued self-righteous muttering that the world is about to blow up. The world is not about to blow up, but behind the extreme literary pose that everything exists to stifle and suppress and exterminate us perhaps lies the belief, as Henry Miller plainly put it in *Tropic of Cancer,* that "For a hundred years or more the world, *our* world, has been dying. . . . The world is rotting away, dying piecemeal. But it needs the *coup de grâce,* it needs to be blown into smithereens. . . . We are going to put it down—the evolution of this world which has died but which has not been buried. We are swimming on the face of time and all else has drowned, is drowning, or will drown."

The setting of this apocalyptic wish is the stated enmity between the self and the world, between the literary imagination and mere reality—a tension which was set up by Romanticism and which Freudianism has sharpened and intensified to the point where the extreme Romantic, the Beat writer, confesses that the world must be destroyed in order that the freedom of his imagination proceed to its infinite goal. Romanticism put so much emphasis on the personal consciousness that eventually the single person came to consider himself prior to the world and, in a sense, replacing it; under Romanticism, the self abandoned its natural ties to society and nature and emphasized the will. The more the single conscious mind saw the world as an object for it to study, the more consciousness was thrown back on itself in fearful isolation; the individual, alone now with his consciousness, preoccupied in regarding himself and studying himself, had to exercise by more and more urgent exertions of will that relationship to the world which made consciousness the emperor of all it could survey—the world was merely raw material to the inquiring mind.

Freud, himself a highly conservative and skeptical thinker with a deeply classical bias in favor of limitation, restraint, and control, could not have anticipated that his critique of repression, of the admired self-control of the bourgeoisie, would in time, with the bankruptcy of bourgeois values, become a philosophy for many of his followers. Freudianism is a critique of Victorian culture; it is not a prescription for living in the twentieth century, in a world where the individual finds himself increasingly alienated from the society to which he is physically tied. Freud once wrote in a letter to Romain Rolland: "Psychoanalysis also has its scale of values, but its sole aim is the enhanced harmony of the ego, which is expected successfully to mediate between the claims of the instinctual life [the id] and those of the external world; thus between inner and outer reality.

"We seem to diverge rather far in the role we assign to intuition. Your mystics rely on it to teach them how to solve the riddle of the universe; we believe that it cannot reveal to us anything but primitive, instinctual impulses and attitudes . . . worthless for orientation in the alien, external world."

It was the Romantics who handed down to modern writers the necessity to think of the world as "alien and external." By now so many writers mechanically think of it this way that it is no wonder that they look for a philosophy of life to the "primitive, instinctual impulses and attitudes," though, as Freud knew, they are "worthless for orientation in the alien, external world." Man cannot cheat his own mind; he cannot bypass the centrality of his own intelligence. Yet is not sole reliance on the "primitive, instinctual impulses" exactly the *raison d'être* of so many Beat poems and novels; of neurotic plays dealing with people whose only weakness, *they* think, is that they are repressed; of literary studies whose whole thesis is that the American novel has always been afraid of sex? What is wrong with such works is not that the single points they make are incorrect, but that they rely upon a single point for a positive philosophy of life. It is impossible to write well and deeply in this spirit of Sisyphus, pushing a single stone up the mountain. It is impossible to write well if you start from an arbitrary point of view, and in the face of everything that is human, complex, and various, push home your *idée fixe*. It is impossible for the haunted, the isolated, the increasingly self-absorbed and self-referring self to transcend itself sufficiently to create works of literature.

Literature grows out of a sense of abundant relationships with the world, out of a sense that what is ugly to everyone else is really beautiful to you, that what is invisible to many men is pressingly alive and present to your writer's eye. We can no longer, by taking thought, transcend the life that consists in taking thought. The English novelist and philosopher Iris Murdoch has recently helped clear the air of desperate self-pity by saying that "We need to return from the self-centered concept to the other-centered concept of truth. We are not isolated free choosers, monarchs of all we survey, but benighted creatures sunk in a reality whose nature we are constantly and overwhelmingly tempted to deform by fantasy. Our current picture of freedom encourages a dream-like facility, whereas what we require is a re-newed sense of the difficulty and complexity of the moral life and the opacity of persons."

By now the self-centered mind fashioned by Romanticism, constantly keeping itself open only to adjurations of absolute freedom and spontaneity, has traveled about as far along the road of self-concern as it can; it has nothing to discover further of itself but fresh despair. The immediate proof of this is in the quality of so much of the literature that has been shaped by Freudianism—only because all other creeds have failed it. It is not possible to write well with one's own wishes as the only material. It is not possible any longer to think anything out without a greater reality than oneself constantly pressing one's words into dramatic shape and unexpected meaning. All our words now are for our own emotions, none for the world that sustains the writer. And this situation is impossible, for it was never the self that literature was about, but what transcended the self, what comes home to us through experience.

Literary Form and Psychic Tension

by FREDERICK J. HOFFMAN

Frederick J. Hoffman's pioneer study, *Freudianism and the Literary Mind,* first appeared in 1945. A second edition was published in 1957 with the addition of an appendix entitled "Psychology and Literature." The title resulted from the fact that the essay was originally delivered at the 1956 English Institute in a symposium on "Peripheries of Literature," Mr. Hoffman's "periphery" being "psychology," or better, psychoanalytic theory applied to the problem of literary form. The present title, selected by the author, is, of course, more precise. Under its older title it was published in the Freud Centenary Number of *Literature and Psychology* (VI, 4, 111–115) and in *Kenyon Review* (Autumn 1957).

Mr. Hoffman holds degrees from Stanford, Minnesota, and Ohio State, and has taught at Chicago, Ohio State, Oklahoma, California (Riverside), and Wisconsin. He is the author of numerous books and articles on literary subjects.

So many attempts have been made to discuss precisely the relationship of psychology with literature or to suggest the usefulness of psychology to criticsm that one needs first of all to see if a new perspective isn't somehow available. I believe we know both the advantage and the limitations of the biographical study of writers; and no one can escape these days the dark presence of Jung's "primordial images." Perhaps we may find our best access to the problem by looking once again at a structure and terminology contributed at the beginning of the century and before by Sigmund Freud and elaborated upon by him in subsequent years.

I refer of course to Freud's definition, description, and analysis of the psychic economy. These involve a series of metaphors, as bold a series as was ever advanced by a cautious scientist. Beginning only with the facts of the unconscious and the conscious mind, Freud saw first of all, or suspected, both the tension between the two and what he called the constancy, or balance, of energy that invariably characterized this tension. From these simple beginnings came the terminology with which we are all now familiar: the id, ego, superego; the unconscious, preconscious, conscious; the pleasure principle and the reality principle, and so on.

Described in Freud's own words,

the ego is that part of the id which has been modified by the direct influence of the external world acting through the Perceptual-Conscious: in a sense it is an extension of the surface-differentiation. Moreover, the ego has the task of bringing the influence of the external world to bear upon the id and its tendencies, and endeavors to substitute the reality-principle for the pleasure-principle which reigns supreme in the id. In the ego perception plays the part which in the id devolves upon instinct. The ego represents what we call reason and sanity, in contrast to the id which contains the passions.[1]

These terms were in the nature of accessory metaphors, introduced as the original insight into psychic tensions required elaboration and its subtleties needed definition. I am aware of the fact that these formulations stem from a desire to assert and affirm the existence of what underlay the conscious, external world, of what we know from having seen or sensed. It is also true that they are the product of a desire to pay a discreet tribute to the language of orthodox science. There is nothing at all unusual or surprising in Freud's characterization of these phenomena; nor was Freud the first to emphasize the need to examine an "unconscious" life or mind. It is perhaps in his admirable and patient *consistency* of attention that the merit of his system lies—

as well as in its availability to almost endless fruitful elaboration.

Once we have established that the unconscious is a positive entity, a specific and viable aspect of the psyche, then we may proceed to describe it. We continue to do so, however, by the ingenious method of analyzing causally the aberrancies and obliquities of the conscious mind; and our major instrument in such analysis is language. We must assume a language norm, a norm of linguistic behavior, linked to a kind of systematic logical or rational form. If there are such norms—if they may be maintained without one's retreating too far into abstractions—then it is possible to examine variants, deviations, subterfuges, psychic "jamming," and to explain them as a part of the strategy of the id, as a verbal consequence of the tension resulting from the flow and counterflow of psychic energy.

Freud's own description of these processes is both precise and illuminating:

By virtue of its relation to the perceptual system, [the ego] arranges the processes of the mind in a temporal order and tests their correspondence with reality. By interposing the process of thinking it secures a postponement of motor discharges and controls the avenues to motility. . . . All the experiences of life that originate from without enrich the ego; the id, however, is another outer world to it, which it strives to bring into subjection to itself. It withdraws libido from the id and transforms the object-cathexes of the id into object-construction. With the aid of the super-ego, though in a manner that is still obscure to us [1927], it draws upon the experiences of past ages stored in the id.[2]

This is what amounts to a psychological analysis of the basic constituents of a literature. In terms of it we may illuminate much of what we discuss in literary criticism as form, texture, metaphor, and symbol. I should like to suggest the following plan for a criticism based upon Freud's initial descriptions of the psychic order. Let us assume that our psychic life may be divided into primary and secondary processes; that these, since they are located differently and react to different kinds of exposure, are in conflict with each other, or more accurately that they cause conflict in the psyche; that basic energies (whether of wish or desire, as Freud maintained, or of some other incentive) are turned back upon themselves, or are permitted only partial expression, or express themselves fully only in extraordinary circumstances; that our understanding of these energies comes from the fact of their being thwarted, controlled, suspended in a state of partial expression; and that, ultimately, the ideal psychic state results from a *balance* of tensions and a *conservation* of psychic energy. A number of important opportunities for the description of our psychic lives occur to us. While the energies are not specifically one thing or another, they may be characterized with a quite satisfactory and useful precision. The push, drive, energy of the id are desire, wish, for pleasure, for specific gratifications; the agency for thwarting the desire is exposed to the reality itself, the external world which indicates its prohibitions by inflicting pain or forcing retreat. An uninhibited drive toward satisfaction of unconscious wishes (or expenditure of libidinal energy) would lead to death. The wish needs instruction in the shock of reality; if the character of inhibition is moderate, the shock will lead to readjustment; if the reality is too suddenly and too brutally enforced, the effect will be a traumatic shock, leading to one of several forms of compulsive behavior. Freud assumes stability in the external world; Hemingway among others did not find it so. But this shock is not limited either to the accidents of uninhibited desire or to the catastrophes of an uncontrolled reality. Repression is in itself a cause of pain; it may, in the interests of protecting the psyche and prolonging life, cause violent dislocations of the psychic system.

However inadequate this may be as a sketch of Freud's superbly exact descriptions, I introduce it here as a preliminary to examining its usefulness as a perspective upon literature. The two have in common what we may call a necessary language—language as the instrument of description becomes in the course of my discussion language as a system of strategies. Language is necessary at first to label and define; next, to put phenomena in order; then to characterize the nature of incentives for labeling and ordering; finally, in the most remarkable of its ranges of use, to effect changes in meaning, to represent situations as more complex than they might be or are or ought to be. In the mind of a person endowed with every resource of language, the phenomena of psychic tension, conflict, drive, repression, are articulated and represented in a discourse at once psychologically just and remarkably subtle. I should like to suggest, therefore, that literature may be viewed and analyzed in terms of the verbal and metaphorical equivalents of the psyche and its behavior. Literature possesses a greater metaphoric freedom than psychology, or perhaps it has the license of its own audacity. But it is actively engaged in providing verbal and metaphoric equivalents of and elaborations upon the simply described behavior of the id, ego, and superego in their dynamic relationships. I can scarcely go on from here, to insist upon exact equivalents; it is perhaps as unwise to find iddities and egocentricities in literature as it is to accept literally biographical peculiarities as definitive explanations of achieved works of art. To locate an author's id, ego, superego, etc., in either characters or lines is to violate the subtlety of their necessary arrangements. My purpose is, instead, to explain the complexities of literary work as the results of symbolic actions which report and reflect on a high level of linguistic articulateness and subtlety the basic tensions, balances, imbalances, repressions, and compensations of psychic energies contained within a system such as Freud has described.

In any application of such a criticism, we can begin with fairly simple definitions. The creative process begins with a relaxation of ego control. There are other examples of such relaxation: drunkenness, forms of schizophrenia, dreams. But the work of the artist differs usually from these in that the regression is deliberate and controlled. The creative artist is *aware* of the regression; one may almost say he *wills* it (there have been cases of poets who have tried to force it by artificial means). The creative mind suspends its work between inspiration and control, or criticism. The artist is aware first of all that he is in a state of suspension; deliberately he has allowed the ego to give in to the flow of energy from the id. As Ernst Kris (with Abraham Kaplan) has put it,

We may speak here of *a shift in psychic level,* consisting in the fluctuation of functional regression and control. When regression goes too far, the symbols become private, perhaps unintelligible even to the reflective self; when, at the other extreme, control is preponderant, the result is described as cold, mechanical, and uninspired.[3]

As Freud has pointed out (in *The Interpretation of Dreams* and elsewhere), in the unconscious which has been affected by the ego's inhibitions reside the potential strategies for circumventing the ego. Such strategies as condensation, displacement, additive substitutes for negations or for the conditional mode are all a product of the id-ego tension. The verbalization of this tension is available in the preconscious. Of basic interest to literary criticism is the fact that impulse and inhibition are herein *mixed,* that multiple meanings and ambiguities are thus a *result* of the conflict between desire and inhibition. An ambiguity may be said to suggest in language the subtlety of an achieved balance. The *complexity* of the human state resides neither in the fully charged impact of desire upon the ego nor in the ego's use of societal prohibitions to stop the impact (each of these by itself is superficial)—but, rather, in the *product* of the conflict. The ego provides the language of discourse in its relationship with the preconscious (which is largely charged with the oughtness and counter-energy of conscience); the id determines the strategies used to mitigate, violate, or circumvent. In a remarkable range of meanings and metaphor, literature records the infinite variety of these exchanges and conflicts.

There are two major considerations relevant to literary

criticism: they are the multiplicity of meanings in literature and the element of form. Form is largely a product of the ego; social and moral forms are related to aesthetic forms; or, rather, aesthetic form is an extension of the logic of social and moral forms. That literary forms have great variety is no more remarkable a fact than that form persists through such variety. Experiment in literary form probably comes from a distrust of traditional form; the container no longer satisfactorily orders the thing contained. Thus an attempt to introduce a "qualitative" form, or to insist upon symbolic as distinguished from rational progression comes at least in part from a dissatisfaction with form as not allowing sufficient texture or as overly inhibiting the opportunity of texture. Texture is itself a variant of form: rhythm both encourages and controls freedom of meaning; a rhyme pattern both enhances the quality of word sounds and sets a limit to their frequency.

More specifically, the forms are the special province of the ego; they are the means of inhibition, the ways of containing creative energy, of balancing its tensions and of securing a maximum of discernibility within the range of particulars. The only way of making oneself understood, in short, of communicating, is to contain the charge of psychic energy within a formal pattern that has initially and psychologically been introduced as a way of *preventing* an uninhibited charge of energy. This process may cost much. A slavish obedience to form for form's sake is of course debilitating and unrewarding. But the tension set up by form and texture leads to articulation and then to containment of the basic energy drives that have existed initially inarticulate and without form. Ernst Kris has given us a very interesting discussion of what he calls "stringencies," a term he uses to define external restraints put upon expression in art.

The level of stringency in works of art—their degree of interpretability—varies markedly from period to period. In some cases ambiguity is fully exploited, and correspondingly great demands are made on the audience; in other cases, there is no more ambiguity than is involved in the work's being aesthetic at all; the demands on the audience are minimal; the interpretations called for are rigidly limited. We may suggest that art is likely to be characterized by low stringency (i.e., high ambiguity and interpretability) where systems of conduct or ideals are in doubt or social values are in process of transition.[4]

This is true especially when those aspects of form which define the thing contained while in the act of containing it no longer serve the ego adequately, whether because they have weakened through an excess of abstraction (the definitions no longer define), or because they have become too arbitrarily fixed (the definitions are too remote from the particulars they are supposed to contain). We may say that any form is the result of a series of accidents. As in any situation where balance serves to make energy intelligible, form in literature is the consequence of the need to compromise with energy by limiting it and allowing it exercise in terms of particular tensions.

Our final discussion of form in literature is by way of transition to its relationship with language and meaning. The major instruments which the ego possesses for the purpose of containing energy are time, space, convention, and logic. The id possesses none of these. They are the means of locating psychic energy within the focus of reality. Each of them is both specific and ambiguous. In simplest terms each arrests energy by shaping it, or shapes it in the act of arresting it. If we could imagine the id with a time sense at all, it would be a future sense—that is, the drive toward total gratification is pure future, and leads, if not inhibited, to death. The ego's function is to arrest future by means of past, to make the present moment a unity of past and future. The result of this process is to slow down the drive toward death; and in consequence, moments are realized and both addition and formal patterns of time are constructed. Similarly, the ego gives spatial concepts to the energy discharge; in the matter of time and space both, the ego localizes, forces the psychic energy into an awareness of *milieu*. Milieu itself is a product of objective temporal and spatial situations. Freud's elaborate discussions of the familial origins and progress of societies should concern us here, but they will have only to be assumed.[5] It may be of some interest here to point to the range of psychoanalytic evaluations of milieu. Freud's is hypothetical, but only in the sense of generalizing historically from proven recurrences; a family-centered milieu is in Freud's case derived from clinical practices, the interpretation based upon inferences from personal cases. I think that here we may see the source of what we may call "family-centered literature," in which formal controls are defined in terms of manners (for instance, *Buddenbrooks* and *The Magic Mountain*). Jung's milieu, though also an inference from a kind of therapeutic procedure, is nevertheless extremely wide in its range of descriptive implication. Neither conception of milieu is especially noted for its relationship to contemporary social or societal fact, a fact that other analysts are eager to assert. The literary implications of both Freud's and Jung's views are allied with universals, but Freud's universals are at least easier to associate with the particulars at their source. To continue with the discussion of the four terms, convention is a form of the human history of time and space as inhibiting factors. It is the most flexible, the least firm of all the forms of awareness which the ego uses to arrest the progress toward uninhibited gratification. Nevertheless, it may achieve great significance in literature. There is often a close link of social and moral convention with literary form. Convention is the social logic of literary usage. Logic itself is the final restriction imposed upon the psychic energy expressed in the id. There are basic logical principles common to an external world from which the ego draws its reserves of inhibition. These principles are largely either negating or qualifying; that is, they exclude (if this, then not this), or negate (not this), or prescribe (this and not this). Every grammatical detail is an index, a sign, of the inhibition which anticipates form; but as such it may also be a clue to the aesthetic means of articulating psychic balance.

In so arbitrarily stating the formal conditions of inhibition, I have tried to set the stage for the final phase of my discussion. I should maintain that ambiguity, word-play, and what Philip Wheelwright has called "plurisignation" are primarily a part of the process constantly occurring in the psyche which seeks to achieve an articulate balance of tensions between desire and preservation. The id is neither logical nor illogical; it is prelogical until it comes in contact with the ego or the ego with it. After that it acquires the devices of logic but makes them serve its own purposes. The *balance* in literature between the logical and the contradictory, between single and multiple meanings, is the substance of the very lively tension existing and verbalized between energy and form. Freud's description of the dream work is now so well known that I don't need to give it in detail; chapter seven of *The Interpretation of Dreams* is its initial formulation, and there are many explanations of it, by Freud and by others. I should like to infer from them what seems to me a statement important to literary criticism: every ambiguity purposefully introduced into literature is in one way or another a compromise between uninhibited energy and extreme formal inhibition. It is impossible to decide the ideal degree of ambiguity, but one may, I think, assume that the forms of ambiguity reflect both degrees of tension and conditions of balance within the psyche. There are levels, of course, of sophistication. In children there is a fairly free play of wish and inhibition, contained within a limited number of metaphorical possibilities. Alice is after all Lewis Carroll's Alice and not Alice's. James's Maisie assumes the complexities of adulthood by necessity. In a great majority of adults the containment of energy is achieved in a relatively small number of rather abstract, though sentimentally overcharged, figures. The kinds of paradox and irony achieved by Donne, Marvell, Herbert, and others represent a highly endowed sense of the ambiguities residing in such tensions. Indeed, in the case of Donne the figures employed to express them reach a very high level of complexity, the purpose of which is both to individualize desire and to give it a degree of sophistication. The ambiguities resulting may be said to come partly from a genuine appreciation of human corruptibility (both moral and physical), partly from a wish to defend desire by means of defying those who would cynically dismiss it, partly from contemporary religious and metaphysical resources for transcendence. Such paradox is a result of the need both to admit a truth and at the same time to use available forms of transcendence in order to deny it; the admission and the denial are fused. Corruption becomes death, but death is contained within forms so successful in negating physical death that it triumphs over cynicism ("Only our love hath no decay," "The Anniversarie," l. 7). Similarly, the paradox of time and eternity may function within a poem; necessities forced upon us by time are denied by transforming the temporal into aspects of eternity. Yet the limits set by time (by which we narrowly view the corruption of the body as it "matures") are in themselves contained within the image of eternity; indeed, were it not for time, we should not *have* eternity. The complex nature of much religious poetry probably results from the interrelationship in each of us between our sense of physical instability and our desire for immortality; as for the latter, each of us has his own variant of it. Immortality is the ultimate formalization of desire; we continue to desire but come to realize that if we persist we shall die. To wish immortality is to hope for a removal of the reality principle, with a considerable gain in refinement of the pleasure principle. In the poetry of Laforgue and Corbière there is occasionally an attempt to set up ideally foreshortened versions of the id and either to satirize them ("Epitaphe") or to use them ("Locations des Pierrots") as a means of satirizing, not the fact of ego-control in itself, but the prevailing accepted forms of control. Satire usually protests against the contemporary ways used by the ego to inhibit. In surrealism, and occasionally in the work of Rimbaud, there is an attempt to represent the id pure—or at least to allow the manifest dream content a free display—with the result that the literature describes not a balance of tension but merely the consequence of a superficial exposure of wish to the idiom of ego.

The greatest range and the finest subtlety of all language exchanges based upon this principle of energy conflict and conservation are found in those types of communication described so brilliantly by Philip Wheelwright, in *The Burning Fountain,* as forms of "expressive language." I should like to use one or two of these, with the apology that I shall shift their context, perhaps even radically, from that of his intention. Mr. Wheelwright defines what he calls the "principle of plurisignation" as meaning "that an expressive symbol tends, on any given occasion of its realization, to carry more than one legitimate reference, in such a way that its proper meaning is a tension between two or more directions of semantic stress." [6] That is, in terms I have chosen to explain it, that the language of the symbol retains the charge and tension of its psychic origins, or of the dynamic shifts and exchanges of the energy which it was before the state was articulated. The many possibilities of stress, of direction, of painful thrust and arrest, are here echoed in the multiplications of meaning within a given image, metaphor, or cluster of images. This symbolic maneuver is accessible to a great variety of strategies: the poet may wish to exploit the irony he sees in his state of acceptance-rejection (that is, he may accept only ostensibly, or reject only ostensibly, but he ironically juxtaposes both acceptance and rejection in his language). I believe we may say that Eliot both accepts and rejects. He sees as well the pathetic consequences of pure acceptance or of pure rejection. Herein lies the almost too easy irony of some of his poems. The polarities are perhaps too neatly obvious; and the deficiencies of both Prufrock and Sweeney are too much derived from circumstances that forbid transcendence. Eliot's great admiration of Dante seems to me to have come from his recognizing in Dante a means of escaping from the dead ends of Prufrock and Sweeney, as well as from the forbidding milieu responsible for them. The *Paradiso* is prefigured in the *Inferno;* a terrestrial inferno, such as Eliot describes in the early poems, can suggest a purgatory and a heaven only by an act of daring transcendence, an act which of course Eliot attempted. Or the poet may wish to express the tragedy of acceptance which lies in its inevitability (that is, acceptance of control is most unwished for but not in the least uncalled for); or he may extend the ambiguity to such an extent that it makes a virtue of transcendence (the effort to create a viable mystic exchange out of a condition of stasis, behavioral or mechanical).

Mr. Wheelwright speaks also of what he calls the "principle of paralogical dimensionality," by which he wishes to suggest "that there are other dimensions or *nodi* of meaning than those of logical universality and existential particularity. . . ." [7] The logical dimension is presumably that which restricts and limits within the strict terms of discernible reality. But, as I see it, this dimension is indispensable as a beginning; one must see what a thing is before he determines the scope and degree of its not being or of its being more. The co-ordinates of reality and desire are first set up, with such dimensional angularity as we are prosaically accustomed to use. The "paralogical dimensionality" of expressive language, as Mr. Wheelwright puts it, is nourished by the dissatisfactions accumulating from this initial effort at compromise. As the dream work refuses to accept either-or, the language of the poet suggests a multiple of meanings from a state of tension. There are several ways in which such a state may be true (effectual, "healthful," conducive of peace), several in which it may be false. These variants are all contained within the single linguistic or metaphoric representation of a state of balanced tension.

Finally, one must consider the problem of associating the most intricate of literary expressions with Jung's archetypes. The access to myth in recent criticism is at least partly a product of research, or of a quest of mythical surrogates for displaced symbols. The elaborate structure provided by Jung for the purpose of linking individual present with collective past is useful only in that it suggests the extremes to which the imagination may go in generalizing immediate necessities and experiences. But archetypes, beyond the service they perform in cataloguing and arranging, are actually the most inflexible of forms. They may, in fact, arrest the process of articulating psychic tensions and they may oversimplify the results. Whatever one may say by way of crediting Jung's ingenuity and the vigor of his imagination, the archetypal process, by enlarging and depersonalizing the expressive experience, threatens to destroy both its individuality and its complexity. The appeal to literature and to literary criticism of Jung's archaic forms and residues is, of course, phenomenally great; and it is necessary to explain just what the archetype does to the act of literary creation.

First, the process of verbalizing, of constructing linguistic expressions of any psycho-dynamic state follows along the lines of its own logic. This is not a transcendent logic; it is as complex as the circumstances require and permit. Within the limits seen and set by Freud, transcendence of the actual condition set up by psychic tensions and balances always remains closely associated with them and takes on their quality. Metaphors used to define such states are always individualized according to terms set down by the experiences determined by them.

It follows that the particularities of psychic experiences lend themselves to the act of universalizing. But the universals follow from a commonalty of basic experience, or of basic sources from which the secondary qualities of experience are drawn. To the degree that they may form clusters about a static symbol, they may be called archetypes. The danger is that one will abandon the particular for the archetypical. Once an experience is defined as "shared archetype," its particulars are threatened by dismissal. This indeed is often Jung's therapeutic aim, as I see it.

The advantages of Jung's archetypal portrayal of the collective psyche for literary criticism come primarily from its being available to an almost infinite range of spectacular inference. If poets unconsciously share archetypal interests, and if critics can bring themselves to commune with poets in the sharing, then the lines of tradition, of a discernible past discernibly associated with a felt present, are blurred. There is a great difference between a tradition of the ritual observance of a fixed symbolic and mythical pattern and the direct, knowledgeable, ingenious, overt *use* of myth in modern literature. To explain present literary circumstance by reference to archetypal patterns is to ignore the peculiarities of present practice and need. To say that basically we are linked to the past by archetypal means is to describe falsely the particular nature of our hunger for transcendence. The desire for credible and trustworthy universals is after all, and peculiarly, a feature of our contemporary behavior. It is not that the *desire* is unique, but that its special properties are. In rationally undermining the foundations of our past belief, we have put ourselves in an especially compromising position. We do not submit to any archetypes entirely, but we do love to entertain all of them, as poetic means and as mythical experiences that are half real and half merely "curious."

This peculiarity of our modern circumstance is especially well served by Jung, who serves artists by rescuing them from an unflattering Freudian diagnosis and giving them the role of seer, prophetic bard, guardian of the temple, neighbor of the mystic. Such a characterization makes any analysis of the literary process such as I have sketched impractical and unnecessary. Inspiration is no longer available to psychological explanation, or at least psychological or indeed any other kind of explanation is unnecessary to it. Jung's elaborate system has tried, therefore, to satisfy a great hunger for transcendence. Transcendence, however, is difficult. Jung has tried to make of it a therapeutic necessity, the extreme of psychiatric indulgence. The language of Jung's discourses moves further and further from Freud's cautions; the psychoanalyst becomes priest, "godlike demon," dispenser of posi-tive power, caretaker of archetypes.

To conclude, Freud's meticulously correct choreography of the unconscious maintains the advantages of its discretion. Language in all of its scope of meanings and half-meanings and super-meanings may fit into his remarkable analysis of the psychic economy. The ambiguities of our language are the push-and-pull of our intelligence, alternating between residence in the id and regretful acceptance of the ego. While we may find types of identity with the past, we are not what we were some thousands of years ago; however tempting it is to suggest archetypal identifications, our psychic peculiarities are in the end available only to the sober testimony of sys-tematic investigation. To say otherwise is to ignore both the dilemma and the specific intelligence of our times.

NOTES

1. *The Ego and the Id* (London, 1927), pp. 29–30.
2. *Ibid.,* pp. 81–82.
3. Ernst Kris, *Psychoanalytic Explorations in Art* (New York, 1952), pp. 253–254.
4. *Ibid.,* p. 262.
5. See *Totem and Taboo, The Ego and the Id, Moses and Monotheism.* See especially Herbert Marcuse, *Eros and Civilization* (Boston, 1955).
6. Philip Wheelwright, *The Burning Fountain* (Bloomington, Indiana, 1954), p. 61.
7. *Ibid.,* p. 64.

The Oedipus Trilogy

by *MARK KANZER*

Mark Kanzer, M.D., a busy practicing psychoanalyst in New York City and an active member of the American Psychoanalytic Association, has also produced a number of literary studies dealing with Shakespeare and Dostoevsky, among others, in addition to Sophocles, on whose plays he has written two other papers as well. The present study, published in 1950 in *Psychoanalytic Quarterly* (XIX, 4, 561–572), is as valuable for the student of literature as it is for the professional psychoanalyst. Its greatest merit is its comprehensive overview of the three plays. They did not, of course, constitute a trilogy in the way that the *Oresteia* of Aeschylus constituted a trilogy, all written at the same time, to be produced at the same festival. The *Antigone,* the last play in the chronology of the trilogy, seems to have been written first, in Sophocles' middle age, *Oedipus the King* in his most mature years, and *Oedipus at Colonus* in his great old age. Yet Dr. Kanzer has succeeded in integrating the three plays in a way which no other critic seems to have attempted.

IN Sophocles' drama *Oedipus Tyrannus* Freud found support for his concept that the drives to kill the father and commit incest with the mother constitute the basic repressed wishes of men.[1] The term, oedipus, thus became momentously linked with the complex which Freud found dominating the stage of phallic libidinal development. He cited the passage from the play which states the frequency of incestuous dreams among men, and compared the action of the tragedy to the processes of psychoanalytic investigation. In the "riddle of the Sphinx," which Oedipus solves, Freud saw the perpetual search of the child for sexual information, thereby elucidating this age-old enigma.

In the ample literature on the oedipus complex, the trilogy of Sophocles has often been used to confirm or dispute Freud's discoveries. Among those who explored the Greek legend were Ferenczi,[2] Jung,[3] Reik,[4] Abraham,[5] and Róheim.[6] Rank, after valuable initial researches in support of Freud,[7] evolved his own theories of psychodynamics and used them for a reinterpretation of the Oedipus dramas.[8] Fromm has discussed the plays in terms of their sociological background and has also arrived at conclusions different from Freud's.[9]

A review of the psychoanalytic literature on the Oedipus trilogy has been published by Mullahy,[10] but it is strangely incomplete, failing to take note of the writings of Ferenczi, Reik, Abraham, and Róheim on this subject. A reading of the plays also reveals much material that has not yet been evaluated psychoanalytically. The intrinsic interest of the dramas as psychological and sociological documents, and the special role which must be accorded them in the history of psychoanalysis, make them worthy of detailed study.

I

Oedipus Tyrannus, the first drama of the trilogy, presents the hero-king of the Thebans confronted with a plague which has afflicted his land. A messenger sent to consult the oracles to determine the cause of this catastrophe returns with word that the unknown criminal who killed the land's former king, Laius, must be discovered and brought to justice if the plague is to cease. It is in the search for this evildoer that the history of Oedipus' misdeeds comes to light. He had been unconsciously guilty of killing his father and wedding his mother. In so doing, he fulfilled prophecies made before his birth which he and his parents vainly sought to avert, a detail which corresponds to the fact that each man is destined

to struggle against his oedipal strivings. At the end of the
drama, Jocasta, the queen and mother-wife, hangs herself,
whereupon Oedipus tears out his own eyes (interpreted by
Ferenczi as symbolic castration).

In the course of the developments which lead to this tragic
climax, we learn that Oedipus has won the throne and the
widowed queen of Laius by solving the riddle of the Sphinx.
This monstrous creature, whose upper portion is a human
female and whose lower parts are those of a lioness, sat upon
a rock and questioned all passers-by, slaying those who could
not solve the problem she propounded. Only Oedipus understood the riddle. According to the version of the legend used
by Sophocles, he then slew her; according to another, she
threw herself in mortification into the sea and was killed.

The riddle of the Sphinx is evidently an allegory of the
problems presented by female sexuality. A full-breasted
woman above, a lioness below, she combines the beloved and
dreaded aspects of femininity which the boy must reconcile
in order to achieve genital potency. Freud emphasized the
relationship of the Sphinx to the mysteries of childbirth.[11]
The legend of Oedipus and the monster also belongs among
many others—Perseus and the Gorgon, Theseus and the
Minotaur, the countless legends of the dragon-slayers—which
symbolically depict the dangers that the young man must
overcome before he may attain his sexual partner. In these
menacing antagonists, components of both parents may be
detected: the father, who would keep the son from women,
and the mother, whose very fulfillment of sexual desires
would bring disaster. The Sphinx is such a combined parental figure. Jung saw in her the "terrible mother"; Rank,
Reik, and Róheim have described her variously as the phallic
mother, the symbol of the parents in intercourse, or as a
disguised homosexual representation of the father. In the
riddle which she propounds, "What has first four legs, then
two, then three?", the correct answer being "Man" (during
the stage of maturation), there are apparent allusions to the
appearance of the limbs during intercourse, to the additional

"limb" which distinguished the male, and perhaps also to pregnancy: "that which is first two becomes three."

It is our conclusion, from a study of the play, that the precipitating cause, the "catastrophe which threatens the land" and leads to the undoing of Oedipus, is the pregnancy of the mother-wife, Jocasta. The birth of a son renews the father's oedipal conflicts. The drama states that a plague "blights the fruitful blossoms of the land" and causes the women to suffer "barren pangs." [12] The symbols of birth are represented through opposites—"sterile blossoms," "barren pangs," maternal death—the hostile and negating images corresponding to a neurotic denial of the actual event. Such reactions are appropriate to the child in the oedipal phase, anticipating the birth of a sibling, or to the expectant father who has not resolved his infantile fixations.

If this surmise as to Jocasta's impending delivery is correct, then we find that the Sphinx has re-emerged from the repressed with the old riddle in a new form: for if the *Oedipus Tyrannus* exposes clearly the parricidal drives of the son, it deals no less unambiguously with the counteroedipal determination of the father to rid himself of the rival son. Laius had sought as unsuccessfully to evade the foreordained parricide as had Oedipus, and had tried to kill his child in infancy. The great cycle of the generations thus completes itself with Oedipus as an expectant father who is destined to seek the destruction of the fruit of his wife's womb. The mature man is able to cope with paternity, but not the neurotic whose wife is also his mother. Oedipus never worked through the relationship to his father which is necessary for adjustment to reality. He never accepted him, never identified with him, as is necessary in superego formation, but merely encompassed his death. There was no identification with the parental role: in the hero the child was preserved unchanged. Oedipus, the arrogant, quick-tempered, arbitrary monarch accustomed to homage, incorporates the infantile fantasy of omnipotence.

Such immaturity must be reflected in the sexual relationship to the mother, and as to the details, a psychoanalytic interpretation of the play leaves little doubt. This mother is assuredly the full-breasted Sphinx, bestial and terrifying below the waist. The chorus refers to her as "the maiden with crooked talons who sang darkly," thus placing her in the category of the phallic mother, the woman with the dentate vagina, and all the other terrifying images of the castrating female. The "dark songs" are a link to the Sirens, dangerous seducers of men. In the relationship of Oedipus to Jocasta, there is no simple erotic drive, as Freud originally postulated, but also the anxieties and hostilities aroused by the preoedipal "bad mother." [13] In the great climax of the play, the sex act is depicted symbolically when the king rushes into the room where the body of the mother is hanging (the womb), seizes the golden brooches from her garments, and repeatedly and passionately stabs his eyeballs from which the blood flows "not with a few slow drops, but all at once in a dark shower." [14] In this fantasy of coitus and orgasm, the sexual act is depicted as a sadistic and castrating attack from the maternal phallus. The brooches of Jocasta are another version of the talons of the Sphinx; in the earlier and more successful encounter, Oedipus had taken the active role and had stabbed her with his sword.

The action of the play, as a whole, is a repetitious depiction of the duel between Oedipus and the Sphinx. In the presence of her true form, the mother, he again carries on a remorseless inquiry into his origin. The tormented queen, foreseeing the disastrous outcome, seeks vainly to divert him. Oedipus takes a peculiarly stubborn and obtuse attitude until the riddle of his birth is solved; then Jocasta kills herself, as had the Sphinx. The core of this mighty tragedy is the determined boy plying his reluctant mother with embarrassing questions.

The legend of the Sphinx casting herself into the sea is another familiar symbol of childbirth, a condensation of sexual surrender and pregnancy. Oedipus, emerging from the death room of the mother, blind, wailing, and helpless, presents an unmistakable representation of rebirth. The religions of the East are pervaded with the fantasy of the mystic identity of father and son. It is the father who enters the womb (funeral chamber) and the son who emerges in a repetitive cycle, as in the advent and the wane of the seasons. In this fantasy of rebirth, the neurotic father finds satisfaction. He averts the threat of the new rival by identifying with him and regressing to infancy. Oedipus, who took his father's place, will now take his son's. The past repeats itself when he is cast from the city by his uncle Creon, just as his father Laius had expelled him after he was born. His only companion and comforter in exile is to be his daughter, Antigone, who will take the place of the mother.

II

The two remaining plays of the Oedipus trilogy seek a more satisfactory solution to the problem of man's relationship to parents and children. Success can be achieved, we know, only by maturation of the ego, which devolves on the formation of the superego and abandonment of infantile fantasies of omnipotence.

The third drama of the trilogy, *Antigone,* was the first to be written, but belongs psychologically in an intermediate position. It deals with the civil war between Polyneices and Eteocles, sons of Oedipus, after his death, wherein both lost their lives. Antigone, their sister, and Creon, maternal uncle and king, are depicted at odds over the disposition of the corpse of Polyneices, which lies outside the city. Here Creon decrees that the body of the rebel shall remain unburied and unsanctified. Antigone defies these orders and inters her brother with her own hands. This is clearly a continuance of the oedipal theme. Polyneices, as Oedipus, finds no forgiveness from Creon, the father substitute. Antigone displaces her loyalty from her father to her brother.

Antigone is sentenced to death by Creon. She is to be shut

up in a stone vault [15] with a small quantity of food. After this judgment has been executed, Creon, disturbed by the pleas and resentment of his son Haemon, who was betrothed to Antigone, and by the warnings of the seer Tiresias, is moved to release his niece. When the tomb is opened, it is found that Antigone has hanged herself. Haemon, who had secretly found his way to her side, slays himself with his own sword. Creon, grief-stricken and penitent, emerges only to find that his wife, Eurydice, has killed herself upon hearing of the death of her son.

The tragic ending of Antigone and Haemon clearly repeats, almost in exact detail, the catastrophe of Jocasta and Oedipus. The Sphinx is thus thrice destroyed. The slayer now is Creon, a new guise for Oedipus. If, in the first play, the husband-king solves his conflict by identification with the newborn babe, in the second he achieves the alternate solution of identification with the father. He is now Creon, the banisher and destroyer of infants. He emerges from the tomb, reborn, while the sons—Haemon, Polyneices, and Eteocles—have all been destroyed.

Oedipus and Creon are complementary: the parricidal son, and the castrating father. Oedipus was rejected at birth by his father, Laius, and in his partial identification (superego) with him can become only a rejecting father. This is the problem inherent in the *Antigone*. It corresponds to a stage in the normal development of the superego in which the boy experiences hostility toward his father, and in retaliation through projection of his own aggression, fears castration by the father. It is the force of this castration anxiety, effecting the resolution of the oedipus complex, which is the unconscious content of the *Antigone*. The boy is faithful to his mother, conspiring with her against his father; but Creon triumphs over Antigone. The son, ashamed of his mother's weakness, thenceforth transfers allegiance to his father. The third play of the trilogy, *Oedipus at Colonus*,[16] is the consummation of this process. The relationship between son and father is not one-sidedly hostile, but has the elements of sympathy and love which are indispensable components of the superego.

This theme may be traced in the action of *Oedipus at Colonus*. The now aged hero, after years of bitter exile, arrives at Colonus where he is kindly received by the enlightened ruler, Theseus, with whose aid he defeats Creon's efforts to separate him from Antigone. Oedipus dies mysteriously, leaving his blessing and the custody of Antigone to his benevolent protector, Theseus, who inherits some strange and undescribed power from the grave of the hero. This unknown resting place of Oedipus is within Theseus himself.[17] He is the good father who shelters the son, and it is in this guise that Oedipus is finally presented: the superego, "which is the heir of the oedipus complex," [18] has completed its development in him. The tired exile has given up his battle against the taboos of mankind; his wounds and defeats have taught him to bow to the reality principle; he cannot stand alone but must accept his status as son, brother, and father among men. In the character of Theseus, he discovers the rewards for surrendering the infantile illusion of omnipotence. A king again, he is now a wise and benevolent ruler. The "custody" of Antigone which he achieves is the possession of the woman he loves, but without violating the social taboos which protect the wife and her children from the unrestrained passions of the Sphinx-killer.

Each play of the trilogy resolves a conflict by the symbolic rebirth of the hero. Oedipus, Creon, and Theseus are the successive avatars the maturing man must assume in his persisting endeavors to answer the riddle of the Sphinx.

III

The Oedipus trilogy is a product of Athenian culture, conceived in the mind of one of its most typical representatives, the dramatist Sophocles. The religious and political traditions of the city bore witness to a profound psychological conflict over adherence to male or female divinities. Studies of mythology and custom suggest that the goddesses had been the objects of ancient worship and had gradually been supplanted by male deities.[19] Typical were the legends about Athena, patroness of the great city, who was the daughter of Zeus, ruler of the gods, and had sprung fully grown from his forehead—symbolizing the intellectual superiority of the male. Her shield bore the head of Medusa, the Gorgon, whose terrible visage turned men to stone. Originally warlike, Athena became patroness of the domestic arts, of spinning and the cultivation of the olive, and was also a symbol of wisdom. The Gorgon-Athena, like the Sphinx, represented the destructive potentialities to the male of female sexuality, but after the triumph of men, she was shorn of her warlike attributes. The head of Medusa [20] on her shield is a remnant of her former power which is left to her, and is also the basis for the new order of things: it is the incest taboo which must be respected if the dangerous Sphinx is not to be reawakened in all her dreaded might.

Not only is the Oedipus legend a version of this revolution in the relations between men and women, but also such typical Athenian legends as the conquest of the Amazonian warriors by Theseus, who took their queen Hippolyta in marriage, and the tale of Orestes, the matricide, who received protection in the city after pursuit by the avenging female goddesses, the Furies. In the time of Sophocles, these myths appealed greatly to the imagination of the people and provided themes for many great plays and works of art of the age. It is noteworthy that in the dramas of Sophocles and his great contemporaries, Aeschylus and Euripides, these legends were used for probing into the moral relationships among men and women within the family and the state. The *Antigone,* for example, explores the conflict between love of family, as represented by Antigone, and duty to the government (Creon). Primary allegiance to the family is doomed with the death of Antigone; however, the ruler also learns that he must not be harsh and autocratic, and suffers personal injury when he fails to respect the ties within the family.

Bachofen,[21] reviewing the Greek myths, concluded that earlier matriarchal forms of society had existed and then yielded to masculine rule. This hypothesis seems reasonable but has little actual historical evidence. Such myths could also be accounted for on the basis of the experiences of each generation of men in giving up the ways of childhood, dominated by the relationship to the mother, and assuming the inevitable duties and responsibilities of adult masculinity. A more serious objection, however, must be made to a second hypothesis of Bachofen. He believed that in the matriarchy, maternal love and natural ties prevailed, while in the patriarchy there was stern authoritarianism. Evolution from matriarchy to patriarchy was brought about not by economic or military necessity, but by the triumph of masculine reasoning over feminine feeling. This theory, which bears the impress of the author's mid-Victorian background (his work appeared in 1861), is not substantiated by modern sociological observations.[22] In contrast may be cited the Trobriand matriarchy, where the men maintain friendly relations with each other but show fear and hostility toward women; or the polyandrous Marquesans,[23] whose dread of wild female spirits suggests the terror in which the Furies, Gorgons, and similar ferocious goddesses were held in Greece.

It is noteworthy that two psychological studies of the Oedipus trilogy,[24] which reproach Freud for lack of sociological orientation, lean heavily on the antiquated views of Bachofen. Rank, developing his thesis from his conception of the central significance of the birth trauma, sees in Oedipus the struggle of men to retain their individuality in the face of the demands made upon them to submit to the authority of the state. The individualist finds difficulty in accepting the role of father or son. This conflict was intensified during the Hellenic period of Greek history when patriarchy flourished. The incestuous element in the Oedipus myth is explained, not as a result of sexual attraction, but as an attempt to insure personal immortality by achieving psychological rebirth from the mother, thereby eliminating both father and son. Psychoanalytic interpretation arrives at some of the same conclusions but sees the struggle of the ego for mastery (Rank's goal of individualism) as inherently linked with infantile libidinal and aggressive aims.

Fromm's "sociological" approach to the oedipus is illustrated by his solution of the riddle of the Sphinx.[25] The question about the number of limbs, he maintains, has no significance except to elicit the answer, "Man." In this response, he sees the implication that the solution to the riddle of man is himself and that in the matriarchal state, represented by Oedipus, the dignity of man is more assured than in the patriarchy. This questionable assumption is rendered even more dubious by the fact that the Sphinx herself has a better claim to representing the matriarchy than has Oedipus,[26] who in overthrowing her begins the process of patriarchal dominance. The emotional and dramatic values of the plays most clearly show the limitations of Fromm's concept. It is difficult to believe that in the life and death encounter between Oedipus and the Sphinx, the monster was moved to throw herself into the sea by an exposition on sociology.

Psychological knowledge that reveals to us, as do the constructions of Freud, the intimate and hidden views of men of Athens two thousand years ago on childbirth, sexual intercourse, and family relationships, obviously provides tools of great value. What sidelights are thrown on the intangibles of history when we learn that phrases of Sophocles' Creon seem to have been borrowed from Pericles, contemporary ruler of Athens,[27] or that the crisis which precipitated the downfall of Oedipus—the plague that afflicted his state—presumably mirrored the anxieties and self-searchings of the Athenians after the outbreak of the disastrous Peloponnesian War! Social forces impinge upon and are transmuted into the idiom of individual experience. It is the unique contribution which psychoanalysis makes to sociology that it can illuminate and decipher this process. In this work of interpretation, the social elements are crystallized from the psychological, just as the events of the day emerge in new significance from the analysis of the dream. A valid psychology is the indispensable prerequisite for any "sociological approach" to such great human documents as the Oedipus trilogy.

The three plays dramatize three stages in the development and resolution of the oedipus complex. Oedipus, Creon, and Theseus represent the same character, but with increasingly successful maturation as he seeks to solve the riddle of the Sphinx—the monster that represents the challenge of sexuality.

NOTES

1. Sigmund Freud, *The Interpretation of Dreams* in *The Basic Writings of Sigmund Freud,* ed. A. A. Brill (New York, 1938), pp. 307–309.
2. Sandor Ferenczi, "Symbolic Representation of the Pleasure and Reality Principles in the Oedipus Myth," in *Contributions to Psychoanalysis* (Boston, 1916).
3. Carl Gustav Jung, *Wandlungen und Symbole der Libido* (Vienna, 1912).
4. Theodor Reik, "Oedipus und die Sphinx," *Imago,* VI, 1920, pp. 95–131.
5. Karl Abraham, "Zwei Beiträge zur Symbolforschung," *Imago,* IX, 1923, pp. 122–126.
6. Géza Róheim, *The Riddle of the Sphinx* (London, 1934); "Teiresias and Other Seers," *Psychoanalytic Review,* XXXIII, 1946, pp. 314–334.
7. Otto Rank, *Das Inzestmotiv in Dichtung und Sage* (Leipzig, 1912).
8. Otto Rank, *Modern Education* (New York, 1932).
9. Erich Fromm, "The Oedipus Complex and the Oedipus Myth," in *The Family: Its Function and Destiny,* ed. Ruth Nanda Anshen (New York, 1948).
10. Patrick Mullahy, *Oedipus—Myth and Complex* (New York, 1948).
11. Sigmund Freud, *Three Contributions to the Theory of Sex* in A. A. Brill, ed., *op. cit.,* p. 595.

12. Sophocles, *Oedipus the King* in *The Complete Greek Drama,* Vol. I, Whitney J. Oates and Eugene O'Neill, Jr. eds. (New York, 1938).

13. Melanie Klein, "Early Stages of the Oedipus Conflict" (1928) in *Contributions to Psychoanalysis, 1921–1945* (London, 1948).

14. Sophocles, *Oedipus the King,* in Whitney J. Oates and Eugene O'Neill, Jr., eds., *op. cit.*

15. Sophocles, *Antigone, ibid.*

16. Sophocles, *Oedipus at Colonus, ibid.*

17. Mark Kanzer, "The Passing of the Oedipus Complex in Greek Drama," *International Journal of Psychoanalysis,* XXIX, 1948, pp. 131–134.

18. Sigmund Freud, *The Ego and the Id* (1923) (London, 1935).

19. Bernice Schultz Engle, "The Amazons in Ancient Greece," *The Psychoanalytic Quarterly,* XI, 1942, pp. 512–554.

20. Sigmund Freud, *New Introductory Lectures on Psychoanalysis* (New York, 1933), p. 38.

21. Johann Jakob Bachofen, *Mutterrecht und Urreligion* (1861) (Leipzig, 1926).

22. Cf. Gregory Zilboorg, "Masculine and Feminine," *Psychiatry,* VII, 1944, 257–296.

23. Abram Kardiner, *The Individual and His Society* (New York, 1939).

24. Erich Fromm, *op. cit.;* Otto Rank, *Modern Education, op. cit.*

25. Erich Fromm, *ibid.*

26. Theodor Reik, *op. cit.*

27. "Sophocles," *Encyclopedia Britannica,* 11th edition, Vols. 25–26.

The Theme of the Three Caskets

by SIGMUND FREUD

Whatever peculiar notions Freud may have had about the authorship of the plays, there is no doubt about his deep devotion to Shakespeare. His writings about literature and the arts were voluminous, as Louis Fraiberg has shown in his "Freud's Writings on Art," first published in *Literature and Psychology* (VI, 4, 116–130), and now the first chapter in his *Psychoanalysis and American Literary Criticism* (Detroit, 1961). The present study, which, it should be noted, contains interpretation based on *King Lear* as well as on *The Merchant of Venice,* was probably first conceived in 1912 and was published in German in *Imago* in 1913 (II, 3, 257–266). It was first translated into English in 1925.

I

Two scenes from Shakespeare, one from a comedy and the other from a tragedy, have lately given me occasion for posing and solving a small problem.

The first of these scenes is the suitors' choice between the three caskets in *The Merchant of Venice*. The fair and wise Portia is bound at her father's bidding to take as her husband only that one of her suitors who chooses the right casket from among the three before him. The three caskets are of gold, silver and lead: the right casket is the one that contains her portrait. Two suitors have already departed unsuccessful: they have chosen gold and silver. Bassanio, the third, decides in favour of lead; thereby he wins the bride, whose affection was already his before the trial of fortune. Each of the suitors gives reasons for his choice in a speech in which he praises the metal he prefers and depreciates the other two. The most difficult task thus falls to the share of the fortunate third suitor; what he finds to say in glorification of lead as against gold and silver is little and has a forced ring. If in psychoanalytic practice we were confronted with such a speech, we should suspect that there were concealed motives behind the unsatisfying reasons produced.

Shakespeare did not himself invent this oracle of the choice of a casket; he took it from a tale in the *Gesta Romanorum,*[1] in which a girl has to make the same choice to win the Emperor's son.[2] Here too the third metal, lead, is the bringer of fortune. It is not hard to guess that we have here an ancient theme, which requires to be interpreted, accounted for and traced back to its origin. A first conjecture as to the meaning of this choice between gold, silver and lead is quickly confirmed by a statement of Stucken's,[3] who has made a study of the same material over a wide field. He writes: "The identity of Portia's three suitors is clear from their choice: the Prince of Morocco chooses the gold casket —he is the sun; the Prince of Arragon chooses the silver casket—he is the moon; Bassanio chooses the leaden casket— he is the star youth." In support of this explanation he cites an episode from the Estonian folk-epic *Kalewipoeg,* in which the three suitors appear undisguisedly as the sun, moon and star youths (the last being "the Pole-star's eldest boy") and once again the bride falls to the lot of the third.

Thus our little problem has led us to an astral myth! The only pity is that with this explanation we are not at the end of the matter. The question is not exhausted, for we do not share the belief of some investigators that myths were read in the heavens and brought down to earth; we are more inclined to judge with Otto Rank [4] that they were projected onto the heavens after having arisen elsewhere under purely human conditions. It is in this human content that our interest lies.

Let us look once more at our material. In the Estonian epic, just as in the tale from the *Gesta Romanorum,* the sub-

ject is a girl choosing between three suitors; in the scene
from *The Merchant of Venice* the subject is apparently the
same, but at the same time something appears in it that is in
the nature of an inversion of the theme: a *man* chooses between three—caskets. If what we were concerned with were
a dream, it would occur to us at once that caskets are also
women, symbols of what is essential in woman, and therefore
of a woman herself—like coffers, boxes, cases, baskets and so
on.[5] If we boldly assume that there are symbolic substitu-
tions of the same kind in myths as well, then the casket scene
in *The Merchant of Venice* really becomes the inversion we
suspected. With a wave of the wand, as though we were in a
fairy tale, we have stripped the astral garment from our
theme; and now we see that the theme is a human one, *a
man's choice between three women.*

This same content, however, is to be found in another
scene of Shakespeare's, in one of his most powerfully moving
dramas; not the choice of a bride this time, yet linked by
many hidden similarities to the choice of the casket in *The
Merchant of Venice.* The old King Lear resolves to divide
his kingdom while he is still alive among his three daughters,
in proportion to the amount of love that each of them expresses for him. The two elder ones, Goneril and Regan,
exhaust themselves in asseverations and laudations of their
love for him; the third, Cordelia, refuses to do so. He should
have recognized the unassuming, speechless love of his third
daughter and rewarded it, but he does not recognize it. He
disowns Cordelia, and divides the kingdom between the
other two, to his own and the general ruin. Is not this once
more the scene of a choice between three women, of whom
the youngest is the best, the most excellent one?

There will at once occur to us other scenes from myths,
fairy tales and literature, with the same situation as their
content. The shepherd Paris has to choose between three
goddesses, of whom he declared the third to be the most
beautiful. Cinderella, again, is a youngest daughter, who is
preferred by the prince to her two elder sisters. Psyche, in

Apuleius's story, is the youngest and fairest of three sisters. Psyche is, on the one hand, revered as Aphrodite in human form; on the other, she is treated by that goddess as Cinderella was treated by her stepmother and is set the task of sorting a heap of mixed seeds, which she accomplishes with the help of small creatures (doves in the case of Cinderella, ants in the case of Psyche).[6] Anyone who cared to make a wider survey of the material would undoubtedly discover other versions of the same theme preserving the same essential features.

Let us be content with Cordelia, Aphrodite, Cinderella and Psyche. In all the stories the three women, of whom the third is the most excellent one, must surely be regarded as in some way alike if they are represented as sisters. (We must not be led astray by the fact that Lear's choice is between three *daughters;* this may mean nothing more than that he has to be represented as an old man. An old man cannot very well choose between three women in any other way. Thus they become his daughters.)

But who are these three sisters and why must the choice fall on the third? If we could answer this question, we should be in possession of the interpretation we are seeking. We have once already made use of an application of psychoanalytic technique, when we explained the three caskets symbolically as three women. If we have the courage to proceed in the same way, we shall be setting foot on a path which will lead us first to something unexpected and incomprehensible, but which will perhaps, by a devious route, bring us to a goal.

It must strike us that this excellent third woman has in several instances certain peculiar qualities besides her beauty. They are qualities that seem to be tending towards some kind of unity; we must certainly not expect to find them equally well marked in every example. Cordelia makes herself unrecognizable, inconspicuous like lead, she remains dumb, she "loves and is silent." [7] Cinderella hides so that she cannot be found. We may perhaps be allowed to equate concealment and dumbness. These would of course be only two instances out of the five we have picked out. But there is an intimation of the same thing to be found, curiously enough, in two other cases. We have decided to compare Cordelia, with her obstinate refusal, to lead. In Bassanio's short speech while he is choosing the casket, he says of lead (without in any way leading up to the remark):

> Thy paleness moves me more than eloquence.[8]

That is to say: "Thy plainness moves me more than the blatant nature of the other two." Gold and silver are "loud"; lead is dumb—in fact like Cordelia, who "loves and is silent." [9]

In the ancient Greek accounts of the Judgement of Paris, nothing is said of any such reticence on the part of Aphrodite. Each of the three goddesses speaks to the youth and tries to win him by promises. But, oddly enough, in a quite modern handling of the same scene this characteristic of the third one which has struck us makes its appearance again. In the libretto of Offenbach's *La Belle Hélène*, Paris, after telling of the solicitations of the other two goddesses, describes Aphrodite's behaviour in this competition for the beauty-prize:

> La troisième, ah! la troisième . . .
> La troisième ne dit rien.
> Elle eut le prix tout de même . . .[10]

If we decide to regard the peculiarities of our "third one" as concentrated in her "dumbness," then psychoanalysis will tell us that in dreams dumbness is a common representation of death.[11]

More than ten years ago a highly intelligent man told me a dream which he wanted to use as evidence of the telepathic nature of dreams. In it he saw an absent friend from whom he had received no news for a very long time, and reproached him energetically for his silence. The friend made no reply. It afterwards turned out that he had met his death by suicide at about the time of the dream. Let us leave the problem of telepathy on one side: [12] there seems, however, not to be any doubt that here the dumbness in the dream represented death. Hiding and being unfindable—a thing which confronts the prince in the fairy tale of Cinderella three times, is another unmistakable symbol of death in dreams; so, too, is a marked pallor, of which the "paleness" of the lead in one reading of Shakespeare's text is a reminder.[13] It would be very much easier for us to transpose these interpretations from the language of dreams to the mode of expression used in the myth that is now under consideration if we could make it seem probable that dumbness must be interpreted as a sign of being dead in productions other than dreams.

At this point I will single out the ninth story in Grimm's *Fairy Tales*, which bears the title "The Twelve Brothers." [14] A king and a queen have twelve children, all boys. The king declares that if the thirteenth child is a girl, the boys will have to die. In expectation of her birth he has twelve coffins made. With their mother's help the twelve sons take refuge in a hidden wood, and swear death to any girl they may meet. A girl is born, grows up, and learns one day from her mother that she has had twelve brothers. She decides to seek them out, and in the wood she finds the youngest; he recognizes her, but is anxious to hide her on account of the brothers' oath. The sister says: "I will gladly die, if by so doing I can save my twelve brothers." The brothers welcome her affectionately, however, and she stays with them and looks after their house for them. In a little garden beside the house grow twelve lilies. The girl picks them and gives one to each brother. At that moment the brothers are changed into ravens, and disappear, together with the house and garden. (Ravens are spirit-birds; the killing of the twelve brothers by their sister is represented by the picking of the flowers, just as it is at the beginning of the story by the coffins and the disappearance of the brothers.) The girl, who is once more ready to save her brothers from death, is now told that as a condition she must be dumb for seven years, and not speak a single word. She submits to the test, which brings her herself into mortal danger. She herself, that is, dies for her brothers, as she promised to do before she met them. By remaining dumb she succeeds at last in setting the ravens free.

In the story of "The Six Swans" [15] the brothers who are changed into birds are set free in exactly the same way—they are restored to life by their sister's dumbness. The girl has made a firm resolve to free her brothers, "even if it should cost her her life"; and once again (being the wife of the king) she risks her own life because she refuses to give up her dumbness in order to defend herself against evil accusations.

It would certainly be possible to collect further evidence from fairy tales that dumbness is to be understood as representing death. These indications would lead us to conclude that the third one of the sisters between whom the choice is made is a dead woman. But she may be something else as well—namely, Death itself, the Goddess of Death. Thanks to a displacement that is far from infrequent, the qualities that a deity imparts to men are ascribed to the deity himself. Such a displacement will surprise us least of all in relation to the Goddess of Death, since in modern versions and representations, which these stories would thus be forestalling, Death itself is nothing other than a dead man.

But if the third of the sisters is the Goddess of Death, the sisters are known to us. They are the Fates, the Moerae, the Parcae or the Norns, the third of whom is called Atropos, the inexorable.

II

We will for the time being put aside the task of inserting the interpretation that we have found into our myth, and listen to what the mythologists have to teach us about the role and origin of the Fates.[16]

The earliest Greek mythology (in Homer) only knew a single Μοῖρα, personifying inevitable fate. The further development of this one Moera into a company of three (or less often two) sister-goddesses probably came about on the basis of other divine figures to which the Moerae were closely related—the Graces and the Horae [the Seasons].

The Horae were originally goddesses of the waters of the sky, dispensing rain and dew, and of the clouds from which rain falls; and, since the clouds were conceived of as something that has been spun, it came about that these goddesses were looked upon as spinners, an attribute that then became attached to the Moerae. In the sun-favoured Mediterranean lands it is the rain on which the fertility of the soil depends, and thus the Horae became vegetation goddesses. The beauty of flowers and the abundance of fruit were their doing, and they were accredited with a wealth of agreeable and charming traits. They became the divine representatives of the Seasons, and it is possibly owing to this connection that there were three of them, if the sacred nature of the number three is not a sufficient explanation. For the peoples of antiquity at first distinguished only three seasons: winter, spring and summer. Autumn was only added in late Graeco-Roman times, after which the Horae were often represented in art as four in number.

The Horae retained their relation to time. Later they presided over the times of day, as they did at first over the times of the year; and at last their name came to be merely a designation of the hours (*heure, ora*). The Norns of German mythology are akin to the Horae and the Moerae and exhibit this time-signification in their names.[17] It was inevitable, however, that a deeper view should come to be taken of the essential nature of these deities, and that their essence should be transposed on to the regularity with which the seasons change. The Horae thus became the guardians of natural law and of the divine Order which causes the same thing to recur in Nature in an unalterable sequence.

This discovery of Nature reacted on the conception of human life. The nature-myth changed into a human myth: the Weather-goddesses became goddesses of Fate. But this aspect of the Horae found expression only in the Moerae, who watch over the necessary ordering of human life as inexorably as do the Horae over the regular order of nature. The ineluctable severity of law and its relation to death and dissolution, which had been avoided in the charming figures of the Horae, were now stamped upon the Moerae, as though men had only perceived the full seriousness of natural law when they had to submit their own selves to it.

The names of the three spinners, too, have been significantly explained by mythologists. Lachesis, the name of the second, seems to denote "the accidental that is included in the regularity of destiny" [18]—or, as we should say, "experience"; just as Atropos stands for "the ineluctable"—Death. Clotho would then be left to mean the innate disposition with its fateful implications.

But now it is time to return to the theme which we are trying to interpret—the theme of the choice between three sisters. We shall be deeply disappointed to discover how unintelligible the situations under review become and what contradictions of their apparent content result, if we apply to them the interpretation that we have found. On our supposition the third of the sisters is the Goddess of Death, Death itself. But in the Judgement of Paris she is the Goddess of Love, in the tale of Apuleius she is someone comparable to the goddess for her beauty, in *The Merchant of Venice* she is the fairest and wisest of women, in *King Lear* she is the one loyal daughter. We may ask whether there can be a more complete contradiction. Perhaps, improbable though it may seem, there is a still more complete one lying close at hand. Indeed, there certainly is; since, whenever our theme occurs, the choice between the women is free, and yet it falls on death. For, after all, no one chooses death, and it is only by a fatality that one falls a victim to it.

However, contradictions of a certain kind—replacements by the precise opposite—offer no serious difficulty to the work of analytic interpretation. We shall not appeal here to the fact that contraries are so often represented by one and the same element in the modes of expression used by the unconscious, as for instance in dreams.[19] But we shall remember that there are motive forces in mental life which bring about replacement by the opposite in the form of what is known as reaction-formation; and it is precisely in the revelation of such hidden forces as these that we look for the reward of this enquiry. The Moerae were created as a result of a discovery that warned man that he too is a part of nature and therefore subject to the immutable law of death. Something in man was bound to struggle against this subjection, for it is only with extreme unwillingness that he gives up his claim to an exceptional position. Man, as we know, makes use of his imaginative activity in order to satisfy the wishes that reality does not satisfy. So his imagination rebelled against the recognition of the truth embodied in the myth of the Moerae, and constructed instead the myth derived from it, in which the Goddess of Death was replaced by the Goddess of Love and by what was equivalent to her in human shape. The third of the sisters was no longer Death; she was the fairest, best, most desirable and most lovable of women. Nor was this substitution in any way technically difficult: it was prepared for by an ancient ambivalence, it was carried out along a primaeval line of connection which could not long have been forgotten. The Goddess of Love herself, who now took the place of the Goddess of Death, had once been identical with her. Even the Greek Aphrodite had not wholly relinquished her connection with the underworld, although she had long surrendered her chthonic role to other divine figures, to Persephone, or to the tri-form Artemis-Hecate. The great Mother-goddesses of the oriental peoples, however, all seem to have been both creators and destroyers—both goddesses of life and fertility and goddesses of death. Thus the replacement by a wishful opposite in our theme harks back to a primeval identity.

The same consideration answers the question how the feature of a choice came into the myth of the three sisters. Here again there has been a wishful reversal. Choice stands in the place of necessity, of destiny. In this way man overcomes death, which he has recognized intellectually. No greater triumph of wish-fulfilment is conceivable. A choice is made where in reality there is obedience to a compulsion; and what is chosen is not a figure of terror, but the fairest and most desirable of women.

On closer inspection we observe, to be sure, that the original myth is not so thoroughly distorted that traces of it do not show through and betray its presence. The free choice between the three sisters is, properly speaking, no free choice, for it must necessarily fall on the third if every kind of evil is not to come about, as it does in *King Lear*. The fairest and best of women, who has taken the place of the Death-goddess, has kept certain characteristics that border on the uncanny, so that from them we have been able to guess at what lies beneath.[20]

So far we have been following out the myth and its transformation, and it is to be hoped that we have correctly indicated the hidden causes of the transformation. We may now turn our interest to the way in which the dramatist has made use of the theme. We get an impression that a reduction of the theme to the original myth is being carried out in his work, so that we once more have a sense of the moving significance which had been weakened by the distortion. It is by means of this reduction of the distortion, this partial return to the original, that the dramatist achieves his more profound effect upon us.

To avoid misunderstandings, I should like to say that it is not my purpose to deny that King Lear's dramatic story is intended to inculcate two wise lessons: that one should not give up one's possessions and rights during one's lifetime, and that one must guard against accepting flattery at its face value. These and similar warnings are undoubtedly brought out by the play; but it seems to me quite impossible to explain the overpowering effect of *King Lear* from the impression that such a train of thought would produce, or to suppose that the dramatist's personal motives did not go beyond the intention of teaching these lessons. It is suggested, too, that his purpose was to present the tragedy of ingratitude, the sting of which he may well have felt in his own heart, and that the effect of the play rests on the purely formal element of its artistic presentation; but this cannot, so it seems to me, take the place of the understanding brought to us by the explanation we have reached of the theme of the choice between the three sisters.

Lear is an old man. It is for this reason, as we have already said, that the three sisters appear as his daughters. The relationship of a father to his children, which might be a fruitful source of many dramatic situations, is not turned to further account in the play. But Lear is not only an old man: he is a dying man. In this way the extraordinary premise of the division of his inheritance loses all its strangeness. But the doomed man is not willing to renounce the love of women; he insists on hearing how much he is loved. Let us now recall the moving final scene, one of the culminating points of tragedy in modern drama. Lear carries Cordelia's dead body on to the stage. Cordelia is Death. If we reverse the situation it becomes intelligible and familiar to us. She is the Death-goddess who, like the Valkyrie in German mythology, carries away the dead hero from the battlefield. Eternal wisdom, clothed in the primeval myth, bids the old man renounce love, choose death and make friends with the necessity of dying.

The dramatist brings us nearer to the ancient theme by representing the man who makes the choice between the three sisters as aged and dying. The regressive revision which he has thus applied to the myth, distorted as it was by wishful transformation, allows us enough glimpses of its original meaning to enable us perhaps to reach as well a superficial allegorical interpretation of the three female figures in the theme. We might argue that what is represented here are the three inevitable relations that a man has with a woman—the woman who bears him, the woman who is his mate and the woman who destroys him; or that they are the three forms taken by the figure of the mother in the course of a man's life—the mother herself, the beloved one who is chosen after her pattern, and lastly the Mother Earth who receives him once more. But it is in vain that an old man yearns for the love of woman as he had it first from his mother; the third of the Fates alone, the silent Goddess of Death, will take him into her arms.

NOTES

1. [A medieval collection of stories of unknown authorship.] (Notes in square brackets are by the translators and editors of the *Standard Edition*.)
2. Georg Brandes, *William Shakespeare* (Paris, 1896).
3. E. Stucken, *Astralmythen der Hebräer, Babylonier und Aegypter* (Leipzig, 1907), p. 655.
4. Otto Rank, *Der Mythus von der Geburt des Helden* (Vienna, 1909), pp. 8 ff.
5. [See *The Interpretation of Dreams* (1900), *Standard Edition*, 5, 354.]
6. I have to thank Dr. Otto Rank for calling my attention to these similarities. [Cf. a reference to this in chapter XII of *Group Psychology* (1921), *Standard Edition*, 18, 136.]
7. [From an aside of Cordelia's, Act I, Scene 1.]
8. "Plainness" according to another reading.
9. In Schlegel's translation this allusion is quite lost; indeed, it is given the opposite meaning: "Dein schlichtes Wesen spricht beredt mich an." ["Thy plainness speaks to me with eloquence."]
10. [Literally: "The third one, ah! the third one . . . the third one said nothing. She won the prize all the same."—The quotation is from Act I, Scene 7, of Meilhac and Halévy's libretto. In the German version used by Freud "the third one" *"blieb stumm"*—"remained dumb."]
11. In Stekel's *Sprache des Traumes* (Wiesbaden, 1911), p. 351, dumbness is mentioned among the "death" symbols. [Cf. *The Interpretation of Dreams*, *Standard Edition*, 5, 357.]
12. [Cf. Freud's later paper on "Dreams and Telepathy" (1922).]
13. Stekel, *loc. cit.*
14. [*Die Märchen der Brüder Grimm* (Leipzig, 1918), 1, 42.]

15. ["Die sechs Schwane," Grimm, 1, 217. (No. 49.)]
16. What follows is taken from Roscher's *Lexikon der griechischen und romischen Mythologie* (1884–1937), under the relevant headings.
17. [Their names may be rendered "What was," "What is," "What shall be."]
18. Roscher, *op. cit.*, quoting L. Preller, ed. C. Robert, *Griechische Mythologie*, 4th edition (Berlin, 1894).
19. [Cf. *The Interpretation of Dreams, Standard Edition*, 4, 318.]
20. The Psyche of Apuleius's story has kept many traits that remind us of her relation with death. Her wedding is celebrated like a funeral, she has to descend into the underworld, and afterwards she sinks into a dream-like sleep (Otto Rank).

On the significance of Psyche as Goddess of Spring and as "Bride of Death," cf. A. Zinzow, *Psyche und Eros* (Halle, 1881).

In another of Grimm's tales ("The Goose-girl at the Fountain" [Die Gansehirtin am Brunnen," 2, 300], No. 179) there is, as in "Cinderella," an alternation between the beautiful and ugly aspect of the third sister, in which one may no doubt see an indication of her double nature —before and after the substitution. This third daughter is repudiated by her father, after a test which is almost the same as the one in *King Lear*. Like her sisters, she has to declare how fond she is of their father, but can find no expression for her love but a comparison with salt. (Kindly communicated by Dr. Hanns Sachs.)

Hawthorne's Symbolism

and Psychoanalysis

by LEON EDEL

Leon Edel, Henry James professor at New York University, has devoted many years to interdisciplinary studies and psychoanalysis, especially as applied to the writing of biography. An eclectic, he refuses to be bound to any psychoanalytic school and maintains that his ground is literature first and foremost. A graduate of McGill University, he pursued his studies at the Sorbonne in Paris, from which he received the *doctorat d'état* for two dissertations on Henry James, the writer with whom his name has become most closely associated. Secretary of the National Institute of Arts and Letters, he is also a Fellow of the American Academy of Arts and Sciences and a Pulitzer prize winner.

The paper here included was originally delivered as a lecture to the Harry Stack Sullivan Society of the William Alanson White Institute of Psychoanalysis in New York City under the title "Literary Symbolism and Psychoanalysis" and has not been published elsewhere. In drawing upon *The Scarlet Letter*, Mr. Edel was guided by the fact that that novel has been so widely read that it serves as a recognizable illustration of the integrity of literary symbolism within a work, while at the same time demonstrating that the work itself is the "objective correlative" of the artist's essential mode of being.

THE common ground of the literary discipline and the discipline of psychoanalysis is man's capacity to create and use symbols. Both the critic and the psychoanalyst are therefore students of symbolism. The psychoanalyst studies symbols as they are evoked for him by his patient—and his purpose is to understand them and to make his patient understand them. The literary critic studies them not to make the poet or the novelist understand himself—although this sometimes can happen—but in the wider sense, that is in the hope of enlarging the general understanding of the literary work. The literary critic is concerned with finding specific and possibly universal meanings in the given work; the psychoanalyst seeks personal meanings in the symbolic work of his patient.

This may seem to be obvious: yet there exists much confusion in discussion of symbols. When, in a literary work, a cave is mentioned, some indoctrinated students begin to talk of wombs; others, facing a concrete structure of words, lose themselves in distant horizons of ritual and myth. I would like to suggest that the psychoanalyst's interest in symbolism involves him in what I would call "biographical symbolism"; whereas in the literary discipline we are interested in the imaginative function of the symbol in a wider sense, that is as an integral part of literary expression. In saying this I do not want to suggest that the two disciplines may not be interested in each other's kind of symbolism. The study of symbolism becomes, for the critic, an end in itself, although the critic, in the very nature of his action—as informer, appreciator, disseminator, teacher—tends to have a kind of public didactic purpose. The didactic purpose of the psychoanalyst is peculiarly intimate: he has only one student at any given hour, and this student, during that given hour, is occupied with studying himself. Otherwise stated, the literary critic seeks the meaning of literary symbolism to read the riddles and the mysteries of the human imagination; the psychoanalyst reads the riddle of biographical symbolism to penetrate the mystery of a particular imagination, and within the closed circle of the analytic situation.

And then the literary critic is concerned, first and foremost, with symbolism on a conscious level; he can only touch peripheral unconscious meanings in a speculative way, and when he does so he crosses the frontier of biography. The psychoanalyst, on the other hand, is concerned essentially with the unconscious meaning of the symbol. In most cases, I suspect, the psychoanalyst finds himself analyzing everyday symbolism or cliché-symbolism, which sometimes is fascinating and sometimes dreary, whereas the critics have the choice of concerning themselves exclusively with the symbolism of unusually imaginative individuals, the exceptional, artistic, creative consciousness. I have always suspected that this may be a partial explanation of the extracurricular activities of so many psychoanalysts and their fascination with the literary act. After dozens of patients have dredged up the commonplace, it must be refreshing to read a poem and to discover an imagination in action. Thus the psychoanalyst turns often to literature for refreshment and sometimes for example as well. The student of literature, on his side, can turn to psychoanalysis for insight into the *process* of the imagination. In this sense the two disciplines may be regarded as distinctly complementary.

I

Symbolism in literature derives its existence from man's faculty, from the dawn of imagination, to note similarities and to make comparisons, to perceive the relatedness of things and to wonder at likenesses. Differences are obvious: a stone is not a tree, a tree is not a stone. But a certain stone, lying in a certain position, may resemble a tree; it may also resemble a crouching animal; and like the inkblot test may suggest many images to the onlooker. Clouds are clouds, but when we look at them on a blue summer's day their whiteness can be resolved by us into many shapes. We all remember that Hamlet and Polonius, studying a cloud, first agreed it was like a camel and then very like a whale; and that Herman Melville, in turn, was preoccupied with the meaning of

the whiteness of the white whale. I speak of image-symbol-
ism, the unstructured suggestion upon which individuals impose structure, or things whose appearance suggests other
appearances. The descriptive label or emblem is obvious.
When I say the word *bread,* we know what that means, although everyone here may think of a different kind of bread:
the sliced and the unsliced, the mediocre reinforced loaf and
the well-baked whole wheat; not to speak of the many shapes
in which bread may be baked. When a novelist describes a
room as yellow, we all know what the room looks like, but
everyone reading that novel will supply his own shade of
yellow. We are concerned not with label-symbols or emblems,
which are the starting point of literature, but with literary
symbolism which is the use of these label-symbols—that is
words and language—employed in such a way as to evoke and
stimulate our imagination and make us see the world around
us in its multiplicity and not as a kind of unilinear creation.
It has always been a truth of great poets that they lend us
their eyes and their ears. Yet it is still *we* who look: and what
we can thank them for is an enlargement of our vision.

American writers, from the first, were aware of the nature
of symbolism. Indeed we marvel a little at the extent of
Edgar Allen Poe's influence on the French symbolists, particularly Baudelaire, who in turn so profoundly influenced
nearly all our great symbolist writers of this century. And
one of the earliest of our novels, indeed, our first major
novel, was built entirely around a single symbol. I allude to
The Scarlet Letter. The letter is the first of the alphabet; and
it is scarlet because scarlet to the Puritans was a color of
shame and profligacy. The letter and its color is worn by
Hester Prynne as symbol of public disgrace and stigma. She
is thereby shown as cast out from the puritan society whose
rules she has violated. We are never told in the novel that
the A stands for adultery. But we know, from the first, that
this is its meaning. Hester has been punished by her community for having borne a child while her husband was away, a
child clearly illegitimate and to which she has given the name

of Pearl, a symbolic name. She must, forever after, wear the letter A, sewn on her dress. She sews it on herself, and makes of it an object of skill and of art. During the course of the novel Hester accepts her punishment and carries her stigma with dignity and fortitude; she continues, on the periphery of her community, to do acts of generosity and kindness, so that ultimately she restores herself to a place within it. And Hawthorne, with his unfailing skill at provoking the imagination to see objects within objects, to look at signs and emblems within signs and emblems, lets drop, at one point of the book (when some persons think they have seen a red letter in the sky, forming the shape of an A), that it stands for Angel. And as the townsfolk recognize Hester's good works and ability, certain of them suggest that the letter has still another meaning.

Hawthorne's passage is worth quoting, for it shows the skill with which he plays upon his symbolic meanings:

In all seasons of calamity, indeed, whether general or of individuals, the outcast of society at once found her place. She came, not as a guest, but as a rightful inmate, into the household that was darkened by trouble; as if its gloomy twilight were a medium in which she was entitled to hold intercourse with her fellow-creatures. There glimmered the embroidered letter, with comfort in its unearthly ray. Elsewhere the token of sin, it was the taper of the sick chamber. It had even thrown its gleam, in the sufferer's hard extremity, across the verge of time. It had shown him where to set his foot, while the light of earth was fast becoming dim, and ere the light of futurity could reach him. In such emergencies, Hester's nature showed itself warm and rich; a well-spring of human tenderness, unfailing to every real demand, and inexhaustible by the largest. Her breast, with its badge of shame, was but the softer pillow for the head that needed one. She was self-ordained a Sister of Mercy; or, we may rather say, the world's heavy hand had so ordained her, when neither the world nor she looked forward to this result. The letter was the symbol of her calling. Such helpfulness was found in her—so much power to do, and power to sympathize—that many people refused to interpret the scarlet A by its original

signification. They said that it meant Able; so strong was Hester
Prynne, with a woman's strength.

And farther along Hawthorne continues this symbolic
play, to the point where certain people seeing the letter on
her bosom, see there, instead of the A, "the effect of the
cross on a nun's bosom"; and for some, the scarlet letter,
losing all its original meaning, comes to stand for Affection.
This is symbolism used in a markedly forceful and ironic
sense. Hawthorne makes us aware again and again of symbolic ironies. The clergyman Dimmesdale, in his churchly
robes, symbolizes all that is pure and godly: all the things by
which we are supposed to know the man of God. Yet it is he
who shares Hester's adultery; and Dimmesdale—his name
surely suggests the man—has neither the courage nor the
dignity to confess and share Hester's punishment. For seven
years he lets her bear her stigma alone, though doubtless the
torment of his conscience and the overpowering guilt he experiences, constitutes a rather terrible private punishment.
The goodness he symbolizes is thus in reality evil: it is the
very opposite of all the things for which the A has come to
stand in Hester's life. The white of Dimmesdale's robes is
really a covering for blackness. A symbol of God to the worshippers, he is in reality a symbol of the Devil. In this way
Hawthorne, with that allegorical—as well as ironic and
whimsical—cast of mind he possessed shows the polarities
possible in symbolic meaning, and shows us indeed that literature, like nature, abhors symbolic rigidity. For is this not
true of all symbols; even the great symbol of Christianity?
Carried by the crusader it was a symbol of violence, persecu-
tion, bloodshed; carried by godly men it is the symbol of
suffering, love, resignation, and of all the enlightened and
humane teachings of Christ. And yet when Christ met his
death, it symbolized punishment and ignominy.

Literary symbolism, in the simple examples I have chosen
from Hawthorne's romantic novel, reveals constantly man's
ability to discover the variousness and diversity in life and

man's power for imaginative connection and association. The great acts of the imagination are those which bring together distinct and separate images, and recognize correspondences which may be universally comprehensible even while at the same time carrying deeply personal meanings for all.

II

Thus far, in using the example of *The Scarlet Letter,* it can be said that I draw exclusively upon my own discipline. The symbols themselves are largely explained in the work in which Hawthorne has woven them. Hawthorne's imaginative use of the first letter of the alphabet embodies a vision of crime and punishment—above all, punishment. The crime was committed long before the novel began; the child of the adulterous union is already born when the curtain is rung up. And the novel shows how literary symbolism can be imaginatively used to give a narrative implicit as well as explicit meaning; and how—if we wish to take heed—symbols refuse to have a single meaning. Moreover the book shows us, I think, in a remarkably poignant way, that symbols cannot be discussed unless we discuss them within their context.

The psychoanalytically oriented reader, however, must ask himself many more questions: he cannot be satisfied with the observations I have made thus far. He would ask them, I believe, automatically: it should be second nature to such a person. The main question he might ask would be: what guilt did Hawthorne experience, and why did he experience it so profoundly that he had to write this kind of novel? It is inevitable that some such question should come to his mind, or some related questions, involving Hawthorne himself as well as his story. For it was Hawthorne who imagined the novel of the Scarlet Letter; the work is his and no one else's; or, to be exact, it was he who selected an historical episode in the old New England annals which gave him the theme of his story. That psychoanalysts should ask such questions, I take quite for granted since I am sure that they, like Hawthorne, insist upon reading symbols in their context. And the symbolism that concerns the psychoanalyst is that which is provided by the individual—in this case Hawthorne. Psychoanalysis, in other words, by its very nature is concerned not with the symbolism of the book alone; it is inherent in its function that it should be concerned rather with the book *as symbol of its creator,* as a reflection of a given human—and creative—consciousness. And this, as I said, involves psychoanalysis first and foremost in biographical symbolism.

There is a school of criticism which argues that to concern oneself with biographical symbolism is to commit a "genetic fallacy": that literature, unlike the dream, is depersonalized once it is given to the world; in other words that psychoanalysis should, properly speaking, keep its hands off the literary work if it is going to involve the creator with his creation. I suppose this school of criticism would have no objection to psychoanalysts discussing the symbolism in the work itself; but they would say that the original context of the work, before it was given to the world, is now something *extrinsic* to it. I find this perfectly valid as a critical distinction; but I think that many of us, in literature, and certainly those in psychoanalysis, must feel that the distinction belongs merely to an order of logic; that it is useful and clarifying and of a highly intellectual nature; but that it need not necessarily be a restriction. I am quite sure that it would be possible for a group of psychoanalysts, if they studied *The Scarlet Letter* minutely, to speculate with a considerable degree of accuracy about the personality of the author, that is of the storyteller. The very form he has given to his tale, the manner in which he has related it to history, the words he has used, his choice of phrase and color, and above all his symbolic images, are all, in the end, symbols of himself, signatures of his inner being. The men of Hawthorne's time understood this very well. Emerson, among his many wise sayings, seems to have understood psychological determinism when he said "nothing is more rare in any man than an act of his own." And a corollary remark, even more pertinent to our present discussion, was set down by Thoreau, Emerson's disciple, when he said that "poetry is a piece of private history, which unostentatiously lets us into the secret of a man's life." Coming a generation later, Henry James formulated this idea concretely when he remarked that the literary artist "is present in every page of every book from which he sought so assiduously to eliminate himself."

I suppose the answer to our restrictive critics is precisely this: that all art is personal and impersonal at the same time, but that we can most truthfully study it when we link the story to the story's creator, the dream to the dreamer. I take this to be axiomatic. It is certainly axiomatic in psychoanalysis: for a psychoanalyst it would be a rather large heresy to interpret dreams in a vacuum.

This said, it might be useful to look into the context of *The Scarlet Letter,* for it is precisely by this linking of text to context that we see the relationship between literary symbolism and psychoanalysis. The data for a life of Nathaniel Hawthorne are abundant and there are several excellent biographies. We have his notebooks and journals; we are to have a large edition of his letters. And I think, if we confine ourselves to his novels and tales, we discover within them patterns and symbolic designs which in themselves offer valuable testimony. In so small a space I cannot rehearse his whole life; but I can select data, as if I were sketching a biographical protrait; and by this process we can see in a general way how *The Scarlet Letter* is symbol for Hawthorne as well as for the personages of his Puritan story.

The common theme of Hawthorne's novels is that of the individual who by some act, or for some reason or circumstance, places himself or is placed outside the boundary of his community. All his efforts are directed, with extraordinary intensity, to the recrossing of that boundary. This is what Hester achieves. In *The Blithedale Romance* it is what the hero questions and seeks when he meets the members of a communal farm and observes their relations with one another and with society; in *The House of the Seven Gables* the theme is reasserted in its clearest terms in the recluse existence of the Pyncheons in their old house, their withdrawal from the community, and their attempt to breach their self-imposed boundary. In *The Marble Faun* there is again a crime, which not only places those involved outside the border of society, but also creates a dilemma for an innocent bystander. In a certain sense Hawthorne and Dostoevsky treat the same subject: and in Hawthorne there is constant recognition that alienation and withdrawal from the group is a lonely and destructive thing, and that individuals who for some reason have become isolated from the world struggle to achieve a reunion with it. Yet this is always, in his work, a profound and painful dilemma.

Hawthorne came of a family which had taken an important role in the life of the colonists of the New World. The first to come to America, Major William Hathorne, persecuted Quakers and caused a Quaker woman to be whipped behind a cart and driven into the forest because she had denounced priests and churches. The second, John Hathorne, was one of the judges in the Salem witchcraft trials. Hawthorne took this heritage deeply to heart. In a celebrated passage in his essay "The Custom House," which is his preface to *The Scarlet Letter,* he recalls his bigoted and cruel ancestors and announces that "I, the present writer, as their representative, hereby take shame upon myself for their sakes, and pray that any curse incurred by them—as I have heard, and as the dreary and unprosperous condition of the race, for many a long year back, would argue to exist —may be now and henceforth removed." The pen would seek to exorcise the memory of the whip and the hangman's halter. It recognized the guilt of family. In a sense, in the very act of prefacing *The Scarlet Letter,* Hawthorne pins "shame upon himself." Even if this preface were a total fiction, the very fact that Hawthorne saw fit to write it reveals a sense of guilt.

Scholars long ago pointed out that Hawthorne was reflecting the puritanism which had produced him and we know how deeply grounded in Calvinism is the idea of ancestral guilt: "In Adam's fall, we sinned all," said the New England primer, and *The Scarlet Letter,* as well as Hawthorne's personal sense of family guilt, certainly reflects the religious roots which guilt acquired among the Puritans. When sin is as permanent as this, what disinfectant can wash it away? Guilt is made a common burden, and an uncommonly heavy one. And I find it biographically significant that when the future writer graduated from college, and before he made his literary reputation, he altered his name from Hathorne to Hawthorne. By using another letter of the alphabet, the "w," he gave his name a different color and meaning. This was a quiet dissociation from those who had borne the earlier name, the name he held to have been dishonored by cruelty, the name that carried with it the burden of a great guilt.

Nevertheless it was his father's name; and his father, Hawthorne had never known. The Hathorne family had fallen from its original high position in the New England community and had become a family of seafarers. Nathaniel was four when his father died of a fever in the Dutch Indies. His mother withdrew into a melancholy widowhood, and Hawthorne spent a comparatively solitary boyhood. Much has been made of the fact that for twelve years after his graduation from Bowdoin, he followed his mother's example and led the life of a semirecluse. Hawthorne himself made much of it. We know he was not entirely a hermit; he ventured forth into the town; he occasionally conversed with his sisters; but he stayed much in his room, wrote and rewrote his stories, burned many of them, and ever after spoke of this period as the time when he had cut himself off from the world in a lonely isolation.

In recent times biographers have tried to show that the image of Hawthorne as a recluse, taking his meals in solitude and leaving his tray outside his door, was a self-created legend, particularly since we know that he did not regard himself as imprisoned; and indeed he took certain trips, wandered along Salem's wharves at night, and enjoyed a certain amount of social life, as he had done during his college days. This is however too simple an adherence to biographical fact: it represents a failure to recognize that it is possible for a man to be outwardly sociable and still feel an abyss between himself and society. Hawthorne could have traveled all over the United States and still have been, in his deeper self, an isolated and alienated being. I think that no matter how much evidence will be discovered to prove Hawthorne a busy outgoing individual, as some biographers seem determined to do, the real evidence of his work and his notebooks shows him always as a spiritual recluse. Passages in his notebooks are particularly eloquent: "A recluse like myself, or a prisoner, to measure time by the progress of sunshine through his chamber." Or the anecdote he sets down about two ladies who vow never to see sunlight because of disappointment in love—each keeping the vow and living in apartments closely shut up and lighted by candles.

Late in life Hawthorne had a repeated dream that he was back at school meeting his contemporaries. In it he felt ashamed and depressed, and this, he wrote, was real to him even after waking up. His own interpretation of the dream must be scrutinized; it was, he said, "one of the effects of that heavy seclusion in which I shut myself up, for twelve years after leaving college, when everybody moved onward and left me behind. How strange that it should come now, when I may call myself famous, and prosperous!—when I am happy, too!—still that same dream of life hopelessly a failure." We wonder at his insistence that he is "happy." The dream shows the power of his continuing state of anxiety.

The themes of Hawthorne thus seem to have at their core individuals who seek escape into the past, and then finding themselves isolated, try to break out into the present. This is perhaps a larger way of looking at the rich, tapestried material of Hawthorne's consciousness. But this living in the past is also punishment; and the attempt to find the present is a way of trying to alter the punishment, to make it assume benign instead of stigmatic form. Hawthorne phrased it well; he had an unerring insight into certain aspects of his dilemma. He spoke of the predicament of his characters, of himself, too, as the "individual ajar with the world"; we find this in a passage from *The Marble Faun:*

This perception of an infinite, shivering solitude, amid which we cannot come close enough to human beings to be warmed by them, and where they turn to cold, chilly shapes of mist, is one of the most forlorn results of any accident, misfortune, crime or peculiarity of character, that puts an individual ajar with the world.

The current of all of Hawthorne's writings is suggested by these words, even though he colored his personal drama by the larger spiritual drama of Man's dissociation from God through his Fall, his divorce from the Garden of Eden through Original Sin.

It is not my purpose to "psychoanalyze" Hawthorne. Such a procedure is impossible. But the biographical symbols help us to gain a larger insight into the relationship between literary and biographical symbolism. What did Hawthorne do when he finally emerged from his long period of self-imprisonment?—a very active imprisonment, to be sure, for he read constantly and wrote endlessly. He entered upon a life of action: editing and hack writing, and publishing tales in various journals. These went into the volume *Twice-Told Tales* and the publication of that book attracted attention to him; led him to meet the Peabody sisters, and to marry one of them. After that he lived in the Old Manse outside Concord, but he had also worked in the Boston Customs House, and had briefly involved himself with the Brook Farm experiment. In five years he had moved from an extreme of solitude to an extreme of communal living. His marriage was the middle course between these; and there came that moment when Hawthorne lived at one end of Concord and at the other lived Emerson, and his neighbor Thoreau. After publishing *Mosses from an Old Manse* he worked in the Salem Custom House; and when he lost this job he occupied his leisure with the writing of *The Scarlet Letter*. Published in 1850, it made him famous.

We need not concern ourselves here with Hawthorne's European years, although his *French and Italian Notebooks* contain valuable material which, examined in the light of psychoanalysis, would greatly extend our vision of the man. I find it interesting to observe, however, that on his return to Concord in 1860 he settled in a house he named The Wayside. The choice of this name seems to me illuminating, as indeed, also the location of the Old Manse where he had lived before, which is also Wayside—and slightly Outside—on the periphery of Concord. It suggests that even after Hawthorne had broken into the circle of men, he still felt himself, or needed to think of himself, as belonging to the perimeter. His settling in The Wayside seemed almost as if his return from the wider world of Europe made of him anew a recluse in his little American corner. He began three books; they were never completed. They remain as a sad and painful record of the final gropings of a man of great gifts and his coming to a halt. He did not live long thereafter. There had been too much "pressing moral anxiety," as Henry James put it.

But what was this anxiety? Biography has not yet given us the answer save in theological terms, or in "constituted temperament." How was the temperament constituted? I have indulged in this biographical excursion only to sug-

gest, in a very rough fashion, the ground upon which biographical symbolism may be approached in the search for
the deepest truths about Hawthorne. The answers lie, as
nearly always in such matters, in areas for which we have
no documents. What records can one find of the childhood
of the writer, in an era so far removed from our own? The
absentee father; the relationship with the mother; the rela
tionship with the sisters? The most authoritative recent
biography of Hawthorne gives us no answers to these questions: it seeks in a frankly conjectural way, "ancestral influ-
ences." Is it not true that most biographies are forced, in
the very nature of things, to skip the years to which we
today attach the most importance? Yet it is precisely at this
point that the two disciplines—those of literature and of
psychoanalysis—can best unite in an act of illumination.

III

They can unite precisely by a kind of irradiation of each
other's symbolism. The literary symbolism should, if it is a
function of the biographical symbolism, contain certain
answers for us which could not be found so long as we study
the literary symbol by itself. We can seek to establish a cor-
relation between religious guilt, family guilt, and the guilt
in Hawthorne's novel; the details of the private guilt are
lacking, and these, more profound than the theological or
the ancestral, could throw the greatest light upon our subject. It would be altogether too easy and too pat to postulate
incest fantasies with mother and sisters: and yet this would
not be a wholly implausible postulate. More important
would be an examination of the data of all of Hawthorne's
novels—and perhaps above all the earliest, *Fanshawe,* which
he published and then withdrew and burned; this should
offer us much valuable evidence. What kind of women are
to be found in his novels? what kind of men? what kind of
human relationships? We have here a network of relation-

ships, not least that which exists between the author and his characters. To be sure this is highly speculative material; and yet it is speculation grounded in the only valid materials which we have: the stories spun out of the consciousness of the creating individual, who happened to be obsessed by problems of guilt and punishment, and the pressing nature of his isolation from his fellowmen.

I do not propose to reach any conclusions in this paper, for I am concerned here not with substance but with definition and method. I have tried first to define the distinct approaches the two disciplines impose upon us in dealing with the symbols of the creative consciousness, and to find the ground upon which they can constructively meet. The least constructive approach occurs when the student of literature tries to read symbols in terms of rigid psychoanalytical interpretation, focused on the biographical symbolism, and offers a *diagnosis* of the creator not essentially as creator, but as an ailing human being.

Hawthorne himself showed, in his work, a deep perception of these matters even though he died half a century before Freud's book on dreams was published. He had a great insight into psychological truth. He recognized always the emblematic character of experience; the fact that life's meanings are all stated in symbols; that in life, as in "the topsy-turvy world of dreams," the impossible and the possible, the credible and the incredible, are not as far apart as we believe. It will suggest a little the character of the writer if we digress to quote a passage from *The Scarlet Letter* which could have been written by a psychoanalyst today in any journal of his profession.

Hawthorne is describing the probing of the doctor, Chillingworth, into the consciousness of Dimmesdale. He writes:

So Roger Chillingworth . . . strove to go deep into his patient's bosom, delving among his principles, prying into his recollections, and probing everything with a cautious touch, like a treasure-seeker in a dark cavern. Few secrets can escape an investigator, who has opportunity and license to undertake such a quest and skill to follow it up. A man burdened with a secret should especially avoid the intimacy of his physician. If the latter possesses native sagacity, and a nameless something more —let us call it intuition; if he show no intrusive egotism, nor disagreeably prominent characteristics of his own; if he have the power, which must be born with him, to bring his mind into such affinity with his patient's, that this last shall unawares have spoken what he imagines himself only to have thought; if such revelations be received without tumult, and acknowledged not so often by an uttered sympathy as by silence, an inarticulate breath, and here and there a word, to indicate that all is understood; if to these qualifications of a confidant be joined the advantages afforded by his recognized character as a physician— then, at some inevitable moment, will the soul of the sufferer be dissolved, and flow forth in dark, but transparent stream, bringing all its mysteries into the daylight.

I would judge this to be an accurate description of the ideal psychoanalyst.

IV

I have focused thus far on the single example of Hawthorne in an attempt to define the relationships between the two disciplines. But one other point must be made. It is required because contemporary literary symbolism has gone far beyond that of Hawthorne and because the problem is now infinitely more complex. I allude to the fact that in literature, as in art, we are given the *personal* symbolism of the artist no longer in the older literary structures, but in forms that place us in the position of individuals doing an exercise in thematic apperception, or—in the case of the plastic arts—taking an inkblot test. The symbolism of literature has in the past been comprehensible: even in the earliest days, when Christ talked in parables and used allegory, and the prophets brought the power of metaphor and simile into their exhortations, there was always distinct clarity—no one doubted their meaning: indeed they used symbolism to reinforce meaning. In our time, symbolism has set itself quite another task. Ever since the French symbolist movement it has sought to evoke, to capture, to render atmosphere, *in order that we may experience this atmosphere ourselves.* Where formerly the artist spoke to the reader, saying whatever he had to say in terms of common discourse—he today says it often in such a way as to invite the reader to collaborate with him, or to discover for himself.

In other words, when the symbolism of art becomes entirely personal—and sometimes it is extremely fascinating in this form, for it is the symbolism of the unconscious reaching us without passing through conscious and intellectual structures—it creates a wholly new situation for the literary critic, although the situation for psychoanalysis remains unchanged. The painter who offers a psychoanalyst a doodle or a writer who offers him a word-salad may tell him much about himself; but if he offers it to the literary critic, the latter finds himself involved simply with symbols, however suggestive and however "abstract," which speak to him solely as sign language. Symbolism here moves away from the concrete to the primitive and the mysterious. And here, I believe, only psychoanalysis can discuss it intelligibly. The literary critic, or the art critic, runs the risk merely of projecting his own personal symbolism into the personal symbolism confronting him.

I recognize that I am thinking (as I say this) much more of painting than of words. But literary symbolism, too, can reach its moment of no return, even while exercising a distinct fascination. When, long ago, the experimenters on the Left Bank issued their Manifesto calling for the "Revolution of the Word" they said that "pure poetry is a lyrical absolute that seeks an *a priori* reality within ourselves alone." I do not quarrel with this, if this is the kind of poetry a poet wishes to write. Nor do I quarrel with their further statement: "The writer expresses: he does not communicate." I quite agree. But as a critic and a biographer I must still cope with what has been expressed. I find myself in such instances either abandoning myself to the sheer sensory enjoyment of the words and the images and the symbols, or turning to psychoanalysis—and finding it sometimes rather helpless also. For at this stage, literature—if it is that—comes to us wholly without context; we are back in the miasma of the id, and only when we have copious data from a given individual, can we begin to discover (by psychoanalytic method) the functioning of this particular id, in this particular way.

If we turn back from such extremes, the experiments of surrealism and of dada, the deliberate turning toward the mere shorthand of the unconscious, we discover that the language of dream is more coherent, often, than these artificial creations and that the unconscious can speak in rather more constructed parables. I think that in dealing with this kind of art, we are committed wholly to biographical symbolism of the most difficult kind. Which perhaps only serves to emphasize that we, in literature, are involved much more with that which man creates, as Lamb said, "being awake"; the discipline of his craft, the awareness of his intellect. And since all our endeavor is to find some order in chaos, some meaning in the stuff of human consciousness as represented by its literary expression, these observations, largely definitional, are offered in the hope that further discussion may perhaps widen the common ground that lies between the disciplines of literary criticism and of psychoanalysis.

Thanatos: The Death Instinct
in Dickens' Later Novels

by LEONARD F. MANHEIM

After taking his bachelor's degree at Columbia with honors in English and political science, Leonard Manheim continued graduate work in both fields, taking an M.A. in English and a law degree. After practicing law for ten years he returned to teaching and scholarship and was awarded a doctorate at Columbia in comparative literature, with specialization in psychoanalytic criticism as applied to the novels of Dickens. He has taught at The City College of New York and the Peabody College for Teachers, and he is now affiliated with the University of Massachusetts. He was the founder of *Literature and Psychology* and has been its editor ever since its inception.

The psychoanalytic theory on which the present study is based is the postulation known as the "death instinct." This postulation is not universally accepted even by psychoanalysts, but it seems to be implied in the later writings of Freud and has been most fully developed in the writings of Karl A. Menninger. Acceptance of the theory seems to be wider today than when this paper was first written. One evidence—possibly one cause—of that has been Norman O. Brown's *Life Against Death* (1959). The present paper was first published in *Psychoanalysis and The Psychoanalytic Review* (XLVII, 4, Winter 1960–1961).

Fevers upon wilful distemper of drinks, and surfets, *Consumptions* upon intemperances, and licentiousness, *Madnes* upon misplacing, or overbending our natural faculties, proceed from our selves, and so, as that our selves are in the plot, and we are not only *passive*, but *active* too, to our owne destruction. . . . There are too many *Examples* of men, that have been their own executioners, and that have made hard shrift to bee so; some have alwayes had poysen about them, in a *hollow ring* upon their finger, and some in their *Pen* that they have used to write with; some have beat out their *braines* at the wal of their prison, and some have eate the *fire* out of their chimneys: and one is said to have come neerer our case than so, to have strangled himself, though his hands were bound, by crushing his throat between his knees; but I doe nothing upon my selfe, and yet am mine owne *Executioner*.

—John Donne, *Devotions (XII)*

W HAT are the drives which furnish the motive force for the constant battle which seethes within the human psyche? Most present-day psychoanalytic theorists hold that these drives are present in a dual aspect: *Eros*, or the Life-Instinct; and *Thanatos*, or the Destruction-Instinct. The term *libido* has been generally applied to the former of these drives; it should properly be applied to the fundamental instinctual unity of which these two drives are but the bipolar manifestations.[1]

It was once suggested by Ferenczi that immediately following the experience of birth, almost as painful for the newborn child as for its parent, there is developed a wish to return to the previous state of wishless tranquility, of unconditional omnipotence such as will never again be experienced, and that from this shock there is developed a wish to return to that previous condition, a wish which is the equivalent of a desire for annihilation.[2] While it is true that such a desire is quite probably strongest in the very earliest stages of life, it is really a component of an innate, persistent, fundamental bipolar drive. The Thanatos drive has never received the same attention from psychoanalysis as has Eros. One difficulty arises from the seeming paradox of a will not to live. But while it is true that a conscious attempt to envisage *nonexistence* (with which we should not confuse *unconsciousness*) is impossible, we forget that the unconscious is not bothered by the logically mutual exclusiveness of the yea and the nay, of being and nonbeing.

The theory has been developed by several eminent followers of Freud, notably Franz Alexander and Karl A. Menninger. In spite of the fact that some heat has been engendered by their disagreements, the literary scholar finds more validity in their points of agreement than in their minutiae of dissent. For him probably the most clearly acceptable and accessible analysis of the Thanatos-urge, the self-aggressive trend, the suicidal impulse, is that of Karl A. Menninger. Menninger divides the drive or "instinct" into three components: a wish to kill, a wish to be killed, and a wish to die. The first of these is present in all forms of psychological aggression, whether sublimated or "raw"; the second is found in all guilt-and-propitiation mechanisms. The third element, the true death wish, is the most difficult to comprehend; yet its presence can be shown by a deep penetration into the motives inherent in life and in literature.[3] For example, it is that very element that makes Thomas Mann's *Death in Venice* the stupendous tale that it is. It starts as a tale of ennui and weariness, but it soon passes that phase. It becomes a tale of psychosexual decay. But even that is not all. It suddenly comes upon us with an almost physical shock that everything that Gustav von Eschenbach has done from the beginning to the end of that story has been designed to bring about, surely and inexorably, his own death.

I

Much of what we shall have to say on this subject will deal with the last two novels written by Dickens, the last complete one and the one which Death left incomplete. Yet there were evidences of even more than the first two of the Thanatos elements in many of the earlier novels, notably in

Old Curiosity Shop, in *Bleak House,* and to a lesser extent in *Dombey and Son* and in *A Tale of Two Cities.* Chesterton, with that faculty which enabled him to grasp so accurately the driving forces at work in Dickens, only to toss away his intuitive discovery a moment later with a paradox or some other piece of mystification, tries to make a case for Dickens' treatment of the Thanatos urge by writing:

His horror is a healthy churchyard horror, a fear of the grotesque defamation called death: and this every man has. . . . [It] is literally a mortal fear, a fear of death; it is not the immortal fear, or fear of damnation, which belongs to all the more refined intellects of our day. In a word, Dickens does, in the exact sense, make the flesh creep; he does not, like the decadents, make the soul crawl.[4]

It is to be presumed that this statement means something more than the mere fact that one G. K. Chesterton suffered from a fear of damnation greater than his fear of death. If it means literally that *Old Curiosity Shop* expresses a literal and monovalent abhorrence and horror of death, it is simply a misstatement. Chesterton must have known full well that what characterizes much of the mood of the novel was its wooing of death. In it death is full of fascination as well as horror; in it death is seen through the eyes of a child, a child whose characteristic attitude toward it is increasingly ambivalent. The horror which is regressive is supplemented by the yearning which is, when we come to consider it, even more regressive.

The question was raised in Dickens' time and has been raised again whether there was any artistic need for the death of Little Nell. The suspicion still persists that the author killed her off for the sole purpose of indulging in an orgy of bathos such as he always brought into his works whenever a child died. But for Dickens the death of Little Nell was in the nature of a compulsion. He wrestled long with himself before he could force himself to write about it; he wrote letters defending his course of action in writing it. Yet, in the light of the violence of the unconscious drive which led to her creation, it is obvious that Nell could never be permitted to attain an age at which the coarseness of the gross world of reality might sully her. She could not long remain as the custodian and exhibitor of the old church without growing up, and then either marrying or becoming an odd old spinster. Either course was repugnant to the author; hence she had to perish.

Little Nell was about fourteen years of age when she died, but for Dickens she was still a child, *the* child, and it is through her eyes that we first see Death's fascination. The customary orgy of bathos is conspicuously missing. There are no deathbed agonies and no dying speeches. Instead there is, for the first time, a studied attempt to encompass the mood of Keats's passion "to cease upon the midnight with no pain." Nell gradually succumbs to her own wish to return to the First Mother, she who had never known any mother, nor any father other than the aged Trent. The scenes in the church and its graveyard, the contrast between Nell's youthful yearnings for Thanatos and the great age and love of life of the old sexton and his assistant all strike a new note in the novels, a note which we shall not find sounded quite so well again until one Hans Castorp identifies his yearning for the Unknown with Schubert's *Der Lindenbaum* as sung on a phonograph record.

The mood is not broken after Nell's death, for the picture of old Trent in a profound state of delusion in which he will not believe that Nell is dead is quite in keeping with the earlier scenes. He first insists that she is only asleep; later he waits for her return to her usual haunts; finally he waits for her in the graveyard in which she is buried. The pictures of age and youth in their relationship to death supplement each other perfectly.

The nuance which distinguishes this mood from that of *Bleak House,* written twelve years later, is subtle, but none the less striking. Those intervening twelve years had included the rise and fall of the analytical impulse which reached its climax in *David Copperfield*,[5] the years of the genesis of the Christmas mythology, the years of a tremendous effort by a handicapped author to lift himself by his own bootstraps. Then, at the end of this period, came the shock of the triple death of father, daughter, and sister.[6] The regressive element in *Bleak House* is no longer one of wistful nostalgia, but one of pugnacious grasping for solace, a mystical retreat into a fairytale world in which the abode of death is confused with the house of life, and the ways of reality become the ways of death and corruption. *Bleak House* actually has more deaths in it than any other Dickens novel. Captain Hawdon, Lady Dedlock's secret love and the father of Esther Summerson, dies in miserable penury; Lady Dedlock herself dies in her mad flight from Inspector Bucket; poor Jo dies of starvation and the aftermath of smallpox; Lady Dedlock's sister dies of natural causes after devoting herself to the austere upbringing of the "tainted" Esther; Tulkinghorn dies, murdered by Hortense; Krook dies of spontaneous combustion; Richard Carstone dies in a "decline"; the brickmaker's wife loses her newborn child. Esther almost dies of smallpox; she goes down into the pit and returns, like Rose Maylie, to comfort the author with the thought that the dream maiden may be altered by illness, yet she cannot ever really perish. Sir Leicester Dedlock passes a night of terror and yearning for his beloved wife, a night that leaves him paralyzed. Much of the action in the novel centers around a cemetery in the heart of London, and there is even a wraith that haunts the Ghost Walk at Chesney Wold.

But the real abode of death is not to be found in these outward and ordinary manifestations of mortality. In its mythological aspect, the death which is a comforter, a release from a troubled world, is that house of which we have already spoken, that house which was known as Peak House before it fell to ruins in the possession of the unhappy Tom Jarndyce, but which became a haven of comfort when John

Jarndyce rescued it, found that it had been renamed Bleak House, and decided that it was to be "bleak" in name only. In that house he presides as father-god with his chosen off-spring. He insists that he be called "guardian" and, wonder-ful to relate, Esther does actually use that term in addressing him. He is aided in his mission to make this haven of refuge a beautiful and comforting place by this same chosen maiden, who is specifically referred to in fairy-tale language as "Dame Durden" and "the little old woman who swept the cobwebs out of the sky." With her keys at her belt, she makes this world of unreality the best of all possible worlds. It is amazing to her—and the reader is supposed to share her amazement—that anyone would care to leave that world. When Richard strays off into the world of reality, the world of law and business, presided over by black-coated Vholeses and Tulkinghorns, he is mourned as if *he* were the one who had died. When Ada leaves the House to marry Richard and to become a member of that outside world, Esther's mourning is so great that she hovers around the marital domicile of the faithless pair and kisses the "hearse-like panels" of their door!

On this level, *Bleak House* becomes a novel of regressive self-immolation, with the "self" carefully hidden under dresses and petticoats.[7] But now Dickens finds that he cannot go all the way. If Esther were really to wed Jarndyce, the father-god, it would not only be a violation of the Oedipus canon; it would also be a complete surrender to the forces of Thanatos, a fulfillment (symbolically) of the third element in the Thanatos wish—the wish to die—and for this Dickens is not yet ready. So Esther is snatched back to half-life to wed the "outsider," Allan Woodcourt, and to live in the house that the "guardian" has provided and fitted out for them, and which shares at least the name of the former heavenly abode. The mythological nature of the elements which went into this novel did not wholly escape even Dickens' conscious attention, for he concludes the preface with the telltale sentence, "In *Bleak House,* I have purposely dwelt upon the romantic side of familiar things." The most familiar thing in the novel is death, and it *is* indeed romanticized.

II

During the next twelve years the wistful backward look is never to be absent from the novels, but never in quite so obvious a form. It makes itself felt largely in the growing influence of the first Thanatos element, the element of destructive aggression, and to a somewhat lesser extent in the secondary or propitiatory element. All three of the elements in the death wish crop up again in newer forms in the last two novels. In *Our Mutual Friend* it is aggression, unrestrained sadism, which is paramount; in *Edwin Drood,* it is the third element, the purest form of the death wish.

During the years when *Our Mutual Friend* was written, death could never have been long absent from the author's mind. Those years were strikingly similar to the years preceding *Bleak House.* In the year 1863 he suffered the loss of a parent and of a child, just as he had in the year 1851. It was in 1863 that his mother died and that the son whom he had sent to India to seek his fortune, rather against the son's will, let it be noted, fell a victim to the rigors of Indian life. During a very short period of time Dickens had lost his friends John Leech and Augustus Egg, and had suffered a great shock in the untimely death of his chief rival as a novelist, Thackeray. It was during the first five years of the sixties that his own health first showed marked signs of deterioration, and it was in June of 1865, when the final chapters of *Our Mutual Friend* were being written, that he was in a frightful railway accident which left its mark upon his already shattered psyche.

If we compare *Our Mutual Friend* with the former novel with which it invites comparison, *Little Dorrit,* we note an even greater change than when we compare *Great Expecta-*

tions with *David Copperfield*. That change seems to be wholly due to this newer phase of undisguised aggression. The most interesting symbol of this aggression and of the whole Thanatos mood which colors the later novels is the all-pervading influence of the river. We return to the river time and again as if we were drawn there obsessively. The beginning of the symbolic use of the river may be found toward the end of *Great Expectations*. Pip, in his frantic efforts to get Abel Magwitch out of the country, rows down the Thames with him in a small boat, with the intention of putting the exile on an ocean liner as it is about to take its final leave of England. Pip, Abel, and Herbert Pocket are obliged to seek shelter in a cabin at the river's edge, and Pip shudderingly views the clothing which has been reclaimed from the corpses which occasionally float by.

The scene, minor as it was in *Great Expectations,* must have meant a great deal to the author, for he hired a steamer to make an excursion between Blackwell and Southend in order to be certain of his "local color." He was so much impressed by what he saw that he made the tavern which he had observed on that trip the model for "The Six Jolly-Fellowship Porters" in *Our Mutual Friend*. The novel starts with the recollection of the weird printed handbills which Dickens had seen, describing bodies found in the river and seeking identification for them. The villainous Rogue Riderhood and his unpleasant daughter, Pleasant, vie with the more virtuous "Gaffer" Hexam and his super-virtuous daughter, Lizzie, for the profits to be derived from the corpses which they find in the river. As a feature of the professional rivalry which has succeeded the breaking-up of their partnership, each of them airily accuses the other of "providing" the corpses which they rob.

It is in this same river that John Harmon, heir to the fantastic Harmon fortune, "dies," to be reborn first as Julius Handford and later as John Rokesmith. When he marries the transformed and chastened Bella Wilfer, he takes her and her cherubic father for a trip on the river in its brighter and

sunnier aspect, ending with a wedding breakfast in an inn
overlooking the river. Riderhood changes his occupation and
becomes a lock-keeper farther up the river. Lizzie flees from
the wicked city and the unwelcome attentions of her beloved
Eugene, and finds employment in a factory not far from this
same lock. It is in and by means of the river that the violent
Bradley Headstone—Headstone, who identifies sleep with
death and shrinks from the daily necessity to return there-
from—seeks to be revenged upon Eugene. Eugene, too, is
reborn from the river, a new and reformed man after his
nick-of-time rescue by Lizzie. Again it is in the waters of the
river that both Headstone and Riderhood meet their de-
served ends in a melodramatic scene of murder and suicide.
The river, in this novel and the next, as it is in all dream-
work and fantasy, is a joint symbol of both birth and death.
Herein lies the key to the glorification of those aggressive
trends which, for the first time in a Dickens novel, mark an
almost complete victory of Hate over Love.

In this glorification of aggression lies the disquieting nature of the novel as a whole, the disconcerting flaw which
many readers have sensed. In each major character there is
marked aggressiveness unneutralized by any adequate component of Eros. The whole trouble with Boffin's pretended
crabbèdness, for example, is that it is so much of a piece with
the tone of the rest of the book that we hesitate to admit
that he could have been shamming all along. (Even Chesterton refers to the "deterioration" of Boffin as if it were real
and not assumed.) Eugene is plagued by ungentlemanly com-
pulsions to rob Lizzie of her virginity and by a corollary
snobbishness which causes him to treat Headstone shame-
fully. He moons about, Sidney Cartonlike, in the clutches of
forces which he detests but which he cannot combat until his
descent into the jaws of death brings about his redemption
and his final *mésalliance*. There is an unlovely aggressiveness
not otherwise to be found in Dickens in the entire Podsnap
circle, particularly in Miss Sophronia Akershem's angling for
Mr. Alfred Lammle and in their attitude toward each other

when they discover that each has been cheated and deceived as to the other's wealth. The picture is not mitigated by Mr. Lammle's summary revenge upon the person of the wholly despicable Fascination Fledgeby, nor in Jenny Wren's application of the mustard poultice to that gentleman's smarting back.

The Wilfer family is another case in point. It is a shock to realize that the harridan of a mother is a direct counterpart of Mrs. Micawber, even to her display of a sign indicating that she is perpetually about to conduct a school for young ladies. Dickens would never have rubbed salt into the wound of Mrs. Micawber's pretensions by having the very sign seized and taken away bcause it had not been paid for. Her unfortunate spouse, clearly identified by being nicknamed "The Cherub," exists only as the butt of the malice of his wife, his younger daughter, and even of his elder daughter in her first phase. Lavinia Wilfer, heiress to all of Bella's abandoned malice, and possessor of a large share of her own, is one of the most unlovely and aggressive young women who ever graced the pages of a Victorian novel.

III

Just as *Our Mutual Friend* subordinates the second, or propitiatory, phase of the Thanatos impulse to the first, or aggressive, phase, so *The Mystery of Edwin Drood* is the clearest representation of the third phase of the death wish. It is most difficult to conceive a genuine wish to die, as opposed to a wish to kill or even a wish to be killed (be punished). For the conscious mind the existence of such a wish must be postulated and inferred from evidence as to the functioning of the Unconscious. Not that the wish has been absent—verbally—from literature. Menninger has mentioned the classic examples of Cowper, of Keats, of Bryant, but he expresses grave doubts that the consciously expressed wish for death is truly an undisguised expression of the genuine death instinct. He admits that it is characteristic of many young and adolescent minds to brood upon the mystery of death, but he insists that if we really wish to find evidence of a death wish, we are more likely to find it in the activities of daredevils like mountain-climbers, automobile-racers, building-scalers, Houdinis, than in the pessimistic musings of melancholy philosophers. Leopardi, Menninger notes, mused on Death but, despite the agony of living with his physical handicaps, he fled in terror from cholera-stricken Naples. Montaigne earned immortality by his meditations on the end of life, but bolted like a rabbit when the pest broke out in Bordeaux.

All the pessimists, from Schopenhauer down, have been convinced of the desirability of death, yet could not escape the necessity of living on.[8]

Yet if there is ever a real yearning for extinction, and if it may be found not only in life-activities but also in self-aggressive trends both in living *and* writing, then we should have little difficulty in finding evidence of such a wish in Dickens' later life and, most particularly, in his final novel. Certainly there is nothing more self-aggressive than the conduct of an entertainer who insists on going through an entire theatrical performance by himself a few minutes after he has seemed too weak to be able to stand upon his feet, who insists on including in his repertoire the account of the murder of Sikes' Nancy because he believes that in his reading he is exerting his own unaided will to hypnotize his audience *en masse*. We have seen more than ample evidence of the existence of the centrifugal and the centripetal aggressive elements in the Thanatos drive. The constant combination of these two, coupled with the other evidence set forth above and below, would seem to indicate the existence, somewhere, of a shadowy wish to "cease to be," to be "unborn," in short, to die.

There is considerable evidence of this trend in *Edwin Drood* as far as it was written; there is even more when we consider two outstanding suggestions that have been made for the novel's completion. Here we are on ground so shifting, yet in an atmosphere so fascinating that a full investigation of all of the possibilities would result in a book on this subject alone. Many such books have indeed been written.[9] Two solutions are to be examined here. One consists of the combination by Edmund Wilson of a dual, but complementary, set of theories; the other is the solution offered with much substantiating evidence by Stephen Leacock. The two sets of theories seem, superficially, to be mutually exclusive, but, taken together, they fit admirably into that atmosphere of ambivalence which always characterizes the drives of the Unconscious, and of unconscious literary creation. Mr. Wilson writes:

As one can revive invisible ink by holding it over a lamp or bring out three dimensions in a photograph by looking at it through certain lenses, so it is possible to recall to life the character of John Jasper as must have been conceived by Dickens.[10]

There are certain definite facts upon which all theories on the conclusion of *Edwin Drood* must be based. We know, for example, that the name character, even though he is "eliminated" somehow early in the tale, was the personality around whom the story was to revolve. Indeed, as Dickens wrote to Forster, his ill-starred pairing with the perverse Rosa Bud was the starting point of the book.

What would you think of the idea of a story beginning this way?—Two people, boy and girl, or very young, pledged to be married after many years—at the end of the book. The interest to arise out of the tracing of their separate ways, and the impossibility of telling what will be done with that impending fate.[11]

The implication of that turgid statement seems to be that, as the work was originally planned, Edwin would be alive when the book ended. Yet Dickens also made it plain beforehand, although he insisted on keeping the actual mechanism of the plot secret, that John Jasper was to end his days and write his final confession while in a cell as a condemned murderer. That Drood was to be the victim was probably implied in Dickens' confidential instructions to his illustrator, Luke Fildes, that Jasper must be pictured with a double-length neck scarf, because he was going to strangle someone with it. Yet the question constantly arises whether or not Edwin Drood was actually supposed to be dead.

Edmund Wilson, in his "explanation," relies on one theory advanced by Howard Duffield,[12] supplemented by another put forth by Aubrey Boyd.[13] These two theories come down to the suggestion that Edwin Drood was actually murdered and that (1) John Jasper performed the deed in his capacity of devotee of the Eastern murder cult of Thuggee, and that (2) he used his powers as a hypnotist to cover up his crime and to cast the blame for it upon another. For both of these suggestions there is ample evidence. The book, so far as we have it, stresses Jasper's addiction to opium used in the fashion of the romanticized Orient. It stresses the oriental birth, education, and appearance of both Neville and Helena Landless. There are hints and foreshadowings which might well develop into the uncovering of the full ritual of a Thug murder. Dickens might well have been trying to outdo Collins on the ground of the latter's newly published *Moonstone*, might have been making great capital out of his reading and publication of Meadows Taylor's "The Confession of a Thug" in *All the Year Round* and of his admiration for *Le Juif errant* by his friend, Eugène Sue, in which latter work a Thug figured. He had probably read the work of an American novelist about Thuggee, published in 1867. Dickens' biographer, Dame Una Pope-Hennessy, expresses her tentative concurrence with this phase of Mr. Wilson's theory.

If Dickens had lived to complete the story we should probably find that the root of the antagonisms between the characters lay in their Eastern past. . . . We see into the minds of all the characters in this book except Jasper's. No inkling as to what he thinks or why he reacts in the strange way he does is given, and just because of this we are tempted to construct theories as to his motives. . . . It might be possible to create a character so far from normal that he acted in certain stages of consciousness as if he were a Thug, while at other times he practiced a kind of animal magnetism by means of which he could suggest thoughts and actions to persons in his entourage.[14]

Could anything be more appropriate in a work in which the supreme god is Thanatos than a plot-structure based on the worship of Kali, the Hindu goddess of destruction to whose service all devotees of Thuggee had pledged their lives? Yet, for all of the circumstantial proof of the Kali-magnetism theme, we are vaguely discontented with this theory. As Dame Una writes,

On the whole, it is not a very satisfactory solution of the mystery to say that John Jasper on one plane of consciousness is a Eurasion [sic] organist who because of his passion for Rosa kills one rival and hunts down another, and on another plane of consciousness is an amateur Thug endeavoring to carry out a ritual sacrifice to Kali.[15]

The theory admittedly covers all of the known facts, but, interestingly enough, so does another theory which is, on a basis of fact alone, quite incompatible with the first. Let us remember, however, that if we suggest that *both* of these plans may have been unconsciously in Dickens' mind, there is no such thing as logical incompatibility in the Unconscious.

Stephen Leacock has collated all of the evidence to show that Edwin Drood is *not* dead.[16] The most important of all is the list of possible titles for the novel which was found among Dickens' notes. They are as follows:

The Loss of James Wakefield	*The Mystery in the Drood*
James' Disappearance	*Family*
Flight and Pursuit	*The Loss of Edwin Drood*
Sworn to Avenge It	*(or Edwin Drude)*
One Object in Life	*The Flight of Edwin Drood*
A Kinsman's Devotion	*Edwin Drood in Hiding*
The Two Kinsmen	*The Disappearance of Edwin*
The Loss of Edwin Brood	*Drood*
(or Edwin Brude)	*Dead? or Alive?*

These titles are so clearly incompatible with the theory that
Edwin Drood is really dead that we should have to assume
that Dickens changed the plan of his novel *after* he had decided on the title. Or perhaps, as we have suggested, both
ideas ran through the author's mind simultaneously, and
neither had yet been eliminated. After all—although Mr.
Leacock does not mention it—it would be a complete violation of the consciously acceptable oedipus pattern that John
Jasper should be allowed actually to kill Edwin Drood. The
"father-and-son" relationship between them is too clear for
such an Abraham-and-Isaac sacrifice to be completely con-
summated. Mr. Leacock reaches the same conclusion on quite
different grounds.

Call up two or three million readers of Dickens' books, past and
present, and ask them without giving them time for second
thought and the answer will be an overwhelming shout of
"Alive!" Surely it is a poor kind of story (speaking generally)
which bears the title *Alive or Dead? A Mystery?* and ends up
with the answer, Dead. Death is too easy. There is no "curious
and new idea"—alas!—about being dead. But the real ingenuity
of the problem that fascinates every writer of mystery fiction is
how to bring the "dead" back, alive and hearty, in the concluding chapters. We have but to remember the joyful resurrection
of Red Riding Hood's Grandmother, and The White Cat, to
realize that this denouement is as old as fiction itself.[17]

The theory fits into the whole pattern with a reassuring
click. We have death plus resurrection as the solution. Mr.
Leacock provides for this resurrection in detail by assuming
that John Jasper has hallucinated the murder of Edwin,
that Edwin has then fled for some reason, probably because
he could not bear a public disclosure of his uncle-father's
animus toward him, possibly because the shock has driven
him into a state of amnesia or fugue. But, according to Dickens, Jasper was to end the book in the condemned cell. Leacock ingeniously suggests that, like Jonas Chuzzlewit, Jasper
fears the discovery of the murder he did not commit and
therefore commits a real murder to cover up his secret. The

suggested victim is to be the unfortunate Neville Landless. Then Jasper can end in the cell, writing or telling the tale of his queer opium dream, perhaps even with a little Kali-worship and animal magnetism thrown in for good measure. Finally Leacock suggests that Drood will marry Helena, that Tartar, the dashing sailor, will be rewarded with Rosa and that Mr. Crisparkle will give up Helena "as becomes a well-bred clergyman." [18] The very neatness of the suggestion adds to its plausibility. It will be Dickens-Crisparkle, the man who goes for long walks and leads an ideal life with an ideal mother, who will give up the latest avatar of the newfound virgin so that a younger man, one who has literally gone down into the pit and has been reborn as clearly as Eugene Wrayburn ever was, may have her.

The complete picture, then, requires the worship of Kali the destroyer *plus* the adoration of Shiva the preserver, death *and* resurrection, dying as the longed-for method of being *un*born and then *re*born. That is the complementary picture we find in these two versions of the solution of *The Mystery of Edwin Drood*.

NOTES

1. See Ruth Munroe, *Schools of Psychoanalytic Thought* (New York, 1955), 80–81; Healy, Bronner, and Bowers, *The Structure and Meaning of Psychoanalysis* (New York, 1930), p. 72; Franz Alexander, "The Need for Punishment and the Death Instinct" in *The International Journal of Psychoanalysis*, Vol. 10 (1929), p. 260; also *Fundamentals of Psychoanalysis* (New York, 1948); Karl Menninger, *Man Against Himself* (New York, 1938), p. 6 *et passim*. See also William J. Ford, "A Note on Hans Castorp" in *Literature and Psychology*, II (1952) 4, 2–5.
2. Sandor Ferenczi, "Stages in the Development of the Sense of Reality" in Van Teslaar's symposium, *An Outline of Psychoanalysis* (New York, 1924), pp. 108–127, especially pp. 111–113. The process is also the subject of comment by Otto Rank and other later psychoanalytic writers.

3. Karl Menninger, *op. cit.* The entire book is devoted to a systematic study of all three elements, with examples taken from clinical practice, from popular writings, and from literature.

4. G. K. Chesterton, *Charles Dickens, A Critical Study* (London, 1925).

5. For an account of the Dickens novels which embody a systematic attempt at self-analysis, see the present writer's "The Personal History of David Copperfield," *American Imago,* 9, 1 (April 1952), pp. 3–25. See also Edgar Johnson, *Charles Dickens: His Tragedy and Triumph* (New York, 1952), the chapters on criticism.

6. John Dickens died on March 31, 1851; Dickens' baby daughter Dora Annie died on April 14, 1851; his sister Fanny died during the same year after a long illness.

7. *Bleak House* as a novel of oedipal propitiation and deeply disguised oedipal aggression is discussed in the present writer's dissertation, *The Dickens Pattern* (New York, 1948), Part III, Section 1. See also the present writer's "The Law as 'Father,' " *American Imago,* 12, 1 (Spring 1955), pp. 17–23.

8. Karl Menninger, *op. cit.,* pp. 75 *et seq.,* citing also writings of Ernest Jones and Franz Alexander, and examples from newspapers and popular biographies.

9. For instance, W. Robertson Nicoll, *The Problem of Edwin Drood* (London, 1912); Montagu Saunders, *The Mystery in the Drood Family* (Cambridge, England, 1914); Richard Baker, *The Drood Murder Case* (The University of California Press, 1953).

10. Edmund Wilson, *The Wound and the Bow* (New York, 1941), p. 85.

11. Forster, *The Life of Charles Dickens* (New York, 1927), Book XI, chapter 2.

12. In "John Jasper—Strangler," *The American Bookman,* February, 1930.

13. In Volume IX of *Humanistic Studies,* published by Washington University.

14. Una Pope-Hennessy, *Charles Dickens* (New York, 1946), p. 258.

15. *Ibid.,* p. 459.

16. Stephen Leacock, *Charles Dickens: His Life and Work* (New York, 1933) , p. 290. The evolution of the name is interesting. The innkeeper of the *Sir John Falstaff* inn, directly across the Dover Road from Dickens' home at Gad's Hill

Place, was named Edwin Trood. Interesting word-conno-
tations are suggested by the elimination of the *true* element and the substitution at first of the idea of *Brooding*,
and later of the portmanteau combination of the original
name with the idea of *dread*, perhaps even *dead*, *drool*,
and *Druid*.

17. *Ibid.*, p. 292.
18. *Ibid.*, p. 301.

Saint and Sinner—Dostoevsky's *Idiot*

by *SIMON O. LESSER*

Although the home base for Simon Lesser's college education was the University of Chicago, he later studied at the Kenyon School of English and Columbia, the Chicago and New York Psychoanalytic Institutes, and the Washington School of Psychiatry. In addition to his most influential work, *Fiction and the Unconscious* (1957), he has specifically applied psychoanalytic criticism to a wide range of authors: Hawthorne and Sherwood Anderson (his most frequently anthologized piece), Kafka, Flaubert, Shakespeare, Richardson, Colette, Homer, Sophocles. His main interest has always been in literature, which he has taught at New York University, The City College of New York, and, most recently, the University of Massachusetts; still, he has found time for forays into rural education and psychology, federal information agencies, motivational research, and television consultation work. The present study, which is one of two which he has written on Dostoevsky, approaches the character of Prince Myshkin in *The Idiot* from a new and startling viewpoint which is, at the same time, wholly consistent psychoanalytically speaking and vividly illuminating from a literary standpoint. It first appeared in *Modern Fiction Studies* (IV, 3, 211–224).

THE theme of *The Idiot* is the inadequacy of mere goodness in the world of today. *The Idiot* is the modern morality story in the same sense that *Hamlet* is the modern rendition of the Oedipus situation.

It is easy to miss the point of the novel entirely because it has, with one conspicuous exception, no great analogues. The exception is *Don Quixote;* and it is not by accident that references to the poor knight find their way into the Russian version of the same story. The perennial theme of modern fiction is that of a great man being torn and finally overcome by some one emotional weakness: lust, ambition, jealousy. Whatever the external situation, the fundamental internal conflict is always between what Freud would call the id— the emotional, instinctual, unsocialized part of our personality—and either the superego, which embodies our ideals and values: our conscience; or the ego: the directing, rational part of our personality, the prudent little judge who mediates between the id and superego and reconciles the demands of both with the demands of reality. In *The Idiot,* as in *Don Quixote,* the fundamental conflict is between the superego and the ego. Myshkin suffers from the noblest and most endearing of all possible weaknesses: an excess of goodness. His fatal flaw is an undeveloped ego: a sense of reality so deficient that it not only prevents him from accomplishing good, but causes him to fail everyone, himself included, in the long run and to leave behind him during his brief encounter with nineteenth century Russian society a trail of defeats and destruction. As Freud—and Dostoevsky—knew, the unbridled superego can be as dangerous as the id. Many of our notions of right and wrong are accepted early and uncritically. They are no safer a guide to the complicated problems of life than our instinctual impulses. Both these impulses and the instructions from the superego must be weighed by the conscious intelligence and related to the objective situation. It is amazing, in a way, that there are not more novels along the lines of *Don Quixote* and *The Idiot*—our own century has of course added *The Trial*—for the harm done by an over-developed and tyrannical superego, in a person with a deficient sense of reality, is a familiar phenomenon in life.

So weak is Myshkin's sense of reality that in the last analysis he *is* an idiot. There are of course ironies on ironies in calling him that. He is morally so superior to, and in many respects so much wiser and more penetrating than, the char-

acters who think of him as an idiot that our first tendency is
to laugh at them. But if we set up the simplest operational
definition of intelligence: self-knowledge and a capacity to
appraise people and situations accurately enough so that one
can thread one's way safely through the jungle of the world,
we see at once that Myshkin is indeed an idiot; a second irony
is the literalness of the title. We balk at perceiving Myshkin's
"idiocy" because his intellectual weaknesses are weaknesses
we admire. We are aware of our own malice and envy, our
tendency to do less than justice to the qualities of almost all
other human beings—all, indeed, but a handful whose ac-
complishments in some curious way feed our own narcissism.
How then can we despise a man who suffers from an excess
of generosity, who "sees the good" in everyone and everything? Or, hating ourselves for our concessions to expediency,
how can we despise a man who is invariably honest and
candid?

We face the same difficulty in taking a critical view of
Myshkin's actions. We know our own timidity and coward-
ice. How can we despise a man who acts spontaneously and,
though frail, even rashly, manifesting no fear? We know how
incapable we are of accepting the words of Jesus about the
lilies of the field; an anxious, wizened old man possesses our
soul and keeps even our charities within bounds. How can
we feel contempt for a man who is unfailingly and excessively generous? Nothing blocks us perhaps from perceiving
the childishness of Myshkin, his probable sexual impotence,
but even this deficiency, particularly since it has a physical
cause, we tend to judge indulgently.

Yet Dostoevsky wants us to see the stupidity and shortcomings of Myshkin: *The Idiot* is the story of the tragedy they
cause. To understand the novel, we must shed our illusions
and view Myshkin's character and conduct with our everyday
eyes. In our hearts we know the futility of pure goodness and
the stupidity of naïve generosity. There is a level, as we shall
see, on which Myshkin's "goodness" is immoral and cruel. It
is admirable perhaps but also foolish to accept everyone and

everything. The *appropriate* reaction to something hateful is hatred. We should shrink from the potential murderer, not welcome him to our circle of friends. We should be on guard against involvements with neurotic people, for example, women whose neurosis feeds our own. We should be sensible enough not to permit our generous and admirable tendencies—kindness, let us say, or candor—to carry us away. There are times when it is prudent to be silent or even to lie—perhaps even do things of dubious propriety, for example, open letters not intended for our eyes but which may contain information it is essential for us to have if we are to act wisely. So much Dostoevsky is saying, it might be maintained, explicitly. One other equally important thing is implied. This is the wrongness of completely repressing our instinctual needs. Myshkin is doubly crippled by his sexual innocence: he is incapable in the end of satisfying either of the women with whom he becomes involved—this is a failure of response—and he has no healthy guiding impulse to give order to his own life.

The complete man would perhaps be an amalgam of the three men whose destinies become interlocked in the first chapter of the novel—idealistic, sensual, prudent. The amalgam is unlovely, but it is man. Anyone who, like Myshkin, tries to deny, or simply lacks, some of the components is doomed, more surely than the mixed and imperfect ordinary man, to defeat and destruction by society.

Of course, there is a final, mocking irony in Dostoevsky's title: in a more perfect world the prince's "idiocy" would be something else again. Before the story proper opens, Myshkin has scored his one notable triumph. He has brought peace and ultimate happiness to the wronged and despised Marie. But, significantly, he has achieved this idyllic victory by influencing the hearts of children, and the woman he helps is herself child-like, making no demands on life; she is surprised and satisfied by pity.

Only in a world of children and Maries, or as Aglaia perceived, in a world where he did not get involved in action at all, could Myshkin possibly succeed and his "idiocy," his unrealistic acceptance of everything, be regarded as entirely admirable.

II

In writing *The Idiot*, Dostoevsky faced the, it would seem, insuperable problem of dramatizing pure goodness and certain *failures* of response—failure, for example, to react adequately to the cruelty perceived in Rogozhin. Now for fictional purposes these qualities have a dubious value, for they seldom lead to action. They suggest the spectator rather than the participant, the person acted upon rather than the person setting a chain of events in motion; and neither of these roles is adequate for the central character of a novel. Making a completely faultless character believable also presented difficulties—and difficulties which had to be solved if *The Idiot* was to be a flesh-and-blood novel, not a bodiless allegory. Perhaps Dostoevsky divined very early during the gestation of the book that his hero's goodness would have to be alloyed with weakness or evil. Otherwise the ultimate failure and even destructiveness of the goodness would possess no narrative significance, would seem unrelated to character; it would represent a basically expository comment on the wickedness of the world.

Dostoevsky's difficulties were resolved when, in developing the eighth plan for *The Idiot*, he selected a Christ-like character for his protagonist and proceeded to endow him with his own variety of masochism. In retrospect it is easy to see that no other kind of hero could have fulfilled Dostoevsky's narrative and dramatic purposes. Myshkin's goodness is based upon masochism, and the masochistic man *invites* reactions and involvements; he has a principle of action, albeit a neurotic one; his passivity is only apparent. Myshkin's goodness, his moral masochism, rests on a denial of his lusts and hatreds; it is an extension of his personal or, using the term broadly, his sexual masochism. A man whose goodness has this kind of underlying structure can be an active and wholly credible agent of destruction.

Inevitably, the people with whom such a character would become most closely involved would be sadistic, full of the passion and hatred he represses. He would be attracted by such people and they by him. The masochistic person seeks people who will use him cruelly; the sadistic, people he can torture. There is even more to it than this. According to Freud, neither masochism nor sadism is ever found in isolation. While one characteristic may be dominant, every masochist or sadist has some element of the opposite tendency in his makeup, so that he is drawn to other sadistic-masochistic people not only by his needs but by his ability to identify and sympathize with them.

Thus we have Rogozhin, Nastasya Filippovna, and Aglaia, the only kind of people with whom Myshkin could have established deep emotional relationships. The nature of the other principal characters in *The Idiot,* and the prince's relation with them, is inherent in his personality structure. The dominant traits of the three principal characters have an almost formal symmetry. Myshkin is apparently an example of pure masochism; in Rogozhin sadism is dominant; Nastasya, vindictive to all men but bent on self-destruction, has both qualities in equal proportion.

There is nothing mechanical about the actual working out of the relationships, however. The relationship between Myshkin and Nastasya is underscored and echoed by the relationship between him and Aglaia. Aglaia is a genteel bourgeois counterpart of the fiercer Nastasya. The relative breadth of Nastasya's reaction to Myshkin, as compared with Rogozhin's, is another asymmetrical factor. She reacts to his moral as well as his sexual masochism, in this respect serving as a link with the novel's minor characters. In the proposal scene which ends Part I, for example, she thrice rebukes Myshkin for regarding her, unrealistically, as an innocent. Rogozhin, the sensual man of instinct, is almost completely

oblivious to the prince's moral masochism. From the time he
first meets him, and expresses distrust of his disclaimer of
interest in women, to the time he expresses his fear that
Myshkin's "pity" may prove a more powerful weapon than
his own passionate, sadistic love, he is almost wholly concerned with the prince as a sexual rival.

Rogozhin's reaction to Myshkin makes up in intensity for
anything it lacks in breadth. The relationship between the
two men frames the book dramatically and cuts to its heart
psychologically. When it is fully understood, *The Idiot* has
yielded its ultimate secrets. The most deeply buried parts of
Myshkin's personality come to light in his relationship with
Rogozhin.

The dominant traits of Rogozhin and Myshkin, and the
nature of the relationship which is to bind them together,
are brought out in the short initial chapter of the novel. The
first word Rogozhin addresses to Myshkin—he of course does
not then know his name—reveals his cruelty. Myshkin's
masochism is disclosed almost as promptly by his willingness
to answer any question, however impertinent or inappropri-
ate. As the two men part after this first meeting, Rogozhin
extends a patronizing invitation to Myshkin and offers him
aid; and the prince—though we later find he possesses considerable means—abjectly accepts the offer.

In this initial chapter we are also given a wealth of information about the woman for whom these men will soon be
bitterly competing, who will serve to ripen the relationship
between them. By the end of Part I of the novel Myshkin
and Rogozhin are destined to be implacable rivals for the
hand of this woman. By the end of Part II, in her cruelty,
confusion, and vacillation, she will have twice run away from
each of them, feeding their hatred for one another at the
same time that she enmeshes each of them more deeply in a
sadistic--masochistic relationship with her. By the end of the
novel, every possibility of a non-tragic solution of the affair
exhausted, the two men—themselves on the verge of destruction—are destined to be reunited over the corpse of this

woman. She, Nastasya Filippovna, has of course been murdered by Rogozhin. It is indicative of the rapidity with which
Dostoevsky develops his plot that by the end of chapter 3, the
probability of this murder has been consciously foreseen by
Myshkin.

The relationship between Myshkin and Rogozhin reaches
its climax in Part II of the novel. The dramatic focus of
chapters 3 to 5 of this part is on the impulse the prince and
Rogozhin feel to kill one another. The prince, of course, represses his murderous impulses, but they are revealed to us
none the less, once our eyes are open, with unmistakable
clarity. Rogozhin's impulses are more obviously revealed and
are of course confirmed in the end by his actual attempt to
kill Myshkin.

The section which brings the relationship of the two men
to a head begins with the prince seeking out Rogozhin in his
gloomy home. In the ensuing conversation the motives each
man has for hating the other—as well as the motives each
has for hating Nastasya—are clearly revealed. With what
anguish we can imagine, Rogozhin tells Myshkin that he is
the one Nastasya loves and that if she marries him, Rogozhin, it will only be as a way of seeking her own destruction.
Rogozhin also shows an awareness of Nastasya's sadism and
of the contempt she feels for him. Nor does he attempt to
deny the sadistic nature of his love for her: he accepts Myshkin's charge that he wants to marry Nastasya only to pay her
back for the torment she has caused him, just as he had previously accepted the charge when it was made by Nastasya
herself. At the end of chapter 4, he announces the decision
against which he is fighting and which is the ultimate source
of his hatred of the prince: he offers to surrender Nastasya to
him. How incapable he is of this renunciation his subsequent
attempt to kill Myshkin reveals.

But the prince is no more capable of finally renouncing
Nastasya than is Rogozhin. He has come to see his friend to
assure him that if it is true, as he has heard, that Rogozhin
and Nastasya have been reconciled and are to be married,

despite his own feeling that the marriage will be ruinous for
her, he will not interfere. Yet that very evening he finds himself irresistibly drawn to the house on the "Petersburg Side"
where he believes Nastasya to be staying. It is a stroke of
genius that his compulsive desire to see her asserts itself at
this time, for his impulse to kill Rogozhin also reveals itself
most clearly on this same day, and it is psychologically and
artistically right that his libidinal and aggressive repressions
should crumble simultaneously. Myshkin's thoughts while
he is walking to Nastasya's also show that no one has sur-
passed Dostoevsky as a psychologist. The prince keeps reassuring himself about the purity of his intentions. He tells
himself that he wishes he could see Rogozhin, so that the two
friends could visit Nastasya together. In fact, he does see him
a few minutes later—Nastasya, it turns out, has gone to Pavlovsk—and is so guilt-ridden he cannot speak to him at all.

Myshkin's desire for Nastasya is of course also the primary
basis of his repressed hostility toward Rogozhin. In the scene
where the prince visits his friend it emerges very clearly that,
just as Rogozhin is suspicious of Myshkin's "pity," so Myshkin
is jealous of Rogozhin's passionate love, a kind of love of
which he feels himself incapable. The scene at Rogozhin's
house also reminds us that Myshkin has a more legitimate
reason for wishing Rogozhin out of the way—his desire to
protect Nastasya against the laxly curbed violence he perceives in his friend.

Myshkin's murderous impulses toward Rogozhin must of
course be revealed to us by unconscious manifestations.
Myshkin cannot become aware of them; a principal purpose
of his epileptic fits, one of which he feels impending, is to
keep such an "idea" from consciousness. Two other factors
may keep a hurried reader of *The Idiot* from becoming aware
of the murderous rage against which Myshkin is struggling.
The first is his apparent innocence of such impulses. The
second is our conscious and sympathetic awareness of the
prince's fear of Rogozhin. Our initial impulse is to assume
that the prince's preoccupation with knives and the subject

of murder stems from this fear, from the need he feels to defend himself. But on closer examination it becomes clear that Myshkin's awareness of Rogozhin's desire to kill him— an awareness for which he reproaches himself—is screening the still more terrible idea that he, Myshkin, wants to kill his friend. He is probably as sensitive as he is to what Rogozhin is feeling because of the murderous hate in his own heart.

The evidence for this hate, when we open our eyes to it, is unmistakable; as though compensating for the fact that he could not be more explicit, Dostoevsky has piled on clue upon clue. It is Myshkin, not Rogozhin, who *twice* unconsciously, in a state of extreme agitation, picks up a knife which is lying on his friend's table. Later that afternoon the prince realizes that for some hours previously "he had at intervals begun suddenly looking for something." The "something" proves to be an item he had seen in a hardware store window—a knife with a staghorn handle. It materializes that he has been haunted all day by thoughts of murder. He has been thinking of Lebedyev's nephew, whom he has confused with the murderer of whom Lebedyev spoke at the time he introduced his nephew to the prince. During dinner he has discussed the crime committed by this murderer with his waiter.

The fact that Myshkin is guilty of the same murderous and erotic impulses which are more nakedly revealed in Rogozhin is of the greatest structural importance. It explains his ability to forgive Rogozhin's attempt upon his life—forgive him, it might almost be said, in advance of the attempt. It is a key to understanding the entire relationship between the prince and Rogozhin. It is basic to our emotional acceptance of the overwhelming final scene of *The Idiot*. Myshkin cannot find it in his heart to reproach Rogozhin for the murder of Nastasya for very much the same reason that Hamlet cannot bring himself to kill Claudius: he is himself filled with guilt. Even consciously he has cause to reproach himself: not only has he failed to protect Nastasya, but his inability even at the very last, at Pavlovsk, to give her up has set in motion the final chain of events leading to her death. Unconsciously he knows that his complicity is far deeper and more encompassing than this. Through his identification with Rogozhin he has acted out the sadism and lust for Nastasya he tries so desperately to deny. Through his identification with her he has responded to those feelings, thus satisfying unacknowledged passive and feminine tendencies. In his own person he has felt homosexual love and murderous hate for Rogozhin and irresistible desire for Nastasya. Though these feelings have been repudiated and repressed, at the core of his being Myshkin knows that he is guilty of lusts and hatreds no less terrible than those to which his passionate companions have yielded.

III

Except for the chapters which have been discussed and much of chapter 1, which summarizes what has happened between the time of the proposal scene and Myshkin's reappearance in St. Petersburg six months later, Parts II and III of *The Idiot* are concerned with Myshkin's efforts to extricate himself from the neurotic triangular situation in which he is involved and to make a reasonably normal adjustment to Russian society. Only failure to perceive this, it seems to me, can account for the charge, in part baseless and in part irrelevant, that this middle section of the novel is diffuse and structurally deficient. It is, of course, less intense than Part I. But this loss of intensity is inevitable, for it is of the essence of Myshkin's efforts to achieve stability that Rogozhin and Nastasya must tend to disappear from his life. Some diffuseness is also inevitable, for Dostoevsky is trying to show us the prince's ability to cope with a wide variety of people and problems, of the sort that a man in his position would not fail to encounter. In this section of the book Dostoevsky is giving his hero his chance. Not until we are convinced that he is incapable of taking advantage of it are we fully prepared for *The Idiot's* tragic conclusion. Considering the prince's position in society, it is essential that he be given a broad test. Considering the nature of the relationships he is attempting to escape and establish, it is essential that the test extend over some period of time.

As a matter of fact, the technical skill and economy with which this portion of the novel are developed cannot be passed by without some comment. The loss of intensity is fully compensated for by an accrual of richness which is the despair of anyone trying to write about the book. We not only see Myshkin's relationships with many characters, but we see those characters live and breathe apart from him—see them in their setting, see their vanities, ambitions, intrigues. *The Idiot's* minor characters are without exception interesting in their own right—so interesting that we may fail to observe the structural role they play. But our knowledge of them, and of the way they treat one another, provides indispensable background information for judging Myshkin's responses. The way Lebedyev tortures General Ivolgin to punish him for his theft shows us, for example, how far the prince goes in the other direction in his indulgence of the old man. The interrelationships of the secondary characters, which are also casually and, it appears, effortlessly revealed to us, are also used to advance the action of the novel; consider, for example, the use made of the relationship between Ganya and Ippolit, and between each of them and Aglaia.

On examination we find that Dostoevsky achieves the rich, realistic, peopled texture of the middle part of the book by focussing on just four families—the Epanchins, Lebedyevs, Ivolgins, and Ptitsyns—and Mrs. Ptitsyn is the already introduced Varya Ivolgin. Even the "Burdovsky incident," while perhaps spun out too much in length, is developed with great economy so far as use of characters is concerned. Burdovsky is—apparently—the bastard son of Myshkin's benefactor, Pavlishtchev, and we have already been introduced to Lebedyev's nephew. The two characters who do not stem from the past, Keller and Ippolit, are used extensively in the further development of the story, and the latter is a friend of Kilya Ivolgin. The Burdovsky affair can by no means be regarded as simply an interpolated incident designed to show Myshkin's attitude toward social problems and ability to handle affairs. All of the characters involved in it have links with the larger movement of the novel.

A final brilliant technical achievement of the middle part of *The Idiot* is the way in which Dostoevsky makes the presence of Nastasya and Rogozhin felt, even though it is essential that their actual appearances on the scene be held to a minimum. The presence of Nastasya in particular is felt with cumulative intensity toward the end of Part III, even though she and Myshkin do not encounter one another face to face until the section's final pages. Without bringing her on the scene often, Dostoevsky, in preparation for the final catastrophe, shows how deeply she and Myshkin are still involved with one another. Her interest in the prince is revealed by their one encounter, the testimony of Rogozhin, and, as Aglaia realizes, in inverted fashion by the several letters she has written Aglaia and her effort to eliminate Yevgeny Pavlovitch as a suitor for that young lady so that she will be free to marry Myshkin. His interest in Nastasya is shown by his intervention to protect her during the altercation at the band concert and, even more portentously, by his dreaming of her while awaiting Aglaia's arrival for their early morning rendezvous.

The main focus of the middle section of *The Idiot*, however, is on Myshkin's efforts to make a normal adjustment to society. These efforts center on his relationship with the Epanchin family, and, above all of course, with Aglaia. Though the Epanchins constitute Myshkin's bridge to the ordinary life of his time and place, it is to be noted that they are by no means a typical bourgeois family. If only because of the warm, impulsive character of Lizaveta Prokofyevna, they have a touch of eccentricity about them and are fully aware of it themselves. Aglaia is no run-of-the-mill specimen of the well-brought-up upper-middle-class young lady. She is not only the most remarkable and beautiful of the three sisters, but in any group, however large, would stand out for her intelligence, high spirit and intrepidity. In the character of the Epanchins and Aglaia, Dostovesky has tilted the scales in Myshkin's favor. If he cannot achieve satisfactory relations with them, his case, it is clear, is hopeless.

Like Nastasya, Aglaia is what Freud would call a castrating type of woman—a type encountered frequently enough in modern fiction and modern life. Her sadism is revealed by her treatment of Yevgeny Pavlovitch and Ganya as well as by her treatment of Myshkin himself. It is recognized by her not too perceptive father. Her mother comments on her daughter's cruelty at the time she drags Myshkin to the Epanchin home when she finds he has misinterpreted a note from Aglaia and again a little later on:

"She is exactly, exactly like me, the very picture of me in every respect," the mother used to say to herself. "Self-willed, horrid little imp: Nihilist, eccentric, mad and spiteful, spiteful, spiteful! Good Lord, how unhappy she will be!"

Aglaia's sadism, however, is tempered and redeemed by her intelligence and her deep and growing love for Myshkin. It may be, too, that only a woman possessed of a certain masculine firmness could take the prince seriously as a suitor. Aglaia is compelled to arrange rendezvous, to make Myshkin face his relationship with herself and Nastasya realistically, to reveal her own love with a nakedness that must have shamed her, to maneuver the prince into proposing to her. Her tendency to tease and torment her "suitor" is understandable enough. Aglaia errs only once, and this error is one we cannot fail to admire: in her determination to clear up the matter of Myshkin's relation with Nastasya once and for all she overreaches herself and sets the stage for *The Idiot's* crushing reversal.

Just as Myshkin's sexual masochism keeps us doubtful, throughout the middle section of the novel, about his ability to establish a good relationship with Aglaia, so his moral masochism makes us question his ability to adjust to society. His behavior in handling the Burdovsky affair is so meek that, on one level, it outrages the Epanchins. He is so lenient in his judgment of Ippolit that even the kindly Prince S. chides him for his lack of realism. He shows no ability to protect himself—does not know when he is being chaffed, readily forgives Keller and Lebedyev for exploiting him, is unwilling to accept reports about intrigues even when there is every reason to credit them. A curious and more disturbing fact is that Myshkin frequently provokes the attack of the very people he tries to help. His motives are mistrusted and his ingenuousness makes it difficult for him to attain his idealistic ends. Without being sure of our ground, we are inclined to wonder if there is not some truth in the charge levelled against him by Lebedyev's nephew:

"Yes, prince, one must do you justice, you do know how to make use of your . . . well, illness (to express it politely); you've managed to offer your friendship and money in such an ingenious way that now it's impossible for an honourable man to take it under any circumstances. That's either a bit too innocent or a bit too clever. . . . You know best which."

While we are troubled by this charge and by the recurring evidence of Myshkin's ineffectuality, on the whole, throughout the middle section of the novel, we are inclined to give him the benefit of the doubt. By and large his relations with people seem to be going along well enough and, as has been mentioned, his shortcomings are amiable ones. Dostoevsky dramatizes this fact: we are inclined to judge the prince in kindly fashion not only because *we* cannot condemn such faults as he reveals, but because we see him much of the time through indulgent and admiring eyes—Kolya's and Vera Lebedyev's, for example, and Madame Epanchin's and Aglaia's. It is the judgment of the latter two, above all, that is decisive. While we have some forebodings, our dominant feeling, at the end of Part III of *The Idiot,* is that we are on the eve of the prince's engagement to Aglaia—and this engagement

does in fact become a reality early in Part IV. Seeing Myshkin through the hopeful, loving eyes of his intended and her
mother—who so much resembles her that, like Aglaia, she
continues to feel warmly toward him even when her mind
tells her he is impossible—we begin to believe that somehow
he may "make out" despite his unworldliness. At the end of
this middle section of the novel the prince's affairs are
apparently prospering.

IV

But of course his situation is really precarious. We have
been prepared openly in the first part of the novel and sub-
terraneously throughout the middle part for the possibility
that the prince will not be able to free himself from Nastasya
or cope with his other problems. He has still hardly demonstrated his capacity for affairs, and what success he has had
may be attributed in part to the happiness and confidence he
feels as a result of his relationship with Aglaia. And her
indulgence softens and extenuates his failures.

Thus Myshkin's worldly success and the solution of his
personal problems both pivot around Aglaia. Ironically, the
consummation of his relationship with her is jeopardized by
the very growth of his love and his partial success in freeing
himself from Nastasya. The compulsive attraction he feels
for Nastasya undoubtedly fades in intensity during the middle portion of the novel. However, simultaneously, his pity
for her grows; he comes to the conclusion that she is mad and
desperately in need of help. At this point in the story there
is no doubt for which woman Myshkin feels the more normal, complete love. But with his fatal flaw of masochism
there is no doubt either that, in any showdown, he will
choose the woman he loves least, the woman for whom he
feels deepest pity, the woman who will bring him most pain.

Myshkin's showdown occurs in chapters 6 to 8 of Part IV.
His ability to make an adjustment to society, being the mat-

ter of lesser intensity, is disposed of first. The decisive test comes during the party which the Epanchins have planned to introduce Myshkin, now formally engaged to Aglaia, to society. In particular they are eager for him to make a good impression on Madame Epanchin's influential friend, Princess Byelokonsky. The party is planned with some apprehension and, even though it pains her to do so, Aglaia does not hesitate to brief her fiancé about how he should conduct himself.

There is a shift of focus here which permits Dostoevsky to show us Myshkin's shortcomings magnified. Whereas before we have seen him much of the time through the clement eyes of the Epanchins, in this scene we see them watching his conduct anxiously. Still another technical device is employed to disclose Myshkin's ineptness. In previous scenes, we have seen the prince in relation to people whom we knew and for whom we felt some sympathy. If he judged them too charitably, we were inclined in turn to be charitable toward him. But most of the people at the Epanchin party we do not know or have only met casually. We have no emotional investment in them, and when Myshkin's judgment of them is absurdly overgenerous, nothing prevents us from perceiving the fact. It is even easier to perceive the stupidity of his view of the party as a whole and of his willingness to whitewash the Russian aristocracy en masse.

Even in this scene, there are some residual traces of ambiguity. Within limits the prince's sincerity and intensity seem admirable precisely because he is with a group that takes nothing very seriously and has long since forgotten the meaning of simple honesty. It is significant, too, that despite the prince's fiasco and the pain he has caused them, both Aglaia and her mother continue to feel warmly toward him. Even at the end of chapter 7, his position is not completely hopeless.

But on the whole Dostoevsky does not spare Myshkin in this scene. In addition to dramatizing his failure, and giving us the negative reactions of such a kindly observer as Adelaida, Dostoevsky intervenes as omniscient novelist at a half dozen points to call attention to the prince's ineptness. In this scene, too, we finally come to see why Myshkin's readiness to forgive defeats its apparent purpose. In judging the Epanchins' guests, he is so indulgent that his ingenuousness has precisely the effect of irony. His appraisal of the aristocracy is so at variance with the facts that it makes his listeners more keenly aware of their shortcomings. Instead of providing expiation, it increases their sense of guilt.

It may be that Dostoevsky is saying that one is not in a position either to blame or forgive another unless one first understands him. It is clear in any case that many of the people drawn to Myshkin want understanding as well as forgiveness, and are disappointed when they receive only the latter.

Perhaps the most obvious example is General Ivolgin. In contrast to Lebedyev, who has tortured Ivolgin in reprisal for his theft and ridiculed him for his lying, Myshkin says nothing about the former and accepts the most outrageous lies with no show of incredulity. At first Ivolgin is delighted and feels a rush of affection for the prince. But that evening he writes him a letter in which he informs him that "he was parting with him, too, forever, that he respected him, and was grateful to him, but that even from him he could not accept 'proofs of compassion which were derogatory to the dignity of a man who was unhappy enough without that.'" On reflection it is easy enough to understand this later reaction. Although the course Myshkin follows is apparently dictated by kindness, what he is doing is playing make-believe with the General. Ivolgin is aware of his tendency to lie; he would probably respond either to a serious analysis of the tendency or the sort of chaffing which suggests that his being found out in a lie has not led to any diminution of affection. The prince's course of disregarding the General's lying is not without a trace of malice, for it implies that it is hopeless to talk to him, that he is beyond redemption. Madame Epanchin's treatment of the General dramatizes the

fact that there is a sensible middle course between the deliberate cruelty of Lebedyev and the unsatisfactory form of
forgiveness offered by Myshkin: she is critical but at the
same time tolerant and, above all, perfectly straightforward.

Even after the fiasco of the engagement party, it is still
theoretically possible for Myshkin to make some sort of adjustment to society, for he still has Aglaia's love. But one of
the purposes of that scene is to prepare us for Myshkin's
graver failure in the climactic scene of the novel where for
the first time he, Nastasya, Aglaia, and Rogozhin come together to work out their destiny. It is one of the ironies of
the book that Aglaia, the most likable of the four central
characters, plays so prominent a part in this catastrophic
meeting. She has suggested the meeting and it is her harsh-
ness to Nastasya which stings her into attempting to prove
her continued power over Myshkin. But of course the decisive failure is his. It is not a moral failure in the usual sense
of the term. It is a neurotic failure, the final triumph of his
masochism. He chooses the woman he most pities, not the
one he most loves.

Once that choice is made, the triangular situation of Part I
is re-established—with one decisive difference. Every possible
solution of the situation of Myshkin, Nastasya, and Rogozhin which does not involve their destruction has now been
eliminated. We are reconciled to a tragic liquidation of their
relationship and even prepared for the specific series of
events which now follow so swiftly—Nastasya's final recoil
from Myshkin, her murder by the tormented Rogozhin, the
prince's forgiveness. It is a measure of Dostoevsky's greatness
that horrible as the final scene of *The Idiot* is—it is a scene
that few writers would attempt—we do not balk at accepting
its truth for a minute.

Freud and the Poet's Eye

by NORMAN N. HOLLAND

Norman Holland holds a doctorate in English from Harvard, which he has supplemented by systematic study of psychoanalytic theory, including work at the Boston Psychoanalytic Institute. His work in psychoanalytic criticism is particularly concerned with the reader's affective response, a process which he calls "affective criticism." He taught courses in comedy, Shakespeare, and psychoanalytic criticism at the Massachusetts Institute of Technology since 1955 and has extended his activities to include television lectures on Shakespeare and on current films. His most recent book is *Shakespeare and Psychoanalysis,* and he has a host of other books, among them *The Shakespearian Imagination* (1964), articles, and lectures to his credit. He is now chairman of the English Department of the State University of New York at Buffalo.

The present essay, which first appeared in *Literature and Psychology* in 1961 (XI, 2, 36–45), combines several of Mr. Holland's varied interests by subjecting Freud himself to psychoanalytic scrutiny in his function as literary critic, particularly with respect to Freud's attitude toward Shakespeare.

FREUD's ambivalence toward writers and artists has long hung as a skeleton in the closet of psychoanalytic criticism. To bring it out again would be tactless, except that it helps anatomize two things: first, the *tone* of the ambivalence, and second, the Master's own character and what in him led to his discovering psychoanalysis. Analyzing Freud's psyche is a doubtful business at best, at worst gross rebellion.

As Freud himself replied when he was shown a hostile book which purported to discover his own complexes:

> You taught me language; and my profit on't
> Is, I know how to curse.[1]

Nevertheless, despite this cautionary tale, I find it hard to forego pointing out that the remark applies equally well to Freud himself. Freud learned *his* language from the poets ("Not I, but the poets discovered the unconscious"); then he faced the other way and called the poets daydreaming children.

Yet, in all of Freud's discoveries and all of his life literature played an important part. At least three of his biographers have insisted that had he not turned to psychology, he would have become a writer.[2] In school, he was fascinated by words and style, and when courting Martha Bernays he wrote to her of vague "literary stirrings." [3] In later life, his friends noted "his astonishing knowledge of literature" and "his memory, especially for Shakespeare." [4] Busy as he was, Freud read voraciously and kept up friendships with a number of literary figures. He seems even to have suggested whimsically that he himself become a novelist so as to do justice to his own case histories.[5] His writings are permeated with literary quotations, examples, and insights, and in describing his own dreams, fantasies, and free associations, he is constantly taken on literary excursions, so intimately was literature woven into his emotional life.

Nevertheless for all his skill and interest in things literary, Freud shows a curious reticence toward artists and writers. At various points in his writings, he insists that "before the problem of the creative writer, analysis must lay down its arms" (and the military metaphor, *"die Waffen strecken,"* is not without point.)[6] "It [analysis] can do nothing toward elucidating the nature of the artistic gift, nor can it explain the means by which the artist works—artistic techniques." [7] Perhaps not, but analysts—and Freud himself—seem to have done quite a bit to break the taboo. Freud's reluctance to probe the writer's "gift" is part of a more general pattern of ambivalence. That is, he admires writers and artists greatly, but at the same time, he compares them invidiously to scientists, calls them children, likens their creations to daydreams, and assigns them venal motives.

What Freud admires in the writer are his powers as a seer, his ability to grasp intuitively truths the psychologist gets at only by hard work. As early as 1895, he wrote, "Local diagnosis and electrical reactions lead nowhere in the study of hysteria, whereas a detailed description of mental processes such as we are accustomed to find in the works of imaginative writers enables me, with the use of a few psychological formulas, to obtain at least some kind of insight." [8] "Creative writers," he wrote in *Delusions and Dreams*, "are valuable allies and their evidence is to be prized highly, for they are apt to know a whole host of things between heaven and earth of which our philosophy has not yet let us dream." [9] Writers could see, for example, the "necessary conditions for loving" before psychologists could.[10] Shakespeare had understood the meaning of slips of the tongue long before Freud, and not only that, he had assumed that his audiences would understand, too.[11] The writer, however, knows these things "through intuition—really from a delicate self-observation," while Freud himself had to "uncover" them through "laborious work." [12]

At the same time, however, he says over and over again (devoting an entire essay, "Creative Writers and Day-Dreaming," to the idea) that art and literature are like a child's game, a glorified daydream, a mild narcotic, an illusion offering an escape from reality into fantasy." [13] "Meaning," he wrote of visual artists, "is but little to these men: all they care for is line, shape, agreement of contours. They are given up to the *Lustprinzip*." [14] It is at this point that critics such as Roger Fry and Lionel Trilling have objected most strenuously. Fry demands that the "pure" appreciation of aesthetic form, not the fantasy or "literary content" be the prime motive behind art.[15] But Freud is, in effect, adamant. The artist adopts his own daydreams to provide others with a sorry substitute for instinctual pleasures that reality forbids. In this roundabout way the artist wins by fantasies what he was too weak to win in reality, "honor, power, and the love of women." [16] His motives and his audience's are venal; there is no such thing as art for art's sake. Trilling has pointed out that writers are preoccupied with reality, but Freud's view seems squarely contrary.[17] Art is pure pleasure principle—"harmless and beneficent; it does not seek to be anything else but an illusion"—while science is "the most complete renunciation of the pleasure principle of which our mental activity is capable." [18] Where the artist tries to fantasy a world into being, the scientist tries to strip fantasies off the world of being.[19]

And yet Freud also felt that artists had a special insight into psychic truth. Freud, Jones says, "seemed to take the romantic view of [artists] as mysterious beings with a superhuman, almost divine, afflatus." "This was occasionally tinged with a trace of envy for their superior gifts." [20] The symptom of the envy is that Freud practically never makes a simple statement of the artist's gifts with the necessary qualifications. Instead, the artist is either exalted as a prophet beyond analysis or reduced to a child daydreaming. He is either a seer of reality or an avatar of the pleasure principle and hence, ultimately, of sexual gratification. These two extreme views, the artist as hedonist and the artist as truth-seeker were, for emotional reasons, closely linked in Freud's own psyche.

Curiosity was the most basic motive in his character. "His insatiable desire," wrote Helen Walker Puner, "was the desire for knowledge." [21] He himself said, "In my youth I felt an overpowering need to understand something of the riddles of the world in which we live." "I was moved . . . by a sort of curiosity, which was, however, directed more towards human concerns than towards natural objects." [22] Over and over again in Freud's early life, alongside the transformation of his infantile curiosity, the theme of knowledge as power, the omnipotence of thoughts, recurs. Late in his life he described one of the chief purposes of analytic thinking as the attempt "to master the matter of the outer world psychically" (and as he pointed out in the *Introductory Lectures*, "matter" tends to stand for *mater*).[23]

Freud's passion [writes Dr. Jones] to get at the truth with the maximum of certainty, was, I again suggest, the deepest and strongest motive in his nature and the one that impelled him toward his pioneering achievements. What truth? And why was the desire so overwhelming? In his study of Leonardo, Freud maintained that the child's desire to know is fed by powerful motives arising in his infantile curiosity about the primary facts of life, the meaning of birth and what has brought it about. It is commonly animated by the appearance of a rival child who displaces him in his mother's attention and to some extent in her love.[24]

Jones points out that there was such a figure in Freud's life, his sister Anna, and he goes on to suggest that knowing the truth meant security to the boy, the security of absolute possession of the mother. Crucial in this search was Freud's half-brother Philipp, much given to jokes, as in the screen-memory of the cupboard,

which for the last twenty-nine years has been turning up from time to time in my conscious memory without my understanding it. I was crying my heart out because my mother was nowhere to be found. My brother Philipp (who is twenty years older than I) opened a cupboard [*Kasten*] for me, and when I found that mother was not there either I cried still more, until she came through the door, looking slim and beautiful.[25]

Symbolically, the cupboard meant pregnancy,[26] the threat of another child (hence the importance of his mother's appearing "slim and beautiful"). Peering into the cupboard symbolized his infantile curiosity about the secrets of pregnancy, known to the witty Philipp, "whom," Jones says, "he suspected of being his mother's mate and whom he tearfully begged not to make his mother again pregnant." [27] (It is not surprising that Freud was later drawn to write about *die Kästchenwahl* in *The Merchant of Venice* or that this screen-memory turns up in the very letter in which Freud penetrated the secret of *Oedipus Rex* and *Hamlet*.)

Eyes and other images of looking run like a *leitmotiv* through Freud's life and works. "His most striking feature," his friend Joan Riviere wrote, "was the forward thrust of his head and critical exploring gaze of his keenly peering eyes." [28] Greatly interested in the visual and verbal arts, he was almost totally uninterested in music.[29] He failed (and was puzzled by his failure) to see the potentialities of cocaine as a local anaesthetic for operations on the eye.[30] Though he saw that blindness symbolized castration, curiously enough, he did not apply his insight to the Oedipus myth until 1914, after it had been pointed out by others, even though he himself had earlier used such phrases as "brings to light" or "seek to close our eyes" when in 1900 he first described the repression in the myth.[31]

Visual metaphors abound in his writings. For example, he described his self-analysis as having "days when a flash of lightning illuminates [*erhellt*] the picture." [32] He described the *Interpretation of Dreams* as "planned on the model of an imaginary walk":

First comes the dark wood of authorities (who cannot see the trees), where there is no clear view and it is very easy to go astray. Then there is a cavernous defile through which I lead my readers—my collection of specimens with its peculiarities, its details, its indiscretions, and its bad jokes—and then, all at once, the high ground and the prospect, and the question: "Which way do you want to go?" [33]

(As he himself might have pointed out for another, his description of his researches symbolizes the same infantile curiosity about female anatomy as the screen-memory of the cupboard.) In anlyzing one of his dreams (the "Three Fates"), he associated with the third Fate his mother's rubbing skin off her hands to give an "ocular demonstration" that we are all made of earth.[34] (The three Fates carry us back again to "The Three Caskets" essay.) On the other hand, at the time of his father's funeral, he dreamed of a placard which said, "You are requested to close the eyes." [35] In still another dream (the "non vixit"), eyes became a kind of weapon: "I then gave P. a piercing look. Under my gaze he turned pale; his form grew indistinct and his eyes a sickly blue—and finally he melted away." [36] In still a third dream (the "botanical monograph," associated with his paper on cocaine and its use in eye operations), he recalled a letter from Fliess which said that he could see *The Interpretation of Dreams* finished; Freud apostrophized, "How much I envied him his gift as a seer [*Sehergabe*]! If only *I* could have seen it lying finished before me!" [37] Eyes here are associated with scientific research, and eyes commonly stand for the aggressive, mastering, masculine way. For Freud especially, they seem to have had this symbolic value. Indeed, in the *New Introductory Lectures,* the mind itself seems to become ocular; Freud's diagram of the hypothetical topology of id, ego, and superego looks exactly like the cross-section of an eye.

To do research is to look *into;* to be a poet, on the other hand, is to be looked *at.* Thus, in the Preface to the first edition of *The Interpretation of Dreams* Freud reluctantly agreed to "reveal to the public gaze more of the intimacies of my mental life . . . than is normally necessary for any writer who is a man of science and not a poet." In his letter to Fliess of May 31, 1897, he pointed out the similarity of creative writing to hysterical fantasying, using the rather Oedipal situation of young Werther as an example. He headed the paragraph, *"Dichtung und* Fine Frenzy," and remarked at the end, "So Shakespeare was right in his juxtaposition of poetry and madness (the fine frenzy)." This is a curious failure to quote. Much closer to Freud's meaning would be other phrases from the same passage like "such seething brains, such shaping fantasies" or the famous

> And as imagination bodies forth
> The forms of things unknown.

Instead, he recalled the phrase "fine frenzy" which does not refer to "madness" as such, but to "The poet's *eye*, in a fine frenzy rolling."

Just as this passage links the lover's sight and the poet's, so for Freud seeing (either in a physical sense or in the metaphorical sense of understanding) is associated with his libidinal drives. (He recalled during his self-analysis a journey at two-and-a-half with his mother "during which we spent a night together and I must have had the opportunity of seeing her *nudam*." [38] Seeing and knowing seem to have had for Freud (as for most men) the value of seeing the mother and, by discovering her secrets, possessing her. They suggest, in short, sexual power. Freud's tendency to endow the artist with greater powers of insight than the scientist means symbolically that the artist has greater sexual abilities because he knows some secret.

Freud did say, on intellectual grounds, that the artist had an especially strong sexual drive: he finds "one of the origins of artistic activity" to be the sublimation of "excessively strong excitations." [39] "The artist is originally a man who turns from reality because he cannot come to terms with the demand for the renunciation of instinctual satisfaction as it is first made." The artist "is one who is urged on by instinctual needs which are too clamorous." "An abstinent artist is scarcely conceivable," he wrote. "An abstinent young intellectual [for example, Freud himself] is by no means a rarity. The young intellectual can by abstinence enhance his powers of concentration, whereas the production of the artist is probably powerfully stimulated by his sexual experience." [40]

Freud's feeling that the ordinary intellectual is subordinate sexually to the artist may have caused what Jones calls "the immense capacity for jealousy he manifested during his engagement." For example, when he was tormented by jealousy on account of one Fritz Wahle (an artist), he wrote:

I think there is a general enmity between artists and those engaged in the details of scientific work. We know that they possess in their art a master key to open with ease all female hearts, whereas we stand helpless at the strange design of the lock and have first to torment ourselves to discover a suitable key to it.[41]

The image of lock and key (aside from its suggestion of phallus and vagina) makes the artist, like the scientist, a discoverer. He is a "psychological explorer of the depths," [42] and "One may heave a sigh at the thought that it is vouchsafed to a few with hardly an effort, to salve from the whirlpool of their emotions the deepest truths, to which we others have to force our way, ceaselessly groping amid torturing uncertainties." [43]

This mingling of admiration and envy for the artist is only one instance of a general ambivalence basic to Freud's personality. "My emotional life," he pointed out in his analysis of the "non vixit" dream (in which eyes became weapons), "has always insisted that I should have an intimate friend and a hated enemy . . . and it not infrequently happened that the ideal situation of childhood has been so completely reproduced that friend and enemy have come together in a single individual." This childhood situation was "his relations in childhood with a nephew who was a year my senior . . . my superior . . . I early learned to defend myself against him." He played Brutus to his senior's Caesar in what Jones calls a "pronouncedly parricidal" duologue of Schiller's. In analyzing the "non vixit" dream, Freud hypothesized a scene in which "the two children had a dispute about some object. . . . Each of them claimed to have *got there before the other*."[44]

As this dream and the other quotations suggest, behind Freud's ambivalence toward artists lies his own drive toward the potency of discovery. Discovery in childhood seemed to promise complete possession of the mother; for the adult it held "honor, power, and the love of women." Yet, both emotionally and intellectually, Freud's discoveries led him to the dispiriting conclusion that artists saw intuitively, easily, what he as scientist had to grope for. "It becomes inevitable," he noted, "that science should concern herself with the same materials [*Materien*] whose treatment by artists has given enjoyment to mankind for thousands of years, though her touch must be clumsier and the yield of pleasure less." [45] In effect, the artist "got there before the other." For ordinary men, Freud reflected in analyzing the "non vixit" dream, isn't "having children our only path to immortality"? In the *Leonardo* essay, however, he notes, "The creative artist feels towards his work like a father," and "What an artist creates provides at the same time an outlet for his sexual desire."

Ultimately, then, the artist is for Freud a kind of hero-king-creator who achieves immortality through his artistic progeny and his discoveries. He is the "great man," more powerfully endowed sexually, who "got there before the other," who "has the master key to open with ease all female hearts, whereas we stand helpless at the strange design of the lock," who "with hardly an effort" gets at "the deepest truths, to which we others have to force our way, ceaselessly groping amid torturing uncertainties." The artist, in short, is the father in the most primal, terrible sense of all. Furthermore, even if the scientist learns the secrets known to the artist, he still cannot become this artist-father: "The knowledge that not even the clearest insight into the factors conditioning the choice of imaginative material, or into the nature of the ability to fashion that material, will ever make writers of us does not in any way detract from our interest." [46]

Freud's ambivalence toward the artist is thus simply the ambivalence of the son for the father. As he himself said in his *Goethe-Preis* essay of 1930, we have a need to establish affective relations with great men, a need to link them with the fathers, teachers, and others whose influence we have felt. At the same time, however, our relation to such fathers and teachers is ambivalent; we admire, but we also resent them.[47] Freud acted out this ambivalence by exalting the artist-father and at the same time shrinking him to a day-dreaming child, the son changing roles with the father as sons, he said, wish to do.

Freud's attitude toward his favorite writer, Shakespeare, serves as a paradigm for this sense of the artist as father and also suggests the importance of Freud's ambivalence toward artists in the discovery of psychoanalysis. Freud vastly admired Shakespeare's plays. He first began to read them at the age of eight, read them over and over again, and all his life, with a facility that professional Shakespearians might envy, he could come up with an apt quotation. His books fairly bristle with illustrations from Shakespeare. His famous analysis of *Hamlet* occurs in the very same letter (October 15, 1897) as his discovery of the Oedipus complex itself. Freud must have been thinking of *Hamlet* and *Oedipus Rex,* almost expecting Sophocles and Shakespeare to guide him in his self-analysis.

The hostile component of his attitude toward Shakespeare took the form of irrationally denying Shakespeare his identity, symbolically "killing" him: "The name *William Shakespeare* is very certainly a pseudonym, behind which a great mysterious stranger [*ein grosser Unbekannter:* the father?] is hidden."[48] Although Jones and James Strachey remonstrated, although Freud knew that scholars thought such pseudonym theories absurd, although he had to give up the convenient fact that "Shakespeare wrote *Hamlet* very soon after his father's death,"[49] Freud persisted in proclaiming the true Shakespeare in a variety of writings.

An early form of attack was to make the bard into a Frenchman. "He insisted," Jones reports, "that his countenance could not be that of an Anglo-Saxon but must be French, and he suggested that the name was a corruption of Jacques Pierre." Shakespeare's name is fairly phallic, and Freud might well have pointed out (were he analyzing someone else) that the name was now, in effect, gelded; he did, of course, point out that destroying a man's name sym-

bolizes destroying the man himself. Also, since he greatly
admired the English, and rather disliked the French, the
attempt to make Shakespeare French is at least covertly an
attempt to degrade him.[50]

In his sixties, Freud rejected the Baconian hypothesis and
attached himself to J. T. Looney's idea that Shakespeare
was Edward De Vere, Earl of Oxford, a man whom Freud
described as "passionately disordered," "somewhat déclassé,"
"an inadequate father who never did his duty by his children," a "squanderer of his inheritance and a miserable
manager of his affairs, oppressed by debts," and a cuckold.
Jones points out that "Something in Freud's mentality led
him to take a special interest in people not being what they
seemed to be," for example, Shakespeare, Moses, and Leonardo's mother and stepmother. Jones calls this tendency
a "variant of the Family Romance," that is, the common
childhood fancy that "these quite ordinary people are not
my parents, only my foster parents. My real parents are
rich and powerful people who guide my destiny from afar."
Jones finds support for his view in the fact that Freud was
in fact confused as to which of the older men around him
in the complicated household of his childhood really was
his father.[51]

Doubting that Shakespeare was Shakespeare, however, was
no isolated aberration or special by-product of Freud's ambivalence toward artists. On the contrary, Freud's Oxford-
ian, Baconian, and Jacques-Pierrian vagaries represent a
basic pattern in his thinking. Jones lists, as related eccentricities, Freud's faith in Lamarckian evolution, telepathy,
and the occult.[52] Freud himself "freely associated" the question of telepathy to the Bacon-Shakespeare controversy, calling them two themes that "always perplexed him to dis-
traction." [53] Jones suggests that these aberrations are possibly
all aspects of a single feeling that "things are not what they
seem to be" behind which lies a wish that "a certain part
of reality could be changed," presumably by just thinking
it changed. That is, telepathy, the occult, or the Lamarckian

belief that acquired mental characteristics can be inherited, are all pretty clearly related to the "omnipotence of thought." Freud is thinking, like the infant or the savage, that wishes can directly change reality.[54]

A less friendly analyst of Freud's personality than Jones, Erich Fromm, points to other elements.[55] Freud had, he says, an extreme dependency on the mother's (or some subsequent woman's) love; it made him, among other things, arrive for trains an hour early—one might mention also his fear of open spaces (agoraphobia) "which troubled me much in my younger years." [56] Fromm also notes a strong urge to replace the father, to supplant existing authorities with his own, to be a world-reformer. Fromm says Freud's strongest need was to dominate his instincts by reason and that doing so, Freud felt, was a condition for becoming, as he wished to do, one of the world's elect. Fromm's analysis suggests another reason why Freud was especially resentful of artists. The artist is a man who most notably does *not* curb his instincts, but wins the mother-woman anyway—and becomes the father-authority anyway.

We can, I think, join these two explanations, Jones' and Fromm's, by recalling that Freud charged insight, thought, and discovery with the value of power, particularly the sexual power of the father, and that he regarded this power as peculiarly the possession of the artist or writer. In his artistic fantasies, the writer "actually becomes the hero, king, creator, favorite, he desired to be without pursuing [like the scientist] the circuitous path of creating real alterations in the outer world." [57] "Art constitutes a region half-way between a reality which frustrates wishes and the wish-fulfilling world of the imagination—a region in which, as it were, primitive man's strivings for omnipotence are still in full force." [58] "Satisfaction is obtained through illusions, which are recognized as such, without the discrepancy between them and reality being allowed to interfere with the pleasure they give." [59] In other words, where the scientist slowly, laboriously achieves his ends by changes in the real

world, the writer merely fantasies a changed world into
being. Telepathy, the occult, and a Lamarckian inheritance
of acquired characteristics bridge this dualism of body and
mind. They occupy a sort of middle ground between the
scientist who changes reality by knowing about it and the
artist who "knows" a reality into being. All three make
wishes more than artistic fantasies—wishes directly affect
the material world of the scientist.

In this context, Freud's reason for rejecting Bacon as the
author of Shakespeare's plays is suggestive: "Then Bacon
would have been the most powerful brain the world has
ever produced, whereas it seems to me that there is more
need to share Shakespeare's achievement among several
rivals than to burden another important man with it." [60]
In effect, Freud is saying it would be intolerable for one
"great man" (or father) to have so much creative potency.
It was much more satisfying for the "great mysterious
stranger" to be Edward de Vere, cuckolded husband and inadequate father. In effect, too, Freud is turning a wish, a
mere "need," into a discoverable fact. Most important, by
rejecting Bacon, Freud reserved the unique role of artist-
scientist for himself.

That is, by creating psychoanalysis, Freud became both
the scientist who changes reality through knowledge *and* the
artist who fantasies a changed reality into being. The letters
to Fliess and the *History of the Psycho-Analytic Movement*
pinpoint the crucial transition. At first, Freud thought neuroses came from actual sexual experiences in childhood.
Then various factors ruled this explanation out: "Analysis
had led back to these infantile sexual traumas by the right
path, and yet they were not true. The firm ground of reality
was gone." [61] And Freud was led to posit what has since
turned out to be the most seminal premise in the mind of
the twentieth century, at once the most broadening and
the most limiting assumption of the Age of Freud: "Psychical reality requires to be taken into account alongside
actual reality." As he first phrased it on September 21, 1897,

there is clear relation to literature in his "definite realization that there is no 'indication of reality' in the unconscious, so that it is impossible to distinguish between truth and emotionally-charged fiction *(die mit Affekt besetzte Fiktion)*".

Thus, the wish to dominate, the faintly resentful imitation of writers, and the development of psychoanalysis are all bound up together in Freud's emotional make-up. In his *History of the Psycho-Analytic Movement,* he used the metaphor of a knife for psychoanalysis and noted that "the situation of analysis involves a superior and a subordinate." [62] (The couch of song and story sounds a faintly sexual note in this domination.) Originally, analysis was called the "cathartic" method and its long-term effect is not unlike the short-term effect of drama.[63] Freud himself recognized the quasi-artistic basis for psychoanalysis' method of free association in a quotation from Schiller he inserted in *The Interpretation of Dreams* in 1909,[64] and in 1920 Freud pointed out that he might have derived the method of free association from an essay of Ludwig Börne's called (significantly), "The Art of Becoming an Original Writer in Three Days." Börne had been a favorite of Freud's when he was fourteen, and other essays by Börne "kept on recurring to his mind for no obvious reason over a long period of years." Yet Freud had forgotten this one. "It seems not impossible," he wrote, "that this hint [that such an essay existed] may have brought to light the fragment of cryptomnesia which in so many cases may be suspected to lie behind apparent originality." [65] The whole method of psychoanalytic thinking, in which "a number of very remarkable facts are brought together into a consistent whole," [66] occupies a middle ground between the sequence-thinking which characterizes science and the *gestalt*-thinking which underlies the organic unity of art.

In saying that psychoanalysis may have had the emotional value of an art for Freud, I do not, of course, mean to imply (as the experimental psychologists secure in their laboratories of amazed rats and pigeonholed pigeons like to do) that psychoanalysis is "unscientific," "merely" an art. Nor, in showing that Freud felt about Shakespeare or any other artist as about a father-figure, have I touched in the slightest the validity of his conclusions. "Explaining" Freud's psyche does not explain *away* Freud; it only shows *why* he said what he said. As a matter of fact, it simply shows that the intellectual system of psychoanalysis is self-consistent: it can explain itself, indeed, did explain itself—in Freud's self-analysis. Finally, in intruding upon the privacy of Freud's psyche, in finding there Oedipal feelings, a striving for omnipotence, a desire for sexual domination, and so on, I do not (consciously) mean to denigrate the greatest mind of our century. I mean simply to show, as psychoanalysis has so often shown for artists, why this particular man was able to think in this particular way and so create the thing he did. As Freud said about psychoanalytic probings of poets, "Such studies are not meant to explain the genius of a poet but to show the motifs which have stirred it up, and the topics imposed on it by fate." [67]

In the movement of Freud's intelligence toward his discoveries, three themes mingled. First, there was the driving curiosity, the unrelenting search for the secrets of man's mind. Second, he was preoccupied (in all his thinking, not just in such eccentricities as his odd views on Shakespearean authorship) with the omnipotence of thoughts, the ability to wish something into being, as in a dream. Third, he identified sight with mind and both with procreative, sexual power. These three themes all merged in the figure of the artist, who knew, who created, who saw. The artist became for Freud a kind of spiritual and intellectual totem, both resented and emulated, and the result was psychoanalysis. Psychoanalysis could probably not have come into being in the heavily physiological atmosphere of medical science at the turn of the century, had it not been for a particular scientist with a particular need to create like an artist and through his intellectual offspring win the immortality that few but artists win. In a very real sense, by discovering psychoanalysis, Freud joined to the probing eye of the scientist the creating eye of the poet. Freud's own vision bodied forth the forms of things unknown and gave them a local habitation and a name.

NOTES

In the notes, I have given the English titles of Freud's works as they appear in the *Standard Edition*. The following abbreviations are used:

GW = Sigmund Freud, *Gesammelte Werke,* 18 vols. (London, 1940–1941).

SE = *The Standard Edition of the Complete Psychological Works of Sigmund Freud,* trans. James Strachey, Anna Freud, Alix Strachey, and Alan Tyson, 24 vols. (London, 1953–   ).

CP = Sigmund Freud, *Collected Papers,* trans. and ed. Joan Riviere, 5 vols. (London, 1924–1950).

Origins = Sigmund Freud, *The Origins of Psychoanalysis: Letters, Drafts and Notes to Wilhelm Fliess, 1887–1902,* eds. Marie Bonaparte, Anna Freud, Ernst Kris, trans. Eric Mosbacher and James Strachey (New York, 1954).

Jones = Ernest Jones, *The Life and Work of Sigmund Freud,* 3 vols. (New York, 1953–1957).

1. Letter from Max Eitingon to Charles Maylan, March 22, 1929; quoted, Jones, III, p. 145.
2. Jones, III, p. 418. Helen Walker Puner, *Freud: His Life and Mind* (New York, 1947), pp. 57–58. Theodor Reik, "Psychoanalytic Experiences in Life, Literature, and Music," in *The Search Within* (New York, 1956), pp. 387–388, quoting Wilhelm Stekel.
3. Jones, III, p. 418.
4. Joan Riviere, "An Intimate Impression," *The Lancet,* September 20, 1939, p. 765, quoted by Jones, II, p. 405.
5. Jones, III, p. 427. Fritz Wittels, *Sigmund Freud, His Personality, His Teaching, and His School,* trans. Eden and Cedar Paul (New York, 1924), pp. 19–20, quoting Wilhelm Stekel. Jones, II, p. 256. Reik (n. 2), pp. 387–388, quoting Stekel.

6. "Dostoevsky and Parricide" (1928); *GW*, XIV, p. 399; *CP*, V, p. 222; *SE*, XXI. In "On the History of the Psycho-Analytic Movement" (1914), Freud compares psychoanalysis to a knife: *GW*, X, p. 112; *CP*, I, p. 358; *SE*, XIV, p. 66.

7. *An Autobiographical Study* (1925 [1924]); *GW*, XIV, p. 91; *SE*, XX, p. 65.

8. With Josef Breuer, *Studies in Hysteria* (1893–1895); *GW*, I, p. 227; *SE*, II, pp. 160–161.

9. *Delusions and Dreams in Jensen's "Gradiva"* (1907); *GW*, VII, p. 33; *SE*, IX, p. 8.

10. "A Special Type of Choice of Object Made by Men" (1910); *GW*, VIII, p. 66; *CP*, IV, p. 192; *SE*, XI, p. 165.

11. *Introductory Lectures on Psycho-Analysis* (1916–1917), Lecture II; *GW*, XI, pp. 31–32; *SE*, XV–XVI; *A General Introduction to Psychoanalysis*, trans. Joan Riviere (New York, 1943) pp. 35–36.

12. Letter to Arthur Schnitzler, May 14, 1922, "Sigmund Freud, Briefe an Arthur Schnitzler," *Die neue Rundschau*, LXVI (1955), pp. 96–97.

13. "Creative Writers and Day-Dreaming" (1908); *GW*, VII, p. 213; *CP*, IV, p. 173; *SE*, IX, p. 143. *Civilization and its Discontents* (1930), *GW*, XIV, pp. 437–438; *SE*, XXI; trans. Joan Riviere (London, 1930), pp. 33–35. *Beyond the Pleasure Principle* (1920); *GW*, XIII, p. 15; *SE*, XVIII, p. 17.

14. Letter to Ernest Jones, Jones, III, p. 412.

15. Roger Fry, *The Artist and Psycho-Analysis* (London, 1924).

16. *Autobiographical Study* (n. 7), *SE*, XX, p. 64. "Formulations on the Two Principles of Mental Functioning" (1911), sec. 6; *GW*, VIII, pp. 236–237; *CP*, IV, p. 19; *SE*, XII, p. 224. *Introductory Lectures* (n. 11), Lecture XXIII, trans. Riviere, pp. 327–328. *Five Lectures on Psycho-Analysis* (1909–1910), Fifth Lecture; *GW*, VIII, p. 52; *SE*, XI, p. 50.

17. Lionel Trilling, "Freud and Literature" (1940, 1947), *The Liberal Imagination* (New York, 1953).

18. *Beyond the Pleasure Principle* (n. 13), *loc. cit.* "Special Type" (n. 10), *loc. cit. New Introductory Lectures on Psycho-Analysis* (1933); *GW*, XV, p. 173; *SE*, XXII; trans. W. J. H. Sprott and James Strachey (New York, 1933), p. 219.

19. "On Psychotherapy" (1905[1904]); *GW*, V, p. 17; *CP*, I, pp. 253–254; *SE*, VII, pp. 260–261.

20. Jones, II, p. 344; III, p. 408.

21. Puner (n. 2), p. 55.

22. "Postscript to a Discussion on Lay Analysis" (1927); *GW*, XIV, p. 290; *CP*, V, p. 208; *SE*, XX, p. 253. *Autobiographical Study* (n. 7); *GW*, XIV, p. 34; *SE*, XX, p. 8.

23. Address delivered in the Goethe House at Frankfort (1930); *GW*, XIV, p. 550; *SE*, p. XXI.

24. Jones, II, p. 433.

25. *Origins*, October 15, 1897.

26. *The Psychopathology of Everyday Life* (1901), Ch. IV; *GW*, IV, pp. 58–60; *SE*, VI, pp. 50–52.

27. Jones, II, p. 434.

28. Riviere (n. 4), *loc. cit.* See also Theodor Reik, *From Thirty Years with Freud,* trans. Richard Winston (New York, 1940), p. 17.

29. Reik (n. 2), pp. 386–388.

30. Jones, I, Ch. VI. Cf. Letter to Fritz Wittels, August 15, 1924, *Letters of Sigmund Freud,* selected and edited by Ernest L. Freud, trans. Tania and James Stern (New York, 1960), pp. 350–351.

31. *The Interpretation of Dreams* (1900), V (D) and VI (E); *GW*, II/III, pp. 269–270 and 403 n.; *SE*, IV, p. 263 and V, p. 398 n.

32. *Origins*, October 27, 1897.

33. *Origins*, August 6, 1899.

34. *Interpretation of Dreams* (1900); V (B-iv); *GW*, II/III, p. 211; *SE*, IV, p. 205.

35. *Ibid.*, VI (C); *GW*, II/III, pp. 322–323; *SE*, IV, pp. 317–318. Also *Origins*, November 2, 1896.

36. *Interpretation of Dreams* (1900), VI (F); *GW*, II/III, p. 424; *SE*, V, pp. 421–422.

37. Ibid., V (A); *GW*, II/III, p. 177; *SE*, IV, p. 172.

38. *Origins*, October 3, 1897.

39. *Three Essays on the Theory of Sexuality* (1905); *GW*, V, p. 140; *SE*, VII, pp. 238–239.

40. " 'Civilized' Sexual Morality and Modern Nervous Illness" (1908); *GW*, VII, p. 160; *CP*, II, p. 92; *SE*, IX, p. 197.

41. Jones, I, p. 111; II, p. 433.

42. Letter to Arthur Schnitzler (n. 12).

43. *Civilization and its Discontents* (1930), Ch. VII; *GW*, XIV, p. 495; *SE*, XXI; trans. Joan Riviere (London, 1930), p. 89.

44. *Interpretation of Dreams* (1900), VI (H); *GW*, II/III, pp. 487–500; *SE*, V, pp. 483–487. Jones, I, p. 23.

45. "Special Type" (n. 10), *loc. cit.*

46. "Creative Writers" (n. 13); *CP*, IV, p. 173; *SE*, IX, p. 143.

47. *Loc. cit.*, n. 23.

48. *An Outline of Psycho-Analysis* (1940[1938]); *GW*, XVII, p. 119 n.; *SE*, XXIII; trans. James Strachey (New York, 1949), p. 96 n.

49. *Autobiographical Study* (n. 7); *GW*, XIV, pp. 89–90, 96 n.; *SE*, XX, pp. 63–64. Jones, II, p. 428; III, p. xii.

50. Jones, I, pp. 13–21, 24, 178–179, and 184.

51. Jones, III, p. 458. *Loc. cit.* n. 23. Jones, III, pp. 428–430; II, p. 433; I, pp. 10–11.

52. Jones, III, pp. xii, 313, and 381.

53. Jones, III, p. 430.

54. Jones, III, pp. 428–430; II, p. 433; I, pp. 10–11; III, p. 313.

55. Erich Fromm, *Sigmund Freud's Mission,* World Perspectives Series, Vol. XXI, ed. Ruth Nanda Anshen (New York, 1959).

56. Theodor Reik, *Listening with the Third Ear* (1948), (New York, 1956), pp. 15–16.

57. "Formulations on the Two Principles of Mental Functioning" (1911), sec. 6; *GW*, VIII, pp. 236–237; *CP*, IV, p. 19; *SE*, XII, p. 224.

58. "The Claims of Psycho-Analysis to Scientific Interest" (1913), sec. II(f); *GW*, VIII, pp. 416–417; *SE*, XIII, pp. 187–188.

59. *Civilization and its Discontents* (1930); *GW*, XIV, p. 438; *SE*, XXI; trans. Joan Riviere (London, 1930), p. 35.

60. Jones, III, p. 428.

61. "History" (n. 6); *GW*, X, p. 54; *CP*, I, pp. 299–300; *SE*, XIV, pp. 17–18.

62. Ibid., *GW*, X, pp. 93, 112; *CP*, I, pp. 337, 358; *SE*, XIV, pp. 49, 66.

63. Ibid., *GW*, X, p. 45; *CP*, I, p. 288; *SE*, XIV, p. 8.

64. *Interpretation of Dreams* (1900), sec. II; *SE*, IV, pp. 102–103.

65. "A Note on the Prehistory of the Technique of Analysis" (1920); *GW*, XII, p. 309; *CP*, V, pp. 103–104; *SE*, XVIII, pp. 264–265.

66. *The Future of an Illusion* (1927); *GW*, XIV, p. 345; *SE*, XXI; trans. W. D. Robson-Scott (London, 1934), p. 40.

67. Preface to Marie Bonaparte, *The Life and Works of Edgar Allan Poe* (London, 1949[1933]; *GW*, XVI, p. 276; *SE*, XXII.

Thomas Mann and Psychoanalysis:

The Turning Point

by JOYCE CRICK

In 1956 a thesis was written at the University of London by Miss Joyce Morgan (now Mrs. Crick) which traced in detail the attitude of Thomas Mann toward psychoanalysis throughout the major part of his literary career. This thesis was brought to the attention of the editors by Mrs. Crick's adviser, the late Professor William Rose, and in 1960 two sections of that thesis (the present paper and a study of *Lotte in Weimar*) were published in *Literature and Psychology* (X, 2, 45–55 and X, 3, 69–75, respectively). In the light of the enormous influence which Thomas Mann had on the development and acceptance of psychoanalytic criticism, it is of unique importance to trace the process by which his original attitude of skepticism and insecurity in the face of the new science changed until it became the motive power for his later panegyrics to Freud. Mrs. Crick has taught at various schools in Germany and England.

> Niemand bleibt ganz der er
> ist, indem er sich erkennt.[1]

THE relationship between Thomas Mann's devious psychology and psychoanalysis, between his so-called "new humanism" and the dry moralism of Sigmund Freud has been so close and intimate that many of Mann's critics and commentators have merely taken it for granted. Certainly during the perilous years that saw the end of the Weimar Republic, Mann wrote two major essays on his great contemporary that were at once an affirmation of his own new-won democratic views, and an identification with the ideas of the founder of psychoanalysis: "Die Stellung Freuds in der modernen Geistesgeschichte" (1929) and "Freud und die Zukunft" (1936). But it would be well to look more closely into what Mann really understood by psychoanalysis, to inquire more exactly when he became acquainted with it and when he came to approve it, and to scrutinise the gap between that acquaintance and that approval—for gap there was, as we shall show.

In a sense, the two men were literary contemporaries; the same year, 1900, saw the appearance of young Thomas Mann's first novel, *Buddenbrooks,* and the first major work of the mature analyst, *Die Traumdeutung.* From then on, psychoanalysis became part of the climate of literary opinion. However, it was not until Mann's own middle life that he came directly to grips with it, and even then, there was a remarkable ambiguity in his attitude.

The forces in his youth urging him towards psychoanalysis were many. The literary world, naturalist and symbolist, was ready for it, and Mann himself was a writer with a foot in each camp. The psychology of his mentors Nietzsche and Schopenhauer turned him in that direction, and his entire *oeuvre* seemed to follow: he knew the significance of the parent figures; he brooded on the artist's necessary renunciation of life; he was aware of the subordination of the intellect to the will, or the unconscious; he was preoccupied with the tension of living and dying that together made up life; the detail of his own keen, devious "debunking" psychology was close to Freud's unmasking of self-deception. Wagner's associative musical technique, which had become the formal principle of his own narrative style, lent itself easily to conveying psychological associations. Everything carried him towards psychoanalysis. And yet . . . and yet . . . he did not accept it easily or immediately. Just after *Der Zauberberg* was published (1924) a number of Mann's smaller essays broach the topic directly, or touch upon it in the course of an argument, but the general picture they

offer is exceedingly equivocal: a concession to psychoanalysis in one place is cancelled by a reservation elsewhere; an admission is called into question by the uneasiness
of the tone in which it is made. So contradictory are Mann's
own statements, that it is exceedingly difficult to establish
with any precision when he first became acquainted with
psychoanalysis. "My relationship to psychoanalysis is as complicated as it deserves," [2] he says, and that seems to set the
tone.

What were the objections that Mann raised to psychoanalysis in these years? They may throw light on the curious
survival of his old ironic distress at psychological insight,
his old *Erkenntnisekel*. They seem to be based on two issues,
social and aesthetic. During the 1920's, when Freudian
ideas began to spread beyond austere medical circles, they
frequently fell into the hands of unsavoury cranks, of the
Krokowski type, which did them little credit. They became
involved and confused in a great many suspect and irrational trains of thought, and came to imply the same dubious
atmosphere as clung to the masculine mysticism of the circle
of Stefan George, Hans Blüher's studies in homosexuality,
the questionable pretensions of the characterology of a Ludwig Klages or a Hans Prinzhorn. All this Mann found more
than distasteful; he thought it dangerous, and in a short
article, "Mein Verhältnis zur Psychoanalyse," written in 1925
at the special request of the Freudian circle itself, and seemingly his first utterance on the subject, he said so. His
objection is made typically, as an afterthought. First he
praises its bold clearsightedness, but then withdraws, making a very considerable reservation:

In psychoanalysis, this remarkable outgrowth of the modern scientific mind, we are justified in seeing something great and admirable, a bold discovery, a deep forward thrust of perception,
an astounding, indeed a sensational, extension of our knowledge
of man. But on the other hand, we may well find that, over-
publicised and abused, it can become an instrument of malicious
enlightenment, a mania for debunking and discrediting, danger-

ous to our deep cultural roots; and to have doubts about this aspect of it does not necessarily mean mere sentimentality.[3]

Its popularisation and misuse was something Mann could not look upon with approval. In *Der Zauberberg* he satirized this tendency in the figure of Dr. Krokowski, and many years later, in *Doktor Faustus,* in the figure of the irrationalist, Dr. Chaim Breisacher. Insofar as these two novels represent the decline of the European intellectual world, psychoanalysis abused plays no small role in hastening the decay.

The second objection Mann had to psychoanalysis was more profoundly personal, affecting him where he was most sensitive: it concerned the nature of the artist. "It [psychoanalysis] is in essence understanding, melancholy understanding, especially when it concerns art and the nature of the artist." [3] Elsewhere and in the same year he says,

As an artist I must confess that I am not wholly satisfied with Freud's ideas; rather, I feel myself disturbed and belittled by them. After all, Freud's ideas penetrate the artist like X-rays, right down to destroying the secret of his creativity.[4]

Now the nature of the artist has always been Thomas Mann's own peculiar problem, and he has felt it to be a moral problem. Coming from a background of powerful mercantile Protestant morality, he cannot but feel distressed at the sovereign transcendence of art over all other categories. The formula, by now almost a cliché, for his kind of artist is the "artist with the bad conscience." It would seem that while in other spheres he was ready to recognise the value of psychoanalysis, in this one respect he was still reluctant. The revival of the old *Erkenntnisekel,* the advances and withdrawals, acceptances and hesitations, so evident in the essays of 1925, probably indicate a struggle with psychoanalysis, and with himself, on this issue. Moreover, he fears that knowledge of the source of art will destroy his art, just as insight into life has made his artist unfit for life. The X-ray metaphor is a significant indication of his distaste, for it recalls the consulting room of Krokowski the analyst in *Der Zauberberg*, the psychical counterpart to Behrens' X-ray chamber, where the most questionable hocus-pocus with the occult also went on. But Mann is unrelenting in his determination that some reckoning must be made. In tortuous and tormented sentences he recalls Aschenbach, in *Der Tod in Venedig*, who deliberately and heroically refused perception if it threatened to inhibit activity, and who closed his eyes to unwelcome knowledge. But this, Mann says now, signifies "nothing less than the illusion that, by shutting its eyes, the world can never, as the saying is, 'get round' the results of the research of Freud and his followers. It most certainly will not get round them. Nor will art do so." [5] The reckoning must certainly be made, but as yet he finds it difficult to make wholly. This passage shows Mann right on the horns of his dilemma: on the one hand nostalgia for the old rejection of insight; on the other the certain knowledge that the perception and understanding provided by psychoanalysis, however unpalatable, must be honestly confronted, even with regard to the artist, the point where he is most vulnerable.

This melancholy and ironical uneasiness at his own understanding, which Mann called *Erkenntnisekel*, goes back further in his career than *Der Tod in Venedig* (1911). He refers it to the period in his life which in his second essay on Freud, "Freud und die Zukunft" (1938), he calls "my Nietzsche-Hamlet-Tonio Kröger-period." And *Tonio Kröger* was written in 1903. Perhaps a brief study of the problems implied in this *Novelle—"mein Eigenstes,"* as he once called it—will show why the *Erkenntnisekel* should have persisted so long as far as psychoanalysis was concerned, although such a study involves the delicate task of deducing an author's spiritual biography from his work.

"To be a poet means to stand in judgment on oneself" was the motto from Ibsen, much in keeping with psychoanalysis, that Mann placed at the head of the volume of *Novellen* in which "Tonio Kröger" was first published, and he has made no secret of the strong autobiographical element in this portrait of the artist as a young man. This may perhaps justify our own biographical approach to it. The streets of Mann's own native town of Lübeck form the background of the *Novelle;* we learn from Mann's autobiographical sketch that there was a real Hans Hansen, whom as a boy he had loved; even the incident of Tonio Kröger's arrest when he returns to his old home is not invented, but really occurred to the author. These details, however, are slight in comparison with the profound personal dilemma in Tonio's psychology itself.

In brief, the *Novelle* presents the dilemma of the writer who is unable to be at ease with the careless aestheticism of his art, which by its nature transcends the limitations, responsibilities, and tensions of everyday life. Metaphysically, Mann's artist is a traveller in the realms of death and suspension of being; physically, this is symbolised by the presence of disease within him; psychologically, it has its correlative in his ineptitude in normal society, his vain love of life and sorrowing awareness of his alienation of guilt. He experiences the autonomous amorality of art as explicitly immoral. He is the artist with the bad conscience. This sense of the artist's inadequacy before life is already in keeping with Freud's idea of art as a compensatory activity. What brings the *Novelle* still closer to Freudian theory, however, are the symbolic terms in which Mann presents the bad conscience with which this uneasy artist regards his sullen craft. The moral world he feels answerable towards is the bourgeois world of his native town, summarised and summed up in the symbolic figure of his father.

The contrast between the decency of ethical life and the wild and irresponsible vagabonding of the artist, who knows death, the contrast central to the *Novelle,* finds its clearest symbol in the contrast between Tonio's parents, the correct and reserved father from the North, and the irresponsible and musical mother from the South. Tonio is torn between his love for his mother and the hidden admission that his father was right. His father is for him his good conscience. And this conscience, symbolised by the father, is with him all his life: "And so he fell into adventures of the flesh, plunged down into sensuality and guilt, and suffered unutterably through it. Perhaps it was the inheritance of his father in him . . . that made him suffer thus." [6] This is a conflict of allegiances on the same pattern as the Oedipus situation, which is at the heart of Freud's entire theory. Naturalistically, the young Tonio Kröger might be described as painfully unable to make his way towards vicarious satisfaction by unconscious self-identification with his father, acknowledging and approving his authority. He recognises his father as the symbol of authority and morality, and even shares his views, but he still clings to his mother, and cannot give up the artistic way of life she has encouraged in him. All his life, it is her way he follows—but with the constant inward reminder of his father's disapproval. And this shift too, from external authority to inward conscience, is also Freudian.

But "Tonio Kröger" is far from being a merely naturalistic tale; its strength is that it is realistic and symbolic at the same time. This is conveyed by the structure of the *Novelle* in which the *Leitmotif* is repeated and developed in the course of the narration, being progressively stripped of its naturalistic connotations and coming to stand as a symbol. The figures of Tonio Kröger's father and mother, as well as being in naturalistic-psychological terms the *cause* of Tonio's adult dilemma, are at the same time the *symbols* of the dilemma of the mature artist caught between conflicting demands of morality and aestheticism. There is little need to dwell on the autobiographical nature of this dilemma. It is well-known that Tonio's parental situation is a stylization of Mann's own: his father was the respected senator; his mother the stranger from South America who never became completely part of the Lübeck world. It would not be an exaggeration to say that every one of Mann's artist-figures, from Hanno Buddenbrook to Adrian Leverkühn, is given a similar parentage. For to Mann himself, the philosophical problem of art is experienced and rendered in terms of the psychological problem of the artist. This, then, was Tonio's bourgeois bad conscience that allowed him no joy in his artistic insight; this was the understanding that made him incapable of any close relationship with the children of life whom he loved. This was Mann's own *Erkenntnisekel*.

It may now perhaps be clear why Mann remained hesitant about psychoanalysis for so long. It came far too close to him on the very problem that lay at the heart of his life and work: the relation of art to morality, or of the artist to the bourgeois world of his fathers. Mann would only be able to accept psychoanalysis as part of a wider change in his view of the world, in which the old antitheses could in some measure be reconciled.

That he did at least attain a new sense of harmony with his Lübeck background is amply witnessed by a speech he made there in 1926, when he returned to share the 700th anniversary of the town's foundation. It is a speech of conciliation with the "Bürger" town he had once so lovingly satirised—and outraged—a quarter of a century earlier. It is an acknowledgment of his roots and his parentage. But the remarkable thing about this recognition is that he uses the language and reaches the conclusions of psychoanalysis. The tone is a little apologetic, it is true, but the context is a recollection of Tonio Kröger:

What I had written as a young man in *Buddenbrooks*, I had written as it were at random, unconsciously. . . . But today we know about the powers of the unconscious and to what a great extent the really decisive things come from this essential source, called by philosophy "the will," and controlled by the intellect only with difficulty and after the event. There came the day and the hour when I understood that the apple never falls far from the tree; that as an artist I was far more "genuine," much more an apple from the Lübeck tree than I had dreamed. . . .

And again later,

How often in life I have observed with a smile—caught myself at it—that it was really the personality of my dead father that was acting as the secret model for what I had done or left undone.[7]

When Mann can say that, he has come a long way toward a sympathetic understanding of the Freudian Oedipus situation; and indirectly, has come a long way towards reconciling the two poles, of Lübeck on the one hand, and its melancholy stylization *Buddenbrooks* on the other.

And this only a year after he said so regretfully of psychoanalysis, "It is in essence understanding, melancholy understanding, especially when it concerns art and the nature of the artist." There is no need to suggest that Mann had undergone a radical conversion in the short interval: this is probably just one more instance of the ambivalence he shows towards psychoanalysis in this period. Mann knows that he cannot ignore psychoanalysis. In the passages quoted from the Lübeck speech he has come a long way towards recognising it, and Schopenhauer's concept of "will" has helped him to do so. But he has still not entirely fitted it into a pattern of thought that will allow him to avow it wholeheartedly. This does not come until he fully apprehends and articulates the duality of its nature; that is, not until his first full salutation of Freud in 1929, "Die Stellung Freuds in der modernen Geistesgeschichte."

But meanwhile it has given him the terms in which he could acknowledge the bourgeois world of his fathers. The passage quoted suggests that there had in the interim been a time of decision and revision for Mann, and gives some indication of when that might have been. "There came the day and the hour . . ." The phrase is a recollection of Mann's literary contribution to the 1914–1918 war: *Die Betrachtungen eines Unpolitischen,* a series of essays written throughout the course of the war and gathered together

under that title in 1918; and his study of Frederick the
Great, *Friedrich und die grosse Koalition* (1914), which bore
the subtitle *Ein Aufsatz für den Tag und die Stunde (An
Essay for the Day and the Hour)*. The latter is an historical
study written out of the urgency of his own contemporary
German situation, and is not without parallels between
Prussia's young assertive power in the eighteenth century,
hemmed in by the Grand Coalition, and the position of
Germany in 1914, confronted by the alliance of the rest of
Europe. It is also, incidentally, a keen psychological study
of Frederick himself, indirect and probing, indeed, attract-
ing the attention of the analyst Hitschmann in *Imago*.
Mann's interpretation of the historical situation of Prussia's rising aggressiveness, too, was psychoanalytic: another
variant of the conflict between the generations, it represented the aggression of the young country as self-defence
against the ancient dynasties around it. This was the kind
of paradoxical psychology typical of Mann's writing, but
it was also a piece of avowed special pleading to disguise
the German aggression of 1914 also as self-defence.

It is less easy to describe in brief the polemics of *Die
Betrachtungen eines Unpolitischen*. It began as an assertion
of the German cultural tradition, as Mann in his love of
country conceived it. It developed as a bitter debate with
those German intellectuals who had given their allegiance
to the French republican tradition—foremost among whom
was his own elder brother, the novelist Heinrich Mann; and
it became Mann's own highly personal coming-to-terms with
the political events and the intellectual trends before and
during the first world war. The one is anguished and more
intemperate than anything else Mann has written. Buried
in the hurly-burly, the naive resentments and newspaper
headlines of contemporary polemics, is a painful self-search,
a dialectic *apologia pro vita sua*. It becomes an examination
of his own past—an examination in historical and philosophical, not psychological terms—but then, as the com-

panion piece on Frederick the Great shows, Mann's understanding of history is largely psychological:

> searching in books, in the distress of the age searching after one's
> furthest origins, after one's legitimate foundations, after the
> hard-driven self's oldest inheritance of mind, searching for
> justification. . . .
>   Who am I? where do I come from that I should be as I am,
> and would not have it otherwise? That is what one is searching
> for in times of affliction of soul. . . . I am a townsman, a burgher,
> child and great-grandchild of German burgher culture. . . .[8]

It is a rediscovery of his origins, of the world of his fathers.
    The events in the world make him realise his own in-
tensely German quality, and how much he is the heir of the
German nineteenth-century tradition, which, with Nietzsche,
he characterises as "honest, but dark." He understands it in
terms of his masters Nietzsche, Schopenhauer and Wagner;
in terms of music, psychological honesty, the irony of the
outsider, the "Bürger" way of life; in a word, of "Lübeck
as a form of spiritual life." This he sets against what he calls
the essentially French qualities of the shallow eighteenth-
century enlightenment, social-democratic politics, and the
rhetoric of the journalist. Constructed in unrelenting antitheses, *Die Betrachtungen eines Unpolitischen* is the last
cry of Thomas Mann, the "German-burgher-conservative,"
against the liberal, literary publicist, champion of France
and the Enlightenment. Under Mann's hand, the antitheses
swell and grow in associations, until, however arbitrarily,
they have encompassed every intellectual trend in Europe
under their several flags: Germany against France, understood as profundity against shallow enlightenment; that old
pair of shadow-boxers, culture against civilization; the romantic nineteenth-century against the clever eighteenth century; poetry against journalism; the artist against the publicist; a sense of the seriousness of life and death against
trivial humanitarianism; the paternalistic state against the

liberal-democratic state; Wagner against Zola, Thomas Mann against Heinrich Mann.

He sets himself to anatomise the German heritage he feels to be so much his own, and so much threatened. In the chapters "Einkehr" and "Bürgerlichkeit" he scrutinises his own past, and the world of his fathers that have made him: the Protestant, mercantile ethics of his patrician family; the pessimistic psychology of Nietzsche and Schopenhauer; the music and aestheticism of Wagner. But his analysis is highly ambivalent. His most Teutonic pages bristle with *Fremdwörter* borrowed from the French; with pain—or is it relief, confirmation, justification—he points out how un-German in fact Nietzsche was, and Schopenhauer, and Wagner. He admits his own part in the breakdown of nineteenth-century ideals, his own debt to France and the eighteenth century. He recognises that his own very existence—he who had written about his Buddenbrook ancestors instead of living their ethical burgher life—is sign and symptom enough that their world is at an end.

Confronted with a time of crisis—and the forty-year-old Mann is fully aware that it is a time of personal as well as of historical European crisis—this book is an attempt to salvage and preserve his past, in face of the change he knows is inevitable and to which he knows he has made his contribution. It is a reckoning of what he will be able to take with him into the future, and what he will have to leave behind. The parting is reluctant, and a last, often strident, assertion of it; homesick, reactionary, valedictory.

This, then, is the day and the hour he refers to in his Lübeck speech, when he had come to assert his "Bürger" parentage. In his passionate reluctance to disavow the past, he felt a sense of solidarity with his fathers and fatherland which for the first time was unalloyed by Tonio Kröger's treacherous irony. The guilt of his own misgivings and betrayal of his "Bürger" world was sloughed off and transferred to his adversary. But his conflict with his brother was really a conflict with another aspect of himself.

Mann's passionate, belated identification with the world of his fathers showed the shadow-side of their morality too. He also gives voice to their complacent "sense of the seriousness of things." The specific issues are illuminating, particularly when we recall the very different views that Mann subsequently held. He urges the death penalty, for example, in the *cause célèbre* of Nurse Edith Cavell.

It meant . . . that out of humane feeling the idea of guilt was almost lost; indeed, that at times, under the weight of scientific opinion, we scarcely dared touch the criminal, and regarded capital punishment as the peak of inhumanity—whereas in the eyes of every serious man the idea of guilt bears not, it is true, a humanitarian stamp, but a most human one, and is by no means destroyed by any deterministic way of thinking; on the contrary, this only adds to its seriousness and solemnity. (p. 453)

This is the tortured style and tormented voice of Naphta, the conservative obscurantist of *Der Zauberberg*. And Mann himself, this precarious new-found bourgeois with his ceremonial respect for guilt, also lends his voice to the violent and ignorant repudiation of something very like psychoanalysis. The author of *Friedrich und die grosse Koalition*, that most psychoanalytical of historical essays, calls psychoanalysis "this Dionysian balderdash," and takes his adversary's psychological interpretation of history to task thus:

But when the German nation endured it [tyrannical rule], when —I quote—"for generations it acquiesced in its humiliations," then this was because (and your journalist's psychology goes very "deep" now—in its own opinion it always goes "deep" when it gets as far as sex and drags up a hodgepodge of Nietzsche and Krafft-Ebing) the cruelty of the tyrants "responded to every perverse instinct." It is clearly a case, as simple as it is repulsive, of an interaction of sadism on the one side and masochism on the other. (pp. 324–325)

And again, "there is nothing on earth in which it [psychology] will not use 'psychological analysis' to discover and isolate dirt of the earth, earthy. . . ." (p. 169) There is a kind of deliberate, polemical ignorance at work here. Mann must know that this kind of bludgeoning directed against his brother—and against Freud, the unnamed "hodgepodge of Nietzsche and Krafft-Ebing"—hits at his own essay on Frederick as well. There is pain in this blindness. And in addition to this intemperate abuse from the new found *Bürger,* a protest against "psychology" is made in the name of the sensitive artist's *Erkenntnisekel* too. Accusation is tempered by self-accusation:

Psychology discourages every stupidity and passion; it discourages life and art—through knowledge. For art becomes impossible—the artist becomes impossible—when they are seen through. The effect of psychology then is by no means to develop our culture; it is rather progressively destructive, producing intellectual-rational civilisation. . . . Of course, one can look at these things in a different way, but for the time being and in their fashion, this ordering of things is incontrovertible. (p. 150)

This, then, was the point Mann had reached at the end of the war, after his bitter self-struggle for an interpretation of his own history with regard to his fathers and his fatherland: a final, belated identification with them, even down to the least liberal detail of their views. The terms of conflict, it is true, are presented with exaggerated sharpness, for there is as much stylisation in the work as confession, but the final impression it leaves is one of valediction. Mann had articulated his attitude, and had freed himself to change it.

The Buddenbrooks world was strong within him. As a young man he had scrutinised it with the distance and mockery of art; Lübeck had responded with horror at the picture he portrayed. But this artist was never the total Bohemian and outcast; he kept his *Bürger* bad conscience. *Der Tod in Venedig* envisages the terrible consequences of repudiating it. In middle life, as an established writer, he came very close to the way of life he had once broken away from. So when the sudden crisis of the war burst upon him, it called forth in him a tremendous sense of identification with the once-rejected past (rejected still by his brother, his other self). The poise of the old ambivalence was broken down, and he threw all the weight of his rhetoric onto the Lübeck scale. This was the end of the old precarious, ironical solution, but it was not yet a new solution, only an interim stage on the way to one. The balance was reestablished later in the polarities of *Der Zauberberg*. In this novel, the old dualities are offered the possibility of synthesis into a greater whole in the famous "Man is the Master of Opposites." [9]

This was the new "humanism" of Mann's middle years, in which his attempt at a compromise between antinomies emerged in his adoption of the attitudes of the "Zivilisationsliterat," but with a deeper foundation upon the *Bürger* cultural tradition. He threw off his sense of artistic isolation; he came to regard art as a reciprocal activity between artist and public. And so as an artist, and *hence* as a responsible citizen, he entered public affairs against his former reactionary desire to support the old régime. He honestly took back some of his more extreme reactionary claims. And all these repudiations of his romantic conservatism were made in the name of psychoanalysis. His first great essay on Freud was a speech in support of the Weimar republic. In *Beyond the Pleasure Principle,* Freud described the death impulse, the desire to return to an earlier, inorganic state, as conservative, and Mann was quick to exploit the political implications of the expression. In "Über die Ehe" (1925), for example, his description of conservatism is in terms of death and regression:

But the worst and the most false in all cases is the will to return to an earlier state of affairs. Our age, in horror at itself, is full of the wish for restoration, wishful dreaming for a return. . . . In vain, there is no going back. Every attempt at flight into outmoded historical forms creates only disease and untruth.[10]

He even takes back his old attitude towards capital punishment and quite expressly calls on psychoanalysis to support him. In a short essay, "Über die Todesstrafe" (1926), he recalls his old conservative attitude, its justification of capital punishment as a recognition of the seriousness of life, and its refusal to share in any shallow and sentimental humanitarianism. But then he goes on to show a complete change of opinion, he now angrily condemns his former attitude as hypocritical, self-deceiving, even Fascist, and he calls to his help a long passage from Freud's anthropological treatise *Totem and Taboo:*

A little psychoanalysis! In his great treatise on *Totem and Taboo,* Freud says, "If one member of the community has succeeded in satisfying the repressed desire, then the same desire must be alive in all his fellows. In order to control this temptation, the one who is actually envied must be destroyed and deprived of the fruit of his daring, and not infrequently the punishment gives its executors the opportunity to commit the same sinful deed themselves, justified as retribution."

There you have it, hypocrites! No Fascist contempt for humanitarian reluctance to shed blood can prevent us from *seeing through you*; the idea that knowledge, understanding, is never to be allowed to inhibit life, will, action, passion, is a Fascist truth and a challenge we must go beyond, to the realisation that it is not the purpose of intellectual decision to give strength to stupidity, and that at a certain stage of cultural maturity and moral sensibility, the ritual killing of the miscreant by those "who did not succeed" becomes a foul mockery, and humanly impossible.[11]

This passage is important, for it marks not only one definite point where psychoanalysis helped to mold Mann's attitude, but also his emergence as an opponent of Fascism, attacking it in the name of of psychoanalysis. However, he has said nothing of Thomas Mann the artist, and of *his* attitude toward psychoanalysis, but only of Thomas Mann, the new-found political man. His creativity is the one issue on which he continues to have reservations. Where it threatens to come too close to him as creative artist he still withdraws. This was a point on which he was never easily reconciled to psychoanalysis, the probing into the sources of the artist's talent. As late as 1947, he takes up the cudgels in defence of the artist against the analyst's searching, in a letter about a certain psychoanalytical study of Stifter and his work:

I have no doubt that previous criticism of Stifter has been too kindly and good-natured to do justice to its extremely strange and often quite frightening subject. But to see him now subjected to the strict psychoanalytical method is still not completely to my taste—not because I find this method lacking in respect, but because I cannot help feeling this point of view to be to some extent rather narrow. I would not like to see depth psychology applied as the one true method to all the great models of literature, and when I consider Sainte-Beuve's essay on Molière, quite innocent of sex-symbols and complexes, I feel happier.[12]

However, apart from this one major reservation, it does seem that in the change in Mann's attitude that followed the dual reckoning of *Die Betrachtungen* and *Der Zauberberg,* psychoanalysis played no small part. Some time in the interval between the publication of *Die Betrachtungen* and the completion of *Der Zauberberg* Mann transcended the point of identification with his Lübeck past which his bitter review had brought him to. He published little in the interim, but he did at this time begin his studies of Goethe, sovereign lord over antinomies, who was later to take the place of Nietzsche and Schopenhauer as his guide and model. His only publications were *Goethe und Tolstoy* (1922), a long critical discussion in which the stress is rather upon Tolstoy than upon Goethe, and two slight domestic idylls, *Gesang vom Kindchen* (1919), written in mock-Goethean hexameters, and *Herr und Hund* (1918), a prose account of Mann's dog Bauschan. While it seems clear enough that Mann's closer acquaintance with psychoanalytic theory after *Der Zauberberg* helped him to articulate his new-found humanism, *Herr und Hund* would suggest that his slighter knowledge of it at an earlier date helped him

to move from the tormented avowal of his past to the vision
of synthesis.

It is perhaps to give this quiet, absurd little sketch a quite
disproportionate importance to suggest that it is in some
sense a transition from *Die Betrachtungen* to *Der Zauberberg*. It is a resolution after discord, calm after crisis, and
what is more, it has a serenity that persists in full consciousness of the "muddy ground, which is the ground of all
life." [13] There is mockery in the little work, mockery of
Hans Castorp, the simple young man who, like Bauschan,
also has his wishful dreams and his years under medical
care; mockery of Mann's own immediate past, and also
mockery of psychoanalysis, which might have offered the
terms of understanding it.

This agreeable, trivial little piece hides perhaps a deeper
irony, for here introduced into the dog's inarticulate world
are a number of hints at the workings of the unconscious
mind which accord to a remarkable degree with Freud's
analytic theory. Bauschan's restless growling sleep, it is suggested, hides dreams that fulfill vain desires of the day:

This dream life was all too obviously just an artificial substitute
for real running and hunting which his nature created for him,
because living with me did not allow him the joy of movement
in the open to the extent that his blood and feeling required.
(p. 250)

Mann even speculates along the lines of Jung's "Collective
Unconscious," possibly anticipating Castorp's dream in the
snow, but still in an ironic doggy context:

At his level surely, the life of the individual is separated more
superficially from that of the species than in our case. Birth and
death signify a less far-reaching shifting of existence. Perhaps the
inheritance of his line is maintained more strongly, so that it is
only an apparent contradiction to speak of inborn experiences,
unconscious memories, which, once called forth, can confuse the
creature about his own personal experiences and make him dissatisfied with them. (pp. 303–304)

There is even a hint at certain unconscious motives which were served by the apparently praiseworthy action of leaving Bauschan, who was sick, at the vet's for some weeks. But here too, the occasion of such remorseful introspection is so slight as to have an ironic effect:

And beyond this, was there perhaps involved the secret wish to be rid of him for a while, a certain curiosity and illegitimate longing to be free from his constant surveillance? (p. 320)

But this was also how Hans Castorp regarded his cousin Joachim. Even Bauschan's gradual forgetting of his "traumatic" hospital experience is described in terms congruent with the Freudian theory of repression, the complete forgetting and driving down into the unconscious of an unpleasant experience:

He forgot. The hateful and for Bauschan's mental capacity meaningless, episode sank down into the past, unrelieved, unresolved by any explanation or understanding, which would have been impossible; but time covered it over, as it sometimes has to do amongst humans, and we live on above it, while the unuttered recedes deeper and deeper into forgetfulness. . . . (p. 324)

The phrases "unrelieved," "unresolved," "unresolved by any explanation or understanding," "the unuttered" seem almost to be satirically directed against the analytic process. "Repressed" is to be preferred to "resolved"; but at least it is understood as such. And the cadence is at least a literary resolution, if not a psychological one.

These examples indicate, if anything, a negative, satirical attitude towards the dawning ideas of psychoanalysis. But that is not the end of the story. Such passages, however ironically, have established in the reader the idea of the unconscious as central to the idyll, and Mann does take it up seriously with his image of the rushing stream. In animated terms he describes a nearby stream, suggesting perhaps the human mind, certainty Bauschan's and perhaps

Hans Castorp's as "the simplest and most faithful of its kind," at whose bottom lies the foul and the rejected:

The stream here is one of the simplest and most faithful of its kind; there is nothing special about it; its character, the friendly average. Of crystal-clear naïveté, without guile or harm, it is far from claiming pretended depths beneath troubled waters; it is flat and clear and harmlessly reveals the tin cans and the corpse of an old boot lying at the bottom in the green mud. (p. 292)

There the note is still light and humorous. However, Mann returns to the motif at the very end of the idyll, and connects it with the motif of Bauschan's "repressed traumatic experience." Both together do suggest that the "muddy ground" is an image for what Schopenhauer called the "Will" and Freud the unconscious mind:

But that is a long time ago now, more than half a year, and the same thing has happened with the veterinary episode. Time and forgetfulness have covered it over and on its muddy ground, which is the ground of all life, we go on living our lives. (p. 350)

The treatment of these hints at psychoanalysis is largely ironical and negative, but we must remember that Mann is often most serious when he is most ironical, and a positive concession is made here at the very end in the solemnity of that interpolated phrase, "which is the ground of all life." Bauschan may have "repressed" the "trauma," but his master is fully conscious of it. The gentle satire of *Herr und Hund* does seem to indicate a temporary transition stage between the painful rejection of "psychology" that was part of *Die Betrachtungen,* and the approval of psychoanalysis that is apparent in the essays grouped around *Der Zauberberg*—an approval, however, which is always modified by Mann's hesitancy in respect of his integrity as an artist. This little work is, as it were, Mann's quiet pause for breath on the passage of self-discovery that led from *Die Betrachtungen* to *Der Zauberberg.*

NOTES

1. Thomas Mann, *Pariser Rechenschaft* (Berlin, 1926), p. 112. Translations of all succeeding quotations are by the author of this paper.
2. "Mein Verhältnis zur Psychoanalyse," *Almanach der Psycho-Analyse, 1926.*
3. Ibid.
4. "Thomas Mann und die Psychoanalyse," *Int. Ztschr. f. Psa.,* XI (1925), 247.
5. "Mein Verhältnis zur Psychoanalyse."
6. "Tonio Kröger," *Novellen II* (Berlin, 1922), p. 27.
7. Thomas Mann, "Lübeck als geistige Lebensform, Rede gehalten zur 700-Jahr-Feier der Freien und Hanse-Stadt im Stadttheater zu Lübeck," *Die Forderung des Tages* (Berlin, 1930), pp. 336–37, 38.
8. Thomas Mann, *Die Betrachtungen eines Unpolitischen,* 19. bis 24. Aufl. (Berlin, 1922), p. 90. The work was written and published as a series of articles between 1915 and 1917, first appearing in book form in 1918.
9. Thomas Mann, *Der Zauberberg* (Berlin, 1924), II, 259.
10. "Über die Ehe," p. 183. This essay was first published as one of many by several hands in the compilation *Das Ehebuch,* ed. Hermann, Graf Kayserling. Other contributors were Alfred Adler and C. G. Jung.
11. Thomas Mann, "Über die Todesstrafe," *Die Forderung des Tages,* p. 386.
12. Thomas Mann, in a letter dated 6.12.47 to Alfred, Freiherr von Winterstein, concerning the latter's psycho-analytical study of Adalbert Stifter. The present writer wishes to thank both writer and recipient for permission to quote.
13. "Herr und Hund," *Novellen II* (Berlin, 1922), p. 345.

Ulysses: A Monologue [1]

by C. G. JUNG

Although the influence of the Zurich School on literary
criticism has been great, and although Jung himself and his
students have made copious use of semiliterary materials
from folklore, there have been few direct comments on
literary works by Jung. It is all the more interesting that
Jung should have been asked, and should have agreed, to
write an introduction to a German translation of *Ulysses.*
For the result has been a view of *Ulysses* which is remarkably fresh and unhackneyed. The genesis of the essay is
described in note 12, page 218, and its publishing history is
set forth in note 1. The present text is from the recently
published Volume 15 of Jung's *Complete Works* in the
Bollingen Series.

THE Ulysses of my title has to do with James Joyce and
not with that shrewd and storm-driven figure of Homer's
world who knew how to escape by guile and wily deeds the
enmity and vengeance of gods and men, and who after a
wearisome voyage returned to hearth and home. Joyce's
Ulysses, very much unlike his ancient namesake, is a passive,
merely perceiving consciousness, a mere eye, ear, nose, and
mouth, a sensory nerve exposed without choice or check to
the roaring, chaotic, lunatic cataract of psychic and physical
happenings, and registering all this with almost photographic accuracy.

Ulysses is a book that pours along for seven hundred and
thirty-five pages, a stream of time seven hundred and thirty-
five days long which all consist in one single and senseless
day in the life of every man, the completely irrelevant six-

teenth day of June, 1904, in Dublin—a day on which, in all truth, nothing happens. The stream begins in the void and ends in the void. Is all this perhaps one single, immensely long, and excessively complicated Strindbergian pronouncement upon the essence of human life—a pronouncement which, to the reader's dismay, is never finished? Possibly it does touch upon the essence, but quite certainly it reflects life's ten thousand facets and their hundred thousand gradations of colour. So far as I can see, there are in those seven hundred and thirty-five pages no obvious repetitions, not a single blessed island where the long-suffering reader may come to rest; no place where he can seat himself, drunk with memories, and contemplate with satisfaction the stretch of road he has covered, be it one hundred pages or even less. If only he could spot some little commonplace that had obligingly slipped in again where it was not expected! But no! The pitiless stream rolls on without a break, and its velocity or viscosity increases in the last forty pages till it sweeps away even the punctuation marks. Here the suffocating emptiness becomes so unbearably tense that it reaches the bursting point. This utterly hopeless emptiness is the dominant note of the whole book. It not only begins and ends in nothingness, it consists of nothing but nothingness.[2] It is all infernally nugatory. As a piece of technical virtuosity it is a brilliant and hellish monster-birth.[3]

I had an uncle whose thinking was always direct and to the point. One day he stopped me on the street and demanded: "Do you know how the devil tortures the souls in hell?" When I said no, he replied, "He keeps them waiting." And with that he walked away. This remark occurred to me when I was ploughing through *Ulysses* for the first time. Every sentence rouses an expectation that is not fulfilled; finally, out of sheer resignation, you come to expect nothing, and to your horror it gradually dawns on you that you have hit the mark. In actual fact nothing happens, nothing comes of it at all,[4] and yet a secret expectation battling with hopeless resignation drags the reader from page to page. The seven hundred and thirty-five pages that contain nothing by no means consist of blank paper but are closely printed. You read and read and read and you pretend to understand what you read. Occasionally you drop through an air-pocket into a new sentence, but once the proper degree of resignation has been reached you get accustomed to anything. Thus I read to page 135 with despair in my heart, falling asleep twice on the way. The incredible versatility of Joyce's style has a monotonous and hypnotic effect. Nothing comes to meet the reader, everything turns away from him, leaving him gaping after it. The book is always up and away, dissatisfied with itself, ironic, sarcastic, virulent, contemptuous, sad, despairing, and bitter. It plays on the reader's sympathies to his own undoing unless sleep kindly intervenes and puts a stop to this drain of energy. Arrived at page 135, after making several heroic efforts to get at the book, to "do it justice," as the phrase goes, I fell at last into profound slumber.[5] When I awoke quite a while later, my views had undergone such a clarification that I started to read the book backwards. This method proved as good as the usual one; the book can just as well be read backwards, for it has no back and no front, no top and no bottom. Everything could easily have happened before, or might have happened afterwards.[6] You can read any of the conversations just as pleasurably backwards, for you don't miss the point of the gags. Every sentence is a gag, but taken together they make no point. You can also stop in the middle of a sentence—the first half still makes sense enough to live by itself, or at least seems to. The whole work has the character of a worm cut in half that can grow a new head or a new tail as required.

This singular and uncanny characteristic of the Joycean mind shows that his work pertains to the class of cold-blooded animals and specifically to the worm family. If worms were gifted with literary powers they would write with the sympathetic nervous system for lack of a brain.[7] I suspect that something of this kind has happened to Joyce, that we have here a case of visceral thinking [8] with severe restriction of cerebral activity and its confinement to the perceptual processes. One is driven to unqualified admiration for Joyce's feats in the sensory sphere: what he sees, hears, tastes, smells, touches, inwardly as well as outwardly, is beyond measure astonishing. The ordinary mortal, if he is a specialist in sense-perception, is usually restricted either to the outer world or to the inner. Joyce knows them both. Garlands of subjective association twine themselves about the objective figures on a Dublin street. Objective and subjective, outer and inner, are so constantly intermingled that in the end, despite the clearness of the individual images, one wonders whether one is dealing with a physical or with a transcendental tapeworm.[9] The tapeworm is a whole living cosmos in itself and is fabulously procreative; this, it seems to me, is an inelegant but not unfitting image for Joyce's proliferating chapters. It is true that the tapeworm can produce nothing but other tapeworms, but it produces them in inexhaustible quantities. Joyce's book might have been fourteen hundred and seventy pages long or even a multiple of that and still it would not have lessened infinity by a drop, and the essential would still have remained unsaid. But does Joyce want to say anything essential? Has this old-fashioned prejudice any right to exist here? Oscar Wilde maintained that a work of art is something entirely useless. Nowadays even the Philistine would raise no objection to this, yet in his heart he still expects a work of art to contain something "essential." Where is it with Joyce? Why doesn't he say it right out? Why doesn't he hand it to the reader with an expressive gesture—"a straight way, so that fools shall not err therein"?

Yes, I admit I feel I have been made a fool of. The book would not meet me half way, nothing in it made the least attempt to be agreeable, and that always gives the reader an irritating sense of inferiority. Obviously I have so much of the Philistine in my blood that I am naïve enough to suppose that a book wants to tell me something, to be under-

stood—a sad case of mythological anthropomorphism projected on to the book! And what a book—no opinion possible—epitome of a maddening defeat of intelligent reader,
who after all is not such a—(if I may use Joyce's suggestive
style). Surely a book has a content, represents something;
but I suspect that Joyce did not wish to "represent" anything. Does it by any change represent *him*—does that explain this solipsistic isolation, this drama without eyewit-
nesses, this infuriating disdain for the assiduous reader?
Joyce has aroused my ill will. One should never rub the
reader's nose into his own stupidity, but that is just what
Ulysses does.

A therapist like myself is always practising therapy—even
on himself. Irritation means: You haven't yet seen what's
behind it. Consequently we should follow up our irritation
and examine whatever it is we discover in our ill temper. I
observe then: this solipsism, this contempt for the cultivated
and intelligent member of the reading public who wants
to understand,[10] who is well-meaning, and who tries to be
kindly and just, gets on my nerves. There we have it, the
cold-blooded unrelatedness of his mind which seems to
come from the saurian in him or from still lower regions—
conversation in and with one's own intestines—a man of
stone, he with the horns of stone, the stony beard, the petri-
fied intestines. Moses, turning his back with stony unconcern on the flesh-pots and gods of Egypt, and also on the
reader, thereby outraging his feelings of good will.

From this stony underworld there rises up the vision
of the tapeworm, rippling, peristaltic, monotonous because
of its endless proglottic proliferation. No proglottid is quite
like any other, yet they can easily be confused. In every
segment of the book, however small, Joyce himself is the
sole content of the segment. Everything is new and yet
remains what it was from the beginning. Talk of likeness
to nature! What pullulating richness—and what boredom!
Joyce bores me to tears, but it is a vicious dangerous boredom such as not even the worst banality could induce. It is

the boredom of nature, the bleak whistling of the wind over the crags of Hebrides, sunrise and sunset over the wastes of the Sahara, the roar of the sea—real Wagnerian "programme music" as Curtius rightly says, and yet eternal repetition. Notwithstanding Joyce's baffling many-sidedness, certain themes can be picked out though they may not be intended. Perhaps he would like there to be none, for causality and finality have neither place nor meaning in his world, any more than have values. Nevertheless, themes are unavoidable, they are the scaffolding for all psychic happenings, however hard one tries to soak the soul out of every happening, as Joyce consistently does. Everything is desouled, every particle of warm blood has been chilled, events unroll in icy egoism. In all the book there is nothing pleasing, nothing refreshing, nothing hopeful, but only things that are grey, grisly, gruesome, or pathetic, tragic, ironic, all from the seamy side of life and so chaotic that you have to look for the thematic connections with a magnifying glass. And yet they are there, first of all in the form of unavowed resentments of a highly personal nature, the wreckage of a violently amputated boyhood; then as flotsam from the whole history of thought exhibited in pitiful nakedness to the staring crowd. The religious, erotic, and domestic prehistory of the author is reflected in the drab surface of the stream of events; we even behold the disintegration of his personality into Bloom, *l'homme moyen sensuel,* and the almost gaseous Stephen Daedalus, who is mere speculation and mere mind. Of these two, the former has no son and the latter no father.

Somewhere there may be a secret order or parallelism in the chapters—authoritative voices have been raised to this effect [11]—but in any case it is so well concealed that at first I noticed nothing of the kind. And even if I had, it would not have interested me in my hopelessly irritated state, any more than would the monotony of any other squalid human comedy.

I had already taken up *Ulysses* in 1929 but had laid it

aside disappointed and vexed. Today it still bores me as it
did then. Why do I write about it? Ordinarily, I would no
more be doing this than writing about any other form of
surrealism that passes my understanding. I am writing about
Joyce because a publisher was incautious enough to ask me
what I thought about him, or rather about *Ulysses*,[12] concerning which opinions are notoriously divided. The only
thing beyond dispute is that *Ulysses* is a book that has gone
through ten editions and that its author is glorified by some
and damned by others. He stands in the cross-fire of discussion and is thus a phenomenon which the psychologist should
not ignore. Joyce has exerted a very considerable influence on
his contemporaries, and it was this fact which first aroused
my interest in *Ulysses*. Had this book slipped noiselessly
and unsung into the shades of oblivion I would certainly
never have dragged it back again; for it annoyed me thoroughly and amused me only a little. Above all, it held over
me the threat of boredom because it had only a negative
effect on me and I feared it was the product of an author's
negative mood.

But of course I am prejudiced. I am a psychiatrist, and
that implies a professional prejudice with regard to all manifestations of the psyche. I must therefore warn the reader:
the tragi-comedy of the average man, the cold shadow-side
of life, the dull grey of spiritual nihilism are my daily
bread. To me they are a tune ground out on a street organ,
stale and without charm. Nothing in all this shocks or moves
me, for all too often I have to help people out of these
lamentable states. I must combat them incessantly and I
may only expend my sympathy on people who do not turn
their backs on me. *Ulysses* turns its back on me. It is un-
cooperative, it wants to go on singing its endless tune into
endless time—a tune I know to satiety—and to extend to
infinity its ganglionic rope-ladder or visceral thinking and
cerebration reduced to mere sense-perception. It shows no
tendency towards reconstruction; indeed, destructiveness
seems to have become an end in itself.

But that is not the half of it—there is also the sympto-
matology! It is all too familiar, those interminable ram-
blings of the insane who have only a fragmentary consciousness and consequently suffer from a complete lack of judgment and an atrophy of all their values. Instead, there is
often an intensification of the sense-activities. We find in
these writings an acute power of observation, a photographic
memory for sense-perceptions, a sensory curiosity directed
inwards as well as outwards, the predominance of retrospective themes and resentments, a delirious confusion of
the subject and psychic with objective reality, a method of
presentation that takes no account of the reader but indulges
in neologisms, fragmentary quotations, sound- and speech-
associations, abrupt transitions and hiatuses of thought. We
also find an atrophy of feeling [13] that does not shrink from
any depth of absurdity or cynicism. Even the layman would
have no difficulty in tracing the analogies between *Ulysses*
and the schizophrenic mentality. The resemblance is indeed so suspicious that an indignant reader might easily
fling the book aside with the diagnosis "schizophrenia." For
the psychiatrist the analogy is startling, but he would nevertheless point out that a characteristic mark of the com-
positions of the insane, namely, the presence of stereotyped
expressions, is notably absent. *Ulysses* may be anything, but
it is certainly not monotonous in the sense of being repetitious. (This is not a contradiction of what I said earlier;
it is impossible to say anything contradictory about *Ulysses*.)
The presentation is consistent and flowing, everything is in
motion and nothing is fixed. The whole book is borne along
on a subterranean current of life that shows singleness of aim
and rigorous selectivity, both these being unmistakable proof
of the existence of a unified personal will and directed
intention. The mental functions are under severe control;
they do not manifest themselves in a spontaneous and erratic
way. The perceptive functions, that is, sensation and intuition, are given preference throughout, while the discrimina-
tive functions, thinking and feeling, are just as consistently

suppressed. They appear merely as mental contents, as objects of perception. There is no relaxing of the general tendency to present a shadow-picture of the mind and the world, in spite of frequent temptations to surrender to a sudden touch of beauty. These are traits not ordinarily found in the insane. There remains, then, the insane person of an uncommon sort. But the psychiatrist has no criteria for judging such a person. What seems to be mental abnormality may be a kind of mental health which is inconceivable to the average understanding; it may even be a disguise for superlative powers of mind.

It would never occur to me to class *Ulysses* as a product of schizophrenia. Moreover, nothing would be gained by this label, for we wish to know why *Ulysses* exerts such a powerful influence and not whether its author is a high-grade or a low-grade schizophrenic. *Ulysses* is no more a pathological product than modern art as a whole. It is "cubistic" in the deepest sense because it resolves the picture of reality into an immensely complex painting whose dominant note is the melancholy of abstract objectivity. Cubism is not a disease but a tendency to represent reality in a certain way—and that way may be grotesquely realistic or grotesquely abstract. The clinical picture of schizophrenia is a mere analogy in that the schizophrenic apparently has the same tendency to treat reality as if it were strange to him, or, conversely, to estrange himself from reality. With the schizophrenic the tendency usually has no recognizable purpose but is a symptom inevitably arising from the disintegration of the personality into fragmentary personalities (the autonomous complexes). In the modern artist it is not produced by any disease in the individual but is a collective manifestation of our time. The artist does not follow an individual impulse, but rather a current of collective life which arises not directly from consciousness but from the collective unconsciousness of the modern psyche. Just because it is a collective phenomenon it bears identical fruit in the most widely separated realms, in painting as well as literature, in sculpture as well as architecture. It is, more-over, significant that one of the spiritual fathers of the modern movement—van Gogh—was actually schizophrenic.

The distortion of beauty and meaning by grotesque ob-jectivity or equally grotesque irreality is, in the insane, a consequence of the destruction of the personality; in the artist it has a creative purpose. Far from his work being an expression of the destruction of his personality, the modern artist finds the unity of his artistic personality in destructiveness. The Mephistophelian perversion of sense into nonsense, of beauty into ugliness—in such an exasperat-ing way that nonsense almost makes sense and ugliness has a provocative beauty—is a creative achievement that has never been pushed to such extremes in the history of human culture, though it is nothing new in principle. We can ob-serve something similar in the perverse change of style under Ikhnaton, in the inane lamb symbolism of the early Christians, in those doleful Pre-Raphaelite figures, and in late Baroque art, strangling itself in its own convolutions. Despite their differences all these epochs have an inner relationship: they were periods of creative incubation whose meaning cannot be satisfactorily explained from a causal standpoint. Such manifestations of the collective psyche dis-close their meaning only when they are considered teleo-logically as anticipations of something new.

The epoch of Ikhnaton was the cradle of the first mono-theism, which has been preserved for the world in Jewish tradition. The crude infantilism of the early Christian era portended nothing less than the transformation of the Roman Empire into a City of God. The rejection of the art and science of his time was not an impoverishment for the early Christian, but a great spiritual gain. The Pre-Ra-phael primitives were the heralds of an ideal of bodily beauty that had been lost to the world since classical times. The Baroque was the last of the ecclesiastical styles, and its self-destruction anticipates the triumph of the spirit of science over the spirit of medieval dogmatism. Tiepolo, for instance, who had already reached the danger zone in his technique, is not a symptom of decadence when considered as an artistic personality, but labours with the whole of his being to bring about a much needed disintegration.

This being so we can ascribe a positive, creative value and meaning not only to *Ulysses* but also to its artistic congeners. In its destruction of the criteria of beauty and meaning that have held till today, *Ulysses* accomplishes wonders. It insults all our conventional feelings, it brutally disappoints our expectations of sense and content, it thumbs its nose at all synthesis. We would show ill will even to suspect any trace of synthesis or form, for if we succeeded in demonstrating any such unmodern tendencies in *Ulysses* this would amount to pointing out a gross aesthetic defect. Everything abusive we can say about *Ulysses* bears witness to its peculiar quality, for our abuse springs from the resentment of the unmodern man who does not wish to see what the gods have graciously veiled from sight.

All those ungovernable forces that welled up in Nietzsche's Dionysian exuberance and flooded his intellect have burst forth in undiluted form in modern man. Even the darkest passages in the second part of *Faust,* even *Zarathustra* and, indeed, *Ecce Homo,* try in one way or another to recommend themselves to the public. But it is only modern man who has succeeded in creating an art in reverse, a backside of art that makes no attempt to be ingratiating, that tells us just where we get off, speaking with the same rebellious contrariness that had made itself disturbingly felt in those precursors of the moderns (not forgetting Hölderlin) who had already started to topple the old ideals.

If we stick to one field of experience only, it is not really possible to see clearly what is happening. It is not a matter of a single thrust aimed at one definite spot, but with an almost universal "restratification" of modern man, who is in the process of shaking off a world that has become obsolete. Unfortunately we cannot see into the future and so we do not know how far we still belong in the deepest sense to the Middle Ages. If, from the watch-towers of the future, we should seem stuck in the medievalism up to the ears, I for one would be little surprised. For that alone would satisfactorily explain to us why there should be books or works of art after the style of *Ulysses*. They are drastic purgatives whose full effect would be dissipated if they did not meet with an equally strong and obstinate resistance. They are a kind of psychological specific which is of use only where the hardest and toughest material must be dealt with. They have this in common with Freudian theory, that they undermine with fanatical one-sidedness values that have already begun to crumble.

Ulysses makes a show of semi-scientific objectivity, at times even employing "scientific" language, and yet it displays a truly unscientific temper: it is sheer negation. Even so it is creative—a creative destruction. Here is no theatrical gesture of a Herostratus burning down temples, but a serious effort to rub the noses of our contemporaries in the shadow-side of reality, not with any malicious intent but with all the guileless naïveté of artistic objectiveness. One may safely call the book pessimistic even though at the very end, on nearly the final page, a redeeming light breaks wistfully through the clouds. This is only *one* page against seven hundred and thirty-four which were one and all born of Orcus. Here and there, a fine crystal glitters in the black stream of mud, so that even the unmodern may realize that Joyce is an "artist" who knows his trade—which is more than can be said of most modern artists—and is even a past master at it, but a master who has piously renounced his powers in the name of a higher goal. Even in his "restratification" Joyce has remained a pious Catholic: his dynamite is expended chiefly upon churches and upon those psychic edifices which are begotten or influenced by churches. His "anti-world" has the medieval, thoroughly provincial, quintessentially Catholic atmosphere of an Erin trying desperately to enjoy its political independence. He worked at *Ulysses* in many foreign lands, and from all of them he looked back in faith and kinship upon Mother Church and Ireland. He used his foreign stopping-places merely as anchors to steady his ship in the maelstrom of his Irish reminiscences and resentments. Yet Ulysses does not strain back to his Ithaca—on the contrary, he makes frantic efforts to rid himself of his Irish heritage.

We might suppose this behaviour to be of only local interest and expect it to leave the rest of the world quite cold. But it does not leave the world cold. The local phenomenon seems to be more or less universal, to judge from its effects on Joyce's contemporaries. The cap must fit. There must exist a whole community of moderns who are so numerous that they have been able to devour ten editions of *Ulysses* since 1922. The book must mean something to them, must even reveal something that they did not know or feel before. They are not infernally bored by it, but are helped, refreshed, instructed, converted, "restratified." Obviously, they are thrown into a desirable state of some sort, for otherwise only the blackest hatred could enable the reader to go through the book from page 1 to page 735 with attention and without fatal attacks of drowsiness. I therefore surmise that medieval Catholic Ireland covers a geographical area of whose size I have hitherto been ignorant; it is certainly far larger than the area indicated on the ordinary map. This Catholic Middle Ages, with its Messrs. Daedalus and Bloom, seems to be pretty well universal. There must be whole sections of the population that are so bound to their spiritual environment that nothing less than Joycean explosives are required to break through their hermetic isolation. I am convinced that this is so: we are still stuck in the Middle Ages up to the ears. And it is because Joyce's contemporaries are so riddled with medieval prejudices that such prophets of negation as he and Freud are needed to reveal to them the other side of reality.

Of course, this tremendous task could hardly be accomplished by a man who with Christian benevolence tried to make people turn an unwilling eye on the shadow-side of things. That would amount only to their looking on with perfect unconcern. No, the revelation must be brought about by the appropriate attitude of mind, and Joyce is again a master here. Only in this way can the forces of negative emotion be mobilized. *Ulysses* shows how one should execute Nietzsche's "sacrilegious backward grasp." Joyce sets about it coldly and objectively, and shows himself more "bereft of gods" than Nietzsche ever dreamed of being. All this on the implicit and correct assumption that the fascinating influence exerted by the spiritual environment has nothing to do with reason, but everything with feeling. One should not be misled into thinking that because Joyce reveals a world that is horribly bleak and bereft of gods, it is inconceivable that anyone should derive the slightest comfort from his book. Strange as it may sound, it remains true that the world of *Ulysses* is a better one than the world of those who are hopelessly bound to the darkness of their spiritual birthplaces. Even though the evil and destructive elements predominate, they are far more valuable than the "good" that has come down to us from the past and proves in reality to be a ruthless tyrant, an illusory system of prejudices that robs life of its richness, emasculates it, and enforces a moral compulsion which in the end is unendurable. Nietzsche's "slave-uprising in morals" would be a good motto for *Ulysses*. What frees the prisoner of a system is an "objective" recognition of his world and of his own nature. Just as the arch-Bolshevist revels in his unshaved appearance, so the man who is bound in spirit finds a rapturous joy in saying straight out for once exactly how things are in his world. For the man who is dazzled by the light darkness is a blessing, and the boundless desert is a paradise to the escaped prisoner. It is nothing less than redemption for the medieval man of today not to have to be the embodiment of goodness and beauty and common sense. Looked at from the shadow-side, ideals are not beacons on mountain peaks, but taskmasters and gaolers, a sort of metaphysical police originally thought up on Sinai by the tyrannical demagogue

Moses and thereafter foisted upon mankind by a clever ruse.

From the causal point of view Joyce is a victim of Roman Catholic authoritarianism, but considered teleologically he is a reformer who for the present is satisfied with negation, a Protestant nourished by his own protests. Atrophy of feeling is a characteristic of modern man and always shows itself as a reaction when there is too much feeling around, and in particular too much false feeling. From the lack of feeling in *Ulysses* we may infer a hideous sentimentality in the age that produced it. But are we really so sentimental today?

Again a question which the future must answer. Still, there is a good deal of evidence to show that we actually are involved in a sentimentality hoax of gigantic proportions. Think of the lamentable role of popular sentiment in wartime! Think of our so-called humanitarianism! The psychiatrist knows only too well how each of us becomes the helpless but not pitiable victim of his own sentiments. Sentimentality is the superstructure erected upon brutality. Unfeelingness is the counter-position and inevitably suffers from the same defects. The success of *Ulysses* proves that even its lack of feeling has a positive effect on the reader, so that we must infer an excess of sentiment which he is quite willing to have damped down. I am deeply convinced that we are not only stuck in the Middle Ages but also are caught in our own sentimentality. It is therefore quite comprehensible that a prophet should arise to teach our culture a compensatory lack of feeling. Prophets are always disagreeable and usually have bad manners, but it is said that they occasionally hit the nail on the head. There are, as we know, major and minor prophets, and history will decide to which of them Joyce belongs. Like every true prophet, the artist is the unwitting mouthpiece of the psychic secrets of his time, and is often as unconscious as a sleepwalker. He supposes that it is he who speaks, but the spirit of the age is his prompter, and whatever this spirit says is proved true by its effects.

Ulysses is a *document humain* of our time and, what is

more, it harbours a secret. It can release the spiritually
bound, and its coldness can freeze all sentimentality—and
even normal feeling—to the marrow. But these salutary
effects do not exhaust its powers. The notion that the devil
himself stood sponsor to the work, if interesting, is hardly
a satisfactory hypothesis. There is life in it, and life is never
exclusively evil and destructive. To be sure, the side of it
that is most tangible seems negative and disruptive; but
one senses behind it something intangible—a secret purpose
which lends it meaning and value. Is this patchwork quilt
of words and images perhaps "symbolic"? I am not thinking
of an allegory (heaven forbid!), but of the symbol as an expression of something whose nature we cannot grasp. In
that case a hidden meaning would doubtless shine through
the curious fabric at some point, here and there notes would
resound that had been heard at other times and places,
maybe in unusual dreams or in the cryptic wisdom of forgotten races. This possibility cannot be contested, but, for
myself, I cannot find the key. On the contrary, the book
seems to me to be written in the full light of consciousness;
it is not a dream and not a revelation of the unconscious.
Compared with *Zarathustra* or the second part of *Faust*, it
shows an even stronger purposiveness and sense of direction.
This is probably why *Ulysses* does not bear the features of
a symbolic work. Of course, one senses the archetypal background. Behind Daedalus and Bloom there stand the eternal
figures of spiritual and carnal man; Mrs. Bloom perhaps con-
ceals an anima entangled in worldliness, and Ulysses himself
might be the hero. But the book does not focus upon this
background; it veers away in the opposite direction and
strives to attain the utmost objectivity of consciousness. It
is obviously not symbolic and has no intention of being so.
Were it none the less symbolic in certain parts, then the
unconscious, in spite of every precaution, would have played
the author a trick or two. For when something is "symbolic," it means that a person divines its hidden, ungrasp-
able nature and is trying desperately to capture in words

the secret that eludes him. Whether it is something of the world he is striving to grasp or something of the spirit, he must turn to it with all his mental powers and penetrate all its iridescent veils in order to bring to the light of day the gold that lies jealously hidden in the depths.

But the shattering thing about Ulysses is that behind the thousand veils nothing lies hidden; it turns neither to the world nor to the spirit but, cold as the moon looking on from cosmic space,[14] leaves the comedy of genesis and decay to pursue its course. I sincerely hope that *Ulysses* is not symbolic, for if it were it would have failed in its purpose. What kind of anxiously guarded secret might it be that is hidden with matchless care under seven hundred and thirty-five unendurable pages? It is better not to waste one's time and energy on a fruitless treasure-hunt. Indeed, there *ought not* to be any thing symbolic behind the book, for if there were our consciousness would be dragged back into the world and spirit, perpetuating Messrs. Bloom and Daedalus to all eternity, befooled by the ten thousand facets of life. This is just what *Ulysses* seeks to prevent: it wants to be an eye of the moon, a consciousness detached from the object, in thrall neither to the gods nor to sensuality, and bound neither by love nor by hate, neither by conviction nor by prejudice. *Ulysses* does not preach this but practices it— detachment of consciousness [15] is the goal that shimmers through the fog of this book. This, surely, is its real secret, the secret of a new cosmic consciousness; and it is revealed not to him who has conscientiously waded through the seven hundred and thirty-five pages, but to him who has gazed at his world and his own mind for seven hundred and thirty-five days with the eyes of Ulysses. This space of time, at any rate, is to be taken symbolically—"a time, times, and half a time"—an indefinite time, therefore; but sufficiently long for the transformation to take place. The detachment of consciousness can be expressed in the Homeric image of Odysseus sailing the straits between Scylla and Charybdis, between the Symplegades, the clashing rocks of the world and the spirit; or, in the imagery of the Dublin inferno, between Father John Conmee and the Viceroy of Ireland, "a light crumpled throwaway," drifting down the Liffey:

Elijah, skiff, light crumpled throwaway, sailed eastward by flanks of ships and trawlers, amid an archipelago of corks, beyond new Wapping street past Benson's ferry, and by the threemasted schooner *Rosevan* from Bridgewater with bricks. . . .

Can this detachment of consciousness, this depersonalization of the personality, can this be the Ithaca of the Joycean Odyssey?

One might suppose that in a world of nothing but nothingness at least the "I"—James Joyce himself—would be left over. But has anyone noticed the appearance, among all the unhappy, shadowy "I's" of this book, of a single, actual ego? True, every figure in *Ulysses* is superlatively real, none of them could be other than what they are, they are themselves in every respect. And yet not one of them has an ego, there is no acutely conscious, human center, an island surrounded by warm heart's blood, so small and yet so vitally important. All the Daedaluses, Blooms, Harrys, Lynches, Mulligans, and the rest of them talk and go about as in a collective dream that begins nowhere and ends nowhere, that takes place only because "No-man"—an unseen Odysseus—dreams it. None of them knows this, and yet all live for the sole reason that a god bids them live. That is how life is—*vita somnium breve* —and that is why the Joycean figures are so real. But the ego that embraces them all appears nowhere. It betrays itself by nothing, by no judgment, no sympathy, not a single anthropomorphism. The ego of the creator of these figures is not to be found. It is as though it had dissolved into the countless figures of *Ulysses*. And yet, or rather for that very reason, all and everything, even the missing punctuation of the final chapter, is Joyce himself. His detached, contemplative consciousness, dispassionately embracing in one glance the timeless simultaneity of the happenings of the sixteenth day of June, 1904, must say of all these appearances: *Tat tvam asi*, "That art thou"—"thou" in a higher sense, not the ego but the self.[16] For the self alone embraces the ego and the non-ego, the infernal regions, the viscera, the *imagines et lares*, and the heavens.

Whenever I read *Ulysses* there comes into my mind a Chinese picture, published by Richard Wilhelm,[17] of a yogi in meditation, with five human figures growing out of the top of his head and five more figures growing out of the top of each of *their* heads. This picture portrays the spiritual state of the yogi who is about to rid himself of his ego so as to pass over into the more complete, more objective state of the self. This is the state of the "moon-disk, at rest and alone," of *sat-chit-ananda*, the epitome of being and not-being, the ultimate goal of the Eastern way of redemption, the priceless pearl of Indian and Chinese wisdom, sought and extolled through the centuries.

The "light crumpled throwaway" drifts towards the East. Three times this crumpled note turns up in *Ulysses*, each time mysteriously connected with Elijah. Twice we are told: "Elijah comes." He actually does appear in the brothel scene (rightly compared by Middleton Murry to the Walpurgis-nacht in *Faust*), where in Americanese he explains the secret of the note:

Boys, do it now. God's time is 12.25. Tell mother you'll be there. Rush your order and you play a slick ace. Join on right here! Book through to eternity junction, the nonstop run. Just one word more. Are you a god or a doggone clod? If the second advent came to Coney Island are we ready? Florry Christ, Stephen Christ, Zoe Christ, Bloom Christ, Kitty Christ, Linch Christ, it's up to you to sense that cosmic force. Have we cold feet about the cosmos? No, Be on the side of the angels. Be a prism. *You have that something within, the higher self.*[18] You can rub shoulders with a Jesus, a Gautama, an Ingersoll. Are you all in this vibration? I say you are. You once nobble that, congregation, and a buck joyride to heaven becomes a back number. You got me?

It's a lifebrightener, sure. The hottest stuff ever was. It's the whole pie with jam in. It's just the cutest snappiest line out. It is immense, supersumptuous. It restores.

One can see what has happened: the detachment of human consciousness and its consequent approximation to the divine —the whole basis and highest artistic achievement of *Ulysses* —suffers an infernal distortion in the drunken madhouse of the brothel as soon as it appears in the cloak of a traditional formula. Ulysses, the sorely tried wanderer, toils ever towards his island home, back to his true self, beating his way through the turmoil of eighteen chapters, and, free at last from the fool's world of illusions, "looks on from afar," impassively. Thus he achieves what a Jesus or a Buddha achieved, and what Faust also strove for—the overcoming of a fool's world, liberation from the opposites. And just as Faust was dissolved in the Eternal Feminine, so it is Molly Bloom (whom Stuart Gilbert compares to the blossoming earth) who has the last word in her unpunctuated monologue, putting a blessed close to the hellish, shrieking dissonances with a harmonious final chord.

Ulysses is the creator-god in Joyce, a true demiurge who has freed himself from entanglement in the physical and mental world and contemplates them with detached consciousness. He is for Joyce what Faust was for Goethe, or Zarathustra for Nietzsche. He is the higher self who returns to his divine home after blind entanglement in *Samsara*. In the whole book no Ulysses appears; the book itself is Ulysses, a microcosm of James Joyce, the world of the self and the self of the world in one. Ulysses can return home only when he has turned his back on the world of mind and matter. This is surely the message underlying that sixteenth day of June, 1904, the everyday of everyman, on which persons of no importance restlessly do and say things without beginning or aim—a shadowy picture, dreamlike, infernal, sardonic, negative, ugly, devilish, but true. A picture that could give one bad dreams or induce the mood of a cosmic Ash Wednesday, such as the Creator might have felt on August 1, 1914. After the optimism of the seventh day of creation the demiurge must have found it pretty difficult in 1914 to identify himself with his handiwork. *Ulysses* was written between 1914 and 1921—hardly the conditions for painting a particularly cheerful picture of the world or for taking it lovingly in one's arms (nor today either, for that matter). So it is not surprising that the demiurge in the artist sketched a negative picture, so blasphemously negative that in Anglo-Saxon countries the book was banned in order to avoid the scandal of its contradicting the creation story in Genesis! And that is how the misunderstood demiurge became Ulysses in search of his home.

There is so little feeling in *Ulysses* that it must be very pleasing to all aesthetes. But let us assume that the consciousness of *Ulysses* is not a moon but an ego that possesses judgment, understanding, and a feeling heart. Then the long road through the eighteen chapters would not only hold no delights but would be a road to Calvary; and the wanderer, overcome by so much suffering and folly, would sink down at nightfall into the arms of the Great Mother, who signifies the beginning and end of life. Under the cynicism of Ulysses there is hidden a great compassion; he knows the sufferings of a world that is neither beautiful nor good and, worse still, rolls on without hope through the eternally repeated everyday, dragging with it man's consciousness in an idiot dance through the hours, months, years. Ulysses has dared to take the step that leads to the detachment of consciousness from the object; he has freed himself from attachment, entanglement, and delusion, and can therefore turn homeward. He gives us more than a subjective expression of personal opinion, for the creative genius is never one but many, and he speaks in stillness to the souls of the multitude, whose meaning and destiny he embodies no less than the artist's own.

It seems to me now that all that is negative in Joyce's work, all that is cold-blooded, bizarre and banal, grotesque and devilish, is a positive virtue for which it deserves praise. Joyce's inexpressibly rich and myriad-faceted language unfolds itself

in passages that creep along tapeworm fashion, terribly boring and monotonous, but the very boredom and monotony of
it attain an epic grandeur that makes the book a *Mahabha-
rata* of the world's futility and squalor. "From drains, clefts,
cesspools, middens arise on all sides stagnant fumes." And in
this open cloaca is reflected with blasphemous distortion
practically everything that is highest in religious thought,
exactly as in dreams. (Alfred Kubin's *Die andere Seite* is a
country-cousin of the metropolitan *Ulysses*.)

Even this I willingly accept, for it cannot be denied. On
the contrary, the transformation of eschatology into scatology
proves the truth of Tertullian's dictum: *anima naturaliter
christiana*. Ulysses shows himself a conscientious Antichrist
and thereby proves that his Catholicism still holds together.
He is not only a Christian but—still higher title to fame—a
Buddhist, Shivaist, and a Gnostic:

(With a voice of waves.) . . . White yoghin of the Gods. Occult
pimander of Hermes Trismegistos. *(With a voice of whistling sea-
wind.)* Punarjanam patsypunjaub! I won't have my leg pulled.
It has been said by one: beware of the left, the cult of Shakti.
(With a cry of stormbirds.) Shakti, Shiva! Dark hidden Father!
. . . Aum! Baum! Pyjaum! I am the light of the homestead, I am
the dreamery creamery butter.

Is not that touching and significant? Even on the dunghill
the oldest and noblest treasures of the spirit are not lost.
There is no cranny in the psyche through which the divine
afflatus could finally breathe out its life and perish in noisome
filth. Old Hermes, father of all heretical bypaths, is right:
"As above, so below." Stephen Daedalus, the bird-headed
sky-man, trying to escape from the all too gaseous regions of
the air, falls into an earthly slough and in the very depths
encounters again the heights from which he fled. "And
should I flee to the uttermost ends of the earth. . . ." The
close of this sentence is a blasphemy that furnishes the most
convincing proof of this in all *Ulysses*. Better still, that nosy-
parker Bloom, the perverse and impotent sensualist, experi-

ences in the dirt something that had never happened to him before: his own transfiguration. Glad tidings: when the eternal signs have vanished from the heavens, the pig that hunts truffles finds them again in the earth. For they are indelibly stamped on the lowest as on the highest; only in the lukewarm intermediate realm that is accursed of God are they nowhere to be found.

Ulysses is absolutely objective and absolutely honest and therefore trustworthy. One can trust his testimony as to the power and nugatoriness of the world and the spirit. Ulysses alone is reality, life, meaning; in him is comprised the whole phantasmagoria of mind and matter, of egos and non-egos. And here I would like to ask Mr. Joyce a question: "Have you noticed that you are a representation, a thought, perhaps a complex of Ulysses? That he stands about you like a hundred-eyed Argus, and has thought up for you a world and an anti-world, filling them with objects without which you could not be conscious of your ego at all?" I do not know what the worthy author would answer to this question. Nor is it any business of mine—there is nothing to stop me from indulging in metaphysics on my own. But one is driven to ask it when one sees how neatly the microcosm of Dublin, on that sixteenth day of June, 1904, has been fished out of the chaotic macrocosm of world history, how it is dissected and spread out on a glass slide in all its tasty details, and described with the most pedantic exactitude by a completely detached observer. Here are the streets, here are the houses and a young couple out for a walk, a real Mr. Bloom goes about his advertising business, a real Stephen Daedalus diverts himself with aphoristic philosophy. It would be quite possible for Mr. Joyce himself to loom up at some Dublin street-corner. Why not? He is surely as real as Mr. Bloom and could therefore equally well be fished out, dissected, and described (as, for instance, in *A Portrait of the Artist as a Young Man*).

Who, then, is Ulysses? Doubtless he is a symbol of what makes up the totality, the oneness, of all the single appearances in *Ulysses* as a whole—Mr. Bloom, Stephen, Mrs. Bloom, and the rest, including Mr. Joyce. Try to imagine a being who is not a mere colourless conglomerate soul composed of an indefinite number of ill-assorted and antagonistic individual souls, but consists also of houses, street-processions, churches, the Liffey, several brothels, and a crumpled note on its way to the sea—and yet possesses a perceiving and registering consciousness! Such a monstrosity drives one to speculation, especially as one can prove nothing anyway and has to fall back on conjecture. I must confess that I suspect *Ulysses* of being a more comprehensive self who is the subject of all the objects on the glass slide, a being who acts as if he were Mr. Bloom or a printing-shop or a crumpled note, but actually is the "hidden dark Father" of his specimens. "I am the sacrificer and the sacrificed." In the language of the infernal regions: "I am the dreamery creamery butter." When he turns to the world with a loving embrace, all the gardens blossom. But when he turns his back upon it, the empty everyday rolls on—*labitur et labetur in omne volubilis aevum.*

The demiurge first created a world that in his vainglory seemed to him perfect; but looking upward he beheld a light which he had not created. Thereupon he turned back toward the place where was his home. But as he did so, his masculine creative power turned into feminine acquiescence, and he had to confess:

> All things ephemeral
> Are but a reflection;
> The unattainable
> Here finds perfection;
> The indescribable
> Here it is done;
> The Eternal Feminine
> Still draws us on.

From the specimen slide far below upon earth, in Ireland, Dublin, 7 Eccles Street, from her bed as she grows sleepy at about two o'clock in the morning of the seventeenth of June, 1904, the voice of easy-going Mrs. Bloom speaks:

O and the sea the sea crimson sometimes like fire and the glorious sunsets and the figtrees in the Alameda gardens yes and all the queer little streets and pink and blue and yellow houses and the rosegardens and the jessamine and geraniums and cactuses and Gibraltar as a girl where I was a Flower of the mountain yes when I put the rose in my hair like the Andalusian girls used or shall I wear a red yes and how he kissed me under the Moorish wall and I thought well as well him as another and then I asked him with my eyes to ask again yes and then he asked me would I yes to say yes my mountain flower and first I put my arms around him yes and drew him down to me so he could feel my breasts all perfume yes and his heart was going like mad and yes I said yes I will Yes.

O *Ulysses,* you are truly a devotional book for the object-besotted, object-ridden white man! You are a spiritual exercise, an ascetic discipline, an agonizing ritual, an arcane procedure, eighteen alchemical retorts piled on top of one another, where amid acids, poisonous fumes, and fire and ice, the homunculus of a new, universal consciousness is distilled!

You say nothing and betray nothing, O *Ulysses,* but you give us the works! Penelope need no longer weave her neverending garment; she now takes her ease in the gardens of the earth, for her husband is home again, all his wanderings over. A world passed away, and was made new.

Concluding remark: I am now getting on pretty well with my reading of *Ulysses*—forward!

NOTES

1. For the genesis of this essay, see n. 12, infra. It was first published in the *Europäische Revue* (Berlin), VIII: 2/9 (Sept., 1932); reprinted in *Wirklichkeit der Seele* (Zurich, 1934). Translated by W. Stanley Dell in *Nimbus* (London), II:1 (June–Aug., 1952), which translation forms the basis of

the present version. The quotations from *Ulysses* are in accordance with the 1st edn. (Paris, 1922), which Jung may have used.

Author's headnote added to version in *Wirklichkeit der Seele:* This literary essay first appeared in the *Europäische Revue*. It is not a scientific treatise, any more than is my *aperçu* on Picasso. I have included it in the present volume because *Ulysses* is an important "document humain" very characteristic of our time, and because my opinions may show how ideas that play a considerable role in my work can be applied to literary material. My essay lacks not only any scientific but also any didactic intention, and is of interest to the reader only as a subjective confession.

2. As Joyce himself says *(Work in Progress):* "We may come, touch and go, from atoms and ifs, but we are presurely destined to be odds without ends." *(Work in Progress* was the working title of *Finnegans Wake*. Passages were published in *transition*).

3. Curtius *(James Joyce und sein Ulysses)* calls *Ulysses* a "Luciferian book, a work of Antichrist."

4. Curtius *(ibid,* p. 60): "A metaphysical nihilism is the substance of Joyce's work."

5. The magic words that sent me to sleep occur at the bottom of p. 134 and top of p. 135: "that stone effigy in frozen music, horned and terrible, of the human form divine, that eternal symbol of wisdom and prophecy which, if aught that the imagination or the hand of sculptor has wrought in marble of soultransfigured and of soultransfiguring deserves to live, deserves to live." At this point, dizzy with sleep, I turned the page and my eye fell on the following passage: "a man supple in combat: stonehorned, stonebearded, heart of stone." This refers to Moses, who refused to be cowed by the might of Egypt. The two passages contained the narcotic that switched off my consciousness, activating a still unconscious train of thought which consciousness would only have disturbed. As I later discovered, it dawned on me here for the first time what the author was doing and what was the idea behind his work.

6. This is greatly intensified in *Work in Progress*. Carola Giedion-Welcker aptly remarks on the "ever-recurring ideas in ever-changing forms, projected into a sphere of absolute irreality. Absolute time, absolute space" *(Neue Schweizer Rundschau,* 1929, p. 166).

7. In Janet's psychology this phenomenon is known as *abaisse-ment du niveau mental.* Among the insane it happens involuntarily, but with Joyce it is the result of deliberate training. All the richness and grotesque profundity of dream-thinking come to the surface when the "fonction du réel," that is, adapted consciousness, is switched off. Hence the predominance of psychic and verbal automatisms and the total neglect of any communicable meaning.

8. I think Stuart Gilbert *(James Joyce's "Ulysses,"* 1930, p. 40) is right in supposing that each chapter is presided over, among other things, by one of the visceral or sensory dominants. Those he cites are the kidneys, genitals, heart, lungs, oesophagus, brain, blood, ear, musculature, eye, nose, uterus, nerves, skeleton, skin. These dominants each function as a *leitmotif.* My remark about visceral thinking was written in 1930. For me Gilbert's proof offers valuable confirmation of the psychological fact that an *abaissement du niveau mental* constellates what Wernicke calls the "organ-representatives," i.e., symbols representing the organs.

9. Curtius *(ibid,* p. 30): "He reproduces the stream of consciousness without filtering it either logically or ethically."

10. Curtius *(ibid,* p. 8): "The author has done everything to avoid making it easier for the reader to understand."

11. Curtius, Stuart Gilbert, and others.

12. The present essay was originally written at the request of Dr. Daniel Brody, publisher of Rhein-Verlag (Zurich), as an introduction to the third edition of the German translation of *Ulysses,* according to information in Ellmann, *James Joyce,* pp. 651 f., subsequently confirmed by Dr. Brody. However, also see *Letters of James Joyce,* p. 294, Joyce to Harriet S. Weaver, Sept. 27, 1930: "The Rheinverlag wrote to Jung for a preface to the German edition of Gilbert's book. He replied with a very long and hostile attack ... which they are much upset about, but I want them to use it." The book referred to was Stuart Gilbert's *James Joyce's "Ulysses": A Study,* a German translation of which appeared in 1932. It is evident however, that Jung wrote his essay not for the Gilbert book but for *Ulysses.* According to Ellmann, "Jung amended his article somewhat and published it separately.... In its modified form it was not devoid of respect, and Jung sent Joyce a copy with a rather flattering letter," quoted by Ellmann on p. 642.

13. Gilbert, p. 2, speaks of a "deliberate deflation of sentiment."

14. Gilbert, p. 355 n.: "to take, so to speak, a God's-eye view of cosmos."

15. Gilbert likewise stresses this detachment. He says on p. 21: "The attitude of the author of *Ulysses* towards his personages is one of serene detachment." (I would put a question-mark after "serene.") P. 22: "All facts of any kind, mental or material, sublime or ridiculous, have an equivalence of meaning for the artist." P. 23: "In this detachment, as absolute as the indifference of Nature herself towards her children, we may see one of the causes of the apparent 'realism' of *Ulysses.*"

16. As Joyce himself says in *A Portrait of the Artist as a Young Man* (1930 ed., p. 245) : "The artist, like the God of Creation, remains within or behind or beyond or above his handiwork, invisible, refined out of existence, indifferent, paring his fingernails."

17. Wilhelm and Jung, *The Secret of the Golden Flower* (1962 ed.), p. 57. The picture is reproduced in *Alchemical Studies.*

18. My italics.

Kafka's *A Country Doctor* —

Microcosm of Symbolism

by STANLEY COOPERMAN

Stanley Cooperman's doctorate is from Indiana; he taught at the University of Oregon and Hofstra University and was a Fulbright lecturer in Iran before going to the Simon Fraser University in British Columbia. He has published widely, with scholarly articles and criticism on such diverse figures as Frank Norris, Dickens, Edward Bellamy, Howells, Kipling, and E. M. Forster. To this he has added fiction and poetry in popular and "little" magazines. The present paper was first published in 1957 in the *University of Kansas City Review* (XXIV, 1, 15–22).

There are so many levels of Kafka criticism that it is difficult to single out one study which is psychoanalytically oriented but which avoids the vice of insistence that every other approach is necessarily wrong. Mr. Cooperman has therefore done well to devote his study of one of Kafka's most difficult short stories to several different possible levels of interpretation of its thorny symbolism.

THE work of Franz Kafka has been a boon to three great interpretive movements: the socio-materialist, the theological-mystic, and the psychological-rationalist. For the first of these groups Kafka is simply another manifestation of the social rot leading to fascism; he is, indeed, part of the fascist mentality itself. E. B. Burgum, for example, went so far as to equate the decay of Kafka as an individual with the decay of pre-fascist German society, adding the rather unkind note that readers who enjoy Kafka are likely to do so in ratio to their own neurosis.

Theological criticism, on the other hand, evolves a perverse *Divine Comedy* from the work of Kafka—the existential search for salvation and grace of a fictionalized Kierkegaard manipulating his own guilt of reconciliation with the absolute. Kafka's religious critics, in brief, fashion his work into the Sacred (and neo-traditional) Wound of Despair—purposelessness, sin, and awareness of the essential absurdity of existence. It is the theology of crisis, which by its acceptance of negation, at last is saved.

Psychological criticism all too often attempts to make of Kafka a simple case history, usually of Oedipus, and seems far closer to the clinical study of neurotic personality than to the appreciation of art. The Freudians are, as usual, the worst offenders in this respect. There is the usual incantation —page after page of A means B and C means D; this is phal-lic and that is female; and whole catalogues from the Freudian dogma. Such criticism not only falls prey to the genetic fallacy, but more serious, attempts to set up mechanical and objective definitions of symbols.

Although we may classify certain areas of fiction as "psychological," it is vital to remember that here art remains the chief goal of our understanding. Psychology, both for an author and his readers, may be used for art or absorbed into it; exclusive concentration on psychiatric theorizing will be disastrous. This is the error made by many critics who, in a great effort to be scientific, treat symbols as though they were chemicals, or constant and quantitative data. Symbolic art is intensely rewarding precisely because there can be no balance-sheet, no bookkeeping method of excerpt and "meaning." Symbols are more than psychiatric short-hand for "complexes." As Albert Camus points out, no matter how exactly we translate a symbol (or believe we do), only the artist himself can restore movement to it. "There is no word-for-word correspondence . . . a symbol always goes beyond him who would use it." We might add that a symbol goes beyond those who would explain or describe it.

An essential factor in successful symbolic art, then, is multi-level meaning which cannot be detached entirely from the work itself. The richer and greater the symbolism, the more complex will be the reader's response on several levels, each of which may be justified. The value of a sensitive eclecticism becomes especially apparent in discussing the work of Franz Kafka. Like other masters of the symbolic, Kafka may be approached from several directions; there is no one approach, and those who read Kafka (and comment on him) in order to grind a particular philosophical ax, run the risk of losing the work itself.

An examination of one of Kafka's shorter pieces—"A Country Doctor"—will demonstrate symbolic method in all its multiplicity. This story is only eight pages long, but it is rewarding from several standpoints. As a microcosm of Kafka's thematic basis and stylistic approach it is invaluable. It is immensely suggestive on the symbolic level, setting up repeated echoes in the mind. Psychologically the story is powerful and rich in possible interpretations. Finally, the technique is superb, showing Kafka at his best.

A familiar characteristic of modern fiction—the absence of traditional plot or story-telling development—is found in "A Country Doctor." There is no precise beginning, middle or end. The primary concern is with the significance of the events rather than with the events themselves. Narration is interior and vertical rather than exterior and horizontal. The reader is plunged immediately into the situation, and must make his way out as best he can; there are, if anything, more unanswered questions at the finish than at the start.

Because both development and conflict are enormously compact—with great symbolic association—any attempt to paraphrase or summarize will be watery; the impact of the prose, as highly charged as poetry, is non-transferable. Try, for example, to tell the story of *Ulysses* and you will of course find there is nothing much to tell. Joyce, of course, was a literary virtuoso, but aside from his word-performance the material of his art is dynamic largely on the psychic and psychological levels.

The unimportance of plotting is basic to "A Country Doctor"; we cannot "tell" the story and communicate more than a superficial orientation. Roughly, this is what occurs: a doctor, about to answer a call from the country, finds that his horse had died, and sends his servant girl to obtain another. She fails, but a groom and two great horses appear mysteriously from an old pigsty. The horses seem satisfactory, but the groom begins making sexual advances to the girl.

The groom ignores the doctor's objections, and the horses begin traveling with amazing speed, bringing him to his patient's house almost immediately. He finds his patient—a young country boy—suffering from a horrible wound which he cannot cure. This is resented by the family and friends, who undress the doctor and place him in bed with the boy, hoping for a cure. Preoccupied with the thought of the servant girl being assaulted by the groom, the doctor dresses and starts back home. The horses, however, travel with agonizing slowness, and the doctor fears his home and place have been usurped.

One must admit that in paraphrase, the story line of "A Country Doctor" is hardly impressive. Yet from this rather loose construction, Kafka gives us an art at once disturbing and subtle, meaningful and elusive—apparently simple yet technically sophisticated.

Like most of Kafka's work, the story unfolds within a single consciousness—a single point of view, which is, moreover, largely passive. The doctor (just as Joseph K. in "The Trial") is a logical little man bickering talmudically with the externals appearing to manipulate his fate. These externals are irrational, irreversible and fantastic, but despite his indignant posturing, the doctor is aware both of the inevitability of the process and his own role in creating it. As Claude-Edmonde Magny points out, there is "the idea of responsibility antedating the action . . . together with the theme of nightmare, the helplessness before the predestined event—the theme of gratuitous catastrophe for which we are nevertheless responsible."

"A Country Doctor" starts with a direct plunge into a situation of anxiety, and from the very first, introduces and confirms an impression of nightmare. The droning sentence structure, acceptance of the obviously impossible, distortions of time and space—in short, the entire nature as well as the contents of narration seem a description or reactivation of dream. "What was it about?" we may imagine a psychiatrist asking. The answer is, in part, given below:

I was in great perplexity; I had to start an urgent journey; a seriously ill patient was waiting for me in a village ten miles off; a thick blizzard of snow filled all the wide spaces between him and me; I had a gig, a light gig with big wheels, exactly right for our country roads; muffled in furs, my bag of instruments in my hand, I was in the courtyard all ready for the journey; but there was no horse to be had, no horse. . . .

Here is the combination which is to grow more striking as the story progresses: the monotone, the simple declarative clauses, the repetition. Then, from a "year-long uninhabited pigsty" come the man—a groom—and two magnificent horses, "their bodies steaming thickly." This is, certainly, fantastic; yet the sudden arrivals are accepted by the doctor-narrator and Rose, the servant-girl. When the groom turns abruptly to Rose, the doctor makes only feeble objection, for the girl has had a "justified presentiment that her fate was inescapable." From this point, the dream-narrative intensifies:

I could just hear the door of my house splitting and bursting as the groom charged at it, and then I was deafened and blinded by a storming rush that steadily buffeted all my senses. But this only for a moment, since, as if my patient's farmyard had opened out before my courtyard gate, I was already there; the horses had

come quietly to a standstill, the blizzard had stopped, and moonlight was all around.

The final effect, again, of realism and logic within surrealism and illogic cannot be reproduced outside the story
itself. Passages such as "guests . . . were coming in, through
the moonlight at the open door, walking on tip-toe, keeping
balance with their outstretched arms," or sequences such as
the stripping of the doctor, the treadmill drifting of the
horses on his return, the culmination of impotency and
frozen horror, leads us into a world where recognizable objects have become distorted beyond endurance. We arrive,
finally, at an anguished sense of wakening from a dream
which has become our own.

"A Country Doctor," like most dream literature, is rooted
firmly in symbolism—so firmly, indeed, that any certain di-
chotomy between the literal and the symbolic vanishes. It is
necessary to accept a simple dream narrative as the literal
level of "A Country Doctor," since only a dream can give it
any literal meaning whatsoever. On this basis, symbolic associations move within a psychological landscape and may be
interpreted psychoanalytically. We are introduced to a situation of anxiety and impotence—the demands of duty cannot
be fulfilled by the doctor. Into this situation comes a potency
figure—the groom—offering what seems to be a solution.
Notice the symbolism of birth permeating the entire "pigsty"
sequence (the darkness, the smell, the groom crawling out
on all fours calling "Brother" and "Sister"). This culminates
in the arrival of the horses, "their legs tucked close to their
bodies, each well-shaped head lowered like a camel's, by sheer
strength of buttocking squeezed out through the door hole
which they filled entirely."

The groom, then, is an ambivalent figure; on the one
hand, he aids the doctor by providing "Brother" and "Sister"
and the means for fulfilling duty; on the other, he is a
"brute" who subjects Rose to her "inescapable fate"—sexual

violation. Rose, later called "the pretty girl who had lived in my home for years almost without my noticing her," is a mother figure, domesticity, the love-object, and "servant." In a sudden and terrible insight, the doctor becomes aware of the violation of this mother figure ("I could just hear the door of my house splitting and bursting as the groom charged at it").

At that moment time is destroyed, the doctor is plunged back into the timelessness of the unconscious, and he meets himself as a youth—the boy with a wound. Here the atmosphere is one of disgust: "The air was almost unbreathable; I wanted to push open a window." This is a phase which appears in many of Kafka's works.

At first this aspect of himself—this youth—seems well, but the doctor is uncomfortable in his diagnosis. The family—especially the father—oppresses him. The situation finally becomes one with obvious Oedipus overtones, as well as self-defense of potency: "In the narrow confines of the old man's mind I felt ill; that was my only reason for refusing the drink. The mother stood by the bedside and cajoled me toward it." On his second examination the doctor discovers the boy's wound, the Oedipus fixation ("a fine wound is all I brought into the world, that was my sole endowment"), and he succumbs to an intense feeling of guilt and failure. He is guilty of the rape of Rose because he has left her to the groom's lust. And he is also guilty—a failure—because he is unable to effect a cure.

The doctor feels completely isolated as the family and friends stare at him: "The family and the village elders stripped my clothes off me; a school choir with the teacher at the head of it stood before the house." Religion cannot help him, his sin is too great ("the parson sits at home and unravels his vestments"). He must get back to Rose and combat the groom; he must escape from the family and the nightmare of religious sanctions ("O be joyful, all you patients . . ."). The result, however, is impotence. He cannot return, or compete with the lustful tyranny of the groom:

"Like old men we crawled through the snowy wastes . . . in my house the disgusting groom is raging; Rose is his victim; I do not want to think about it any more . . . I cannot reach it." The doctor's narration ends on a note of complete impotency, and the dream stops.

This—a slice of dream life—is one of many possible psychological interpretations. However, it by no means limits the meanings of "A Country Doctor," since the story is rich in associations operating through, but beyond the literal dream level. From another standpoint, the story need not be considered in terms of psychology, but rather as a poetic evocation of the individual buffeted by chaos in an age where all outlines are blurred, and faith has turned to frost. The basic conflict, as in "The Trial," may be considered that of evil breaking suddenly into a rational, well-ordered life (perhaps a life which is over-regulated: "I was the district doctor and did my duty to the uttermost") and finally paralyzing it. The doctor is impotent when faced with the Sacred Wound —which, as Herbert Tauber points out, is the "awakened consciousness of the shattered condition of life."

Viewed in this light, the story becomes a symbolic restatement of the classic existential situation. On the one hand, we have a respectable and adjusted life; on the other, the swift insight, the crisis erupting within the placidly flowing sequence of "duties" and prosaic tasks. "I could see no way out," the doctor cries, and his words are an echo of the philosophers of crisis from Kierkegaard to Sartre.

Suddenly, without warning, the dark, irrational and diabolic forces represented by the beast-groom and the great horses take command. They drive the doctor deeply and instantaneously face to face with the insoluble—the "fear and trembling"—the moment when reasons fail, when "the center will not hold," when nothing is left but the scarlet wound—the beautiful wound—of awareness.

Rose's rape by the dark force of the groom represents the smashing of all that is near, protecting, feminine. But the guilt is strongly the doctor's in this violation; he has failed to realize the true value of Rose ("the pretty girl who had lived in my house for years without my noticing her"); everyday life has become formulistic, conventional, devoid of passion or awareness. As a result of this failure, the doctor is incapable of coping with the crisis when it comes—again, like the other isolated heroes (or victims) of existential literature. His failure delivers him to the disgusting wound and the bitter cold.

Faced with the wound (which represents his own ruined state and so cannot be cured) the doctor is isolated, completely alone before a suddenly meaningless and hostile universe. The traditional answers are gone; they can no longer serve ("the parson sits at home and unravels his vestments"). Although the secular self must be relied upon ("the doctor is supposed to be omnipotent"), it provides neither meaning nor answer ("old country doctor that I am"), and, when the usual prosaic days and nights are shattered ("bereft of my servant girl"), there is nothing but sterility, the empty shell of what once were solutions ("strip his clothes off; then he'll heal us . . . O be joyful all you patients").

The nightmare ending is the doctor's chaotic spiritual state after meeting the wound: a wasteland of panicked effort and treadmill motion, a vain attempt to prevent the inevitable crisis. He is caught, now, between "neither—nor" in a ruined secularism ("earthly vehicle"), driven by a desperate necessity for something beyond himself ("unearthly horses"). But it is too late; he is incapable of making the choice made by those who meet the Wound but who arrive finally at acceptance through faith. And so he rides through the snowy wastes, the nightmare storm, an absurd and anguished figure ("I cannot reach it") in a shattered world ("It cannot be made good, not ever").

The two interpretations I have presented concern the same work, and in addition rely to a great extent on the same symbols. But they are not mutually exclusive; in the symbolic art of Kafka two methods of criticism may, and indeed must, occupy the same space at the same time. Kafka is ambiguous and difficult, but his material—the stuff of the human soul—would be violated if he presented a single dimension of meaning. The work has many truths, a weaving and reweaving of many themes, and it cannot be approached bluntly or singlemindedly. We must synthesize, separate and reform with every method at our disposal, without sneering at one method or completely discounting another. This may involve considerable difficulty. It has often been pointed out, however, that in the art of reading fiction, as in the art of living, our satisfactions increase as we are willing to hazard our resources.

Psychiatrist and Saint in

The Cocktail Party

by RICHARD B. HOVEY

Richard B. Hovey took his A.B. degree at the University of Cincinnati and his doctorate at Harvard. His dissertation at Harvard finally led to his publication in 1959 of the "mental biography" entitled *John Jay Chapman—An American Mind.* He now teaches at the University of Maryland, where he conducts a graduate seminar on the relations between literature and psychology. He is at work on a study of Hemingway.

The present paper was presented at the annual meeting of the Modern Language Association Discussion Group on Literature and Psychology in 1959 and was published at the time in *Literature and Psychology* (IX, 3 & 4, 51–55). It is in part an investigation into unconscious elements in the structure of Eliot's most popular play, but its main function is to evaluate Eliot's ambivalence toward psychiatry and dynamic psychology in his portrayal of the psychiatrist Sir Henry Harcourt-Reilly.

WHETHER *The Cocktail Party* should be asked to bear the addition of one more pebble to the mountain of commentary already heaped upon it is a nice question. It is one I shall not try to answer. I am content that Eliot's play means many things to many men. We have been interested in its poetry, its dramaturgy, its characterizations, its symbols, its myths, its theology, and its parallels to the *Alcestis.* What is also obvious about *The Cocktail Party* is that it contains more overt and explicit psychologizing than do any of Eliot's other plays. Here we have a temptation for the psychology-minded reader, and I am not going to resist it. Although Mr. Eliot might frown and remind us that in one of his *Four Quartets* he classed Freudian methods along with palmistry, astrology, and "the usual pastimes and drugs," [1] I entertain a hope that to bring to this play a few insights borrowed from psychoanalysis will explain why it continues to tease our imagination. In fact, I am going to argue that in *The Cocktail Party* Mr. Eliot's inadequate understanding of dynamic depth psychology points up a limitation of his insight into Christianity.[2]

But let us begin with the obvious. The narrative of the play, based on a double triangular situation, is easy to follow. The marriage of the childless, middle-aged couple Edward and Lavinia Chamberlayne is going on the rocks. Edward has been seeking happiness in a love affair with young Celia Coplestone; his wife has been flirting with young Peter Quilpe, and Peter's love for Celia is unreturned. Matters come to a head when Lavinia temporarily leaves her husband. Whereupon, the tangled lives of these worldlings are set upon clearer courses by the professional counsel of "a very great doctor," Sir Henry Harcourt-Reilly. With his help Edward and Lavinia are adjusted toward a workable marriage; and Celia, recognizing the emptiness of her affair with Edward, discovers within herself and answers a religious vocation to enter an order of missionary nuns—a vocation which eventuates in her martyrdom. Evidently the spiritual intent of the play is to contrast secular with sacred love. Its moral is uttered by the doctor when he remarks of human existence:

> The best of a bad job is all any of us can make of it—
> Except, of course, the saints.

Such a dictum, to be sure, is consistent with the pronouncements Eliot has regularly made about Christianity and the modern world since his conversion to the Church of England. It is also self-evident that Sir Henry Harcourt-Reilly is

pivotal to the action of the play and that he serves as Eliot's
raisonneur. But what has not been so obvious to some readers is that we might begin by calling Sir Henry a psychiatrist.
With Eliot's nudging, we know of course that Sir Henry
sometimes behaves like the Hercules of the *Alcestis.*[3] Sometimes, too, he talks like a priest. Yet to be satisfied with
either of the two latter labels exclusively is to be led astray
by a partial truth. For Sir Henry in fact functions as a psychiatrist: he does give to emotionally disturbed persons professional counsel which helps them toward self-knowledge.
The crucial role given to Sir Henry indicates on Eliot's part
a recognition of how important as a guide to life depth psychology has become to us moderns. Actually, about two decades before *The Cocktail Party* appeared, Eliot admitted that
the new psychology might have "very great utility" in reviving "truths long since known to Christianity, but mostly
forgotten and ignored," and in putting them into "a form
and language understandable by modern people to whom the
language of Christianity is not only dead but undecipher-
able." [4] Out of this seed-idea, it seems, *The Cocktail Party*
was to grow. It is also our clue that in Eliot's conception of
Sir Henry Harcourt-Reilly Christianity and psychoanalysis
meet for their reciprocal illumination or obscuration. Our
test, then, is the manner in which Sir Henry handles his cases,
those of Celia and the Chamberlaynes. About his conduct we
ask two questions: how competent is he as a medical man?
and how valid is he as an agent of Christian truths?

In his treatment of Celia, Sir Henry at first glance may
seem to be depicted as a plausible psychiatrist and possibly
a wise Christian as well. He has uncommon insight into spiritual matters. He is humble enough to recognize the limitations of his science and of his healing art. Seemingly he can
distinguish—as do both the psychiatrist and the enlightened
clergyman today—between the normal and the neurotic use
of religion. Sir Henry demonstrates that it is never the psychiatrist's business to alter the religious practices and beliefs
of his patients unless these are distorted by the patient's ill-

ness. And he is aware that psychiatric treatments may involve value judgments.

Also at first glance Celia's case seems not over-complicated. In her consultation with the doctor, Eliot is at great pains to persuade us that no pathology has gone into the making of Celia's personality or into the decision she reaches to renounce this world and its earth-bound loves. Though she is distressed by Edward Chamberlayne's lack of sufficient courage to divorce his wife and though she sees herself duped by the vanity of human wishes, Celia is neither heart-broken nor embittered. Her "honest mind" perceives that she has lost nothing but an illusion. She can, in fact, describe only two symptoms: her sense that every human being is isolated and her sense of sin. To Sir Henry she admits she would prefer to suppose something were really wrong with herself because that feeling would be easier to endure than an awareness of something wrong with the world. Indeed, Celia tells the doctor that she doubts if her case deserves serious consideration.

But when Sir Henry's response to this last remark is to call Celia a "most uncommon" patient, we begin seriously to question his medical competence. For every psychiatrist knows how routine it is for many of his patients to have such an attitude toward themselves. True, we may accept Eliot's view when he has Celia explain that her modern, liberal upbringing has taught her to disbelieve in sin—to regard sin as merely "bad form" or else as "mental kinks" or "psychological." Our doubts increase, however, as soon as Sir Henry informs Celia that she is "most unusual" to have a sense of sin. If by sense of sin Eliot means sense of guilt, then at this juncture he permits his psychiatrist to speak nonsense. Plenty of psychiatric patients are burdened, either consciously or unconsciously, with a crippling sense of guilt magnified beyond anything which their most grievous faults could merit. To be sure, psychiatrists seldom use the word *sin;* yet they hardly deny the reality which that word designates. Sin is what a psychiatrist deals with hourly, and he is as fully aware of the

evil in human hearts as Mr. Eliot is. The psychiatrist struggles with that evil in the form of his patients' unconscious or
half-conscious impulses toward hatred and destruction of
themselves and of others.

For the moment, though, let us pass over the objection
and grant that Eliot tries to define a sense of sin beyond what
is ordinarily human and which is outside the province of
psychiatry. Let us accept at face value Celia's confession that
her sense of sin comes from a feeling of

> . . . emptiness, of failure
> Towards someone, or something, outside myself;
> And I feel I must . . . atone.

This insight she gained when she realized that she and Edward were strangers, each of them using the other for his
own purposes merely:

> That's horrible! Can we only love
> Something created by our own imagination?
> Are we all in fact unloving and unlovable?
> Then one is alone, and if one is alone
> Then lover and beloved are equally unreal
> And the dreamer is no more real than his dreams.

Celia must escape such despair. She desires to be cured—

> Of a craving for something I cannot find
> And of the shame of never finding it.

Sir Henry tells her that she is curable but must choose her
own form of treatment. In brief, if she wishes secular love, he
can "reconcile" her to "the human condition"; or else she
may take the way toward divine love. Celia chooses the latter.

If we are sympathetic to religion, we can agree with Eliot
that there are indeed saints, persons whom nothing but sacred love will satisfy, geniuses in religion who are meant for
it and called to it in single-minded devotion. Through Celia,
Eliot exemplifies a text from *Deuteronomy*, repeated in
Matthew: "Thou shalt love the Lord thy God with all thy

heart, and with all thy soul, and with all thy mind. This is the first and great commandment."

So a saint is made. In the two hours' traffic of the stage, Eliot tries to show how by an inward metamorphosis a worldling becomes a creature of the spirit—how Celia is "transhumanized." Yet Eliot's saint never stings us to tears, never makes us believe in the reality of her vision or in the genuineness of her renunciation. Besides the obvious reasons why she does not, I suggest some others. For one thing, Celia has never experienced nor even glimpsed what psychoanalysis would call mature love—on, if you will, a non-supernatural basis. Sir Henry fails to point out that she has had no opportunity to explore the possibilities of such love—a love which, though not "transhumanized," has its disciplines, sometimes exquisite, sometimes severe, and also has its mysteries.[5] Out of the fever and fantasies of an adulterous amour, Celia could not and did not learn that mature love is an emptiness; she could and did learn only the vanity of vanity, the vacuum of reciprocal self-deceptions.

Apparently, Eliot lacks William James's kind of interest in the varieties of religious experience. At any rate, depth psychology pretends to no formulas for inducing the religious experience or for making a saint. Perhaps Eliot wants us to regard Celia's transformation as a mystery, a mystery rising out of the ambiguous relations of good with evil. Perhaps, to Eliot, Celia's adultery is an example of the paradox of the fortunate fall, in that it enabled her to achieve sainthood. If, however, Eliot were to rest his case on the grounds that he purposed here to make saint-making a mystery, then we are disappointed that he has not made it enough of a mystery. Instead, he has psychologized it—ineptly. For, both as a psychiatrist and a spokesman for orthodox Christianity, Sir Henry should have asked a further question: was there not something neurotic which in the first place impelled the cultivated, attractive, and sensitive Celia to become enamoured of so unlikely a lover as the middle-aged, narcissistic Edward Chamberlayne? Never raising this question, Sir Henry is content to help Celia free herself from the illusions of the affair. He remains quite unconcerned with those (probably oedipal) self-deceptions which preceded it.

I submit, then, that Eliot's zeal for sacred love, his urgency to preach on "the first and great commandment," has led him into special pleading.

In *The Cocktail Party* the case for secular love is presented in the marital problems of the Chamberlaynes. Since the characterization of the husband is fuller, I shall focus on Edward rather than on his wife. Seeking in his affair with Celia an escape from a boring wife, Edward encounters his crisis when, pressed to prove the genuineness of his love for Celia by divorcing his wife, he feels no longer able to decide or act for himself. His predicament exposes Edward's weaknesses and leads him to Sir Henry's consultation room. He has symptoms aplenty. His complaints about the emptiness of desire and his melancholy awareness of growing older remind us of Prufrock and Gerontion. Though he wants psychiatric help, in the doctor's presence Edward displays the usual resistance. What he calls his nervous breakdown naturally has its neurotic use: "to escape from himself—and get the better of his wife." In such a plight his former self-image is shattered, he feels lonely, and he is confused by self-deceptions. Edward has become alienated from his real self: that is, he cannot put a right value on himself; so he vacillates between thinking too well and thinking too ill of himself. He applauds himself as a passionate lover while he brands himself as a mediocrity. The truth is that Edward is so full of love for himself that none is left over for others. His worry that he is incapable of loving disturbs Edward as much, says Sir Henry, as "the fear of impotence" disturbs "cruder men." [6] Edward exploits love to bolster his self-esteem; he wants the world to have proof that a woman loves him. As we might expect, Edward is also a passive creature; he drifted into his marriage to Lavinia; and on his honeymoon lacked initiative and decisiveness. What looked like considerateness toward his wife was not an expression of unselfishness but a mask for his passivity. He complains that she always makes him feel insignificant. In fact, Edward fears his wife and variously calls her an "angel of destruction," a "python," and an "octopus." [7]

All of this adds up to a full-blown neurosis, and Eliot is to be congratulated on the clarity of his insight and on the fidelity with which he presents the symptoms.[8] But how does his Sir Henry, who supposedly comprehends all these things, adjust the Chamberlaynes toward a workable marriage? How, in particular, does he handle Edward?

For help in relieving a neurosis like his, Edward needs to tell his troubles to someone who can understand and sympathize. To be guided toward an image of himself more in accord with reality, he needs someone who will care about his best potentialities and rightly value what is best in him. Of course Edward must also come to recognize his weaknesses and faults and sins, and to see through his self-deceptions. He requires a psychiatrist who will make an alliance with the healthy part of Edward's personality for the purpose of defeating the unhealthy or neurotic part. To escape from the prison of self-absorption, Edward needs as a temporary support that controlled and rigorously disciplined—we might almost say scientific—love the psychiatrist must give his patients. In the re-education of his heart Edward has to be freed enough so as to learn to love others. In sum, he must come to think well of himself in a non-neurotic way if he is ever to think well—or lovingly—of others.

What Edward gets from Eliot's psychiatrist is the opposite of all this. His wanting to talk out his troubles Sir Henry at once labels "the luxury of an intimate disclosure." Very promptly Sir Henry tells him:

> Resign yourself to be the fool you are.
> That's the best advice that *I* can give you.

Almost the next thing Sir Henry does is to assure Edward that "humiliation" may be "an experience of incalculable value." In the consultation room, as soon as Edward starts to recall a childhood experience, Sir Henry shuts him up by remarking that such memories would be "largely fictitious." Gratuitously, he adds that to interpret Edward's dreams "would only go to flatter your vanity." When Edward says, "I am obsessed by the thought of my own insignificance," we can respect Sir Henry for refusing a quack cure by immediately flattering Edward. Yet it never dawns on this psychiatrist that his patient can stand in need of any compassion whatsoever. And when he deplores—like one who doth protest too much—"the endless struggle" of human beings "to think well of themselves," we suspect that Sir Henry himself is hipped—hipped on a theory about Christian humility.[9] For the crux of his treatment is to induce in Edward a far deeper self-contempt than the poor fellow already suffers from.

With dispatch the doctor diagnoses and prescribes. He informs the Chamberlaynes that they have much in common— "the same isolation":

> A man who finds himself incapable of loving
> And a woman who finds that no man can love her.

This fact they are directed to regard—

> as the bond which holds you together,
> While still in a state of unenlightenment. . . .
> You could accuse each other of your own faults
> And so could avoid understanding each other.

No doubt, the description fits too many marriages—a shared neurosis. And of course Sir Henry is describing what psychoanalysis calls "projection." Anyhow, the prescription for the Chamberlaynes is that they reverse the proposition: each should try to understand the other, and each should accuse himself of his own faults. In sum, they are to "make the best of a bad job." Their only hope of enlightenment, Sir Henry explains cryptically, is that as this phase is forgotten, their condition "will alter." Naturally, we cannot quarrel with the advice to try to understand one another. But love is indispensable to such understanding.[10] And though in the last act of the play (two years later), Edward and Lavinia display considerateness toward each other, Sir Henry never expresses any hope that they will learn to love. Indeed, he could not: because the other half of his advice makes self-accusation—even, as we have seen with Edward, self-contempt—a foundation-stone for marriage. What Eliot's psychiatrist misses is that self-accusation, through projection, can be an excellent weapon against an enemy—or a spouse.

Again we find Eliot engaged in special pleading. In truth, his conception of Christian love is strangely limited. We recall that, according to Matthew, when Jesus defined sacred love, he was being quizzed by a sharp, pharisaical lawyer who hoped to confound him. Hence the Master's precision when he followed his definition of the first commandment with these words: "And the second is like unto it, 'Thou shalt love thy neighbor as thyself.' On these two commandments hang all the law and the prophets." In Jesus' teaching that we are to love our neighbors as we love ourselves, we have no corollary like Eliot's preachment of self-contempt. On this point the wisdom of Christianity and the wisdom of psychoanalysis join. The psychoanalyst knows that as self-hatred grows the ability to love dies. Sir Henry does not know this.

His trouble—like Eliot's and yours and mine—began in Eden. I mean of course original sin. For Eliot, it is a dogma, to be maintained with intellectual rigor. To the non-orthodox Christian, original sin points to a psychological and moral truth about our drives toward destruction. Why Eliot so insists upon the dogma or why—granted that pride heads the list of the seven deadly sins—Eliot makes his psychiatrist so eager to annihilate Edward Chamberlayne's petty vanities, I leave you to decide. Until Eliot's biography is written we can have no sure answer. I suspect, however, that Eliot's sense of original sin, his worry over self-love and pride, his personal reticence, and the overplus of intellectuality in his poems and plays and in his Christianity [11]—all these, I suspect, are related to one another in his hidden heart. Literary history sees in Eliot a revolt from the romantic tradition and can explain his banishment of romantic extravagance as well as our relish in the irony with which Eliot riddles emotional sloppiness.[12] Yet we can also read in Eliot's works the biography of his inner life [13]—at least enough of it to find a man who distrusts emotion, who would not or could not commit his heart to the ties of human love. It is true that in *The Cocktail Party,* when Celia must choose between sacred and profane love, Sir Henry tells her that "Neither way is better. Both ways are necessary." But we know this comes from his head, not his heart.[14] A few moments later he worries about the domestic life the Chamberlaynes have gone back to:

> To the stale food mouldering in the larder,
> The stale thoughts mouldering in their minds.
> Each unable to disguise his own meanness. . . .
> Mirror to mirror, reflecting vanity.

Not until *The Elder Statesman* do we meet a different Eliot. Possibly, future readers will find this play more appealing as a biographical document than as a work of art. Here, for the first time, is the tenderness which has always been missing from Eliot's plays and poems. The heartwarming love of Monica and Charles reveals a new and kindlier view of human nature. Here Eliot suggests that in a human relationship, which those of us who are neither saints nor martyrs can share, there may be a way out of the valley of the hollow men. To trust oneself, to trust that self in another person, is to break down the bars of self-isolation. Such a surrender of the heart requires the act of faith which the elder statesman, Lord Claverton, makes when he declares:

> If a man has one person, just one in his life,
> To whom he is willing to confess everything . . .
> Then he loves that person, and his love will save him.

So the mask of Gerontion has dropped. All homage to Eliot that in his green old age he came upon this truth! The pity is that he did not find it sooner.

NOTES

1. In "The Dry Salvages," T. S. Eliot, *The Complete Poems and Plays* (New York, 1950), pp. 135–136.

2. In this paper the terms *psychology, psychiatry,* and *psychoanalysis* and their derivatives are used virtually as synonyms. For the purpose of my central argument, differentiating these terms one from another is not relevant. Nor is it relevant or necessary here to consider the disagreements among Freud, Jung, Adler, Horney, Fromm, Karl Menninger, etc.

3. See T. S. Eliot, "Poetry and Drama," *Atlantic Monthly,* vol. 187 (Feb., 1952), p. 36. Eliot of course has not denied that Sir Henry Harcourt-Reilly is a psychiatrist. See Foster Hailey, "An Interview with T. S. Eliot," *The New York Times,* April 16, 1950, sec. II, p. 1, cols. 5–7, and p. 3, cols. 4–6. See also Robert B. Heilman, "*Alcestis* and *The Cocktail Party,*" *Comparative Literature,* vol. 5 (Spring 1953), pp. 105–116.

4. In *The Listener* of Mar. 30, 1932—as quoted by Elizabeth Drew in her *T. S. Eliot: The Design of His Poetry* (New York, 1949), p. 7—Eliot's ambivalence is indicated by this, the concluding sentence from the passage quoted: "Psychology is an indispensable handmaid to theology; but I think a very poor housekeeper."

5. For definitions and discussions of what I call "mature love" here, see books like Karl Menninger, *Love Against Hate* (New York, 1942) and Erich Fromm, *The Art of Loving* (New York, 1956). My point is that Celia does not know what she is renouncing: she has never followed—i.e., experienced—the argument for mature love.

6. Eliot's lack of understanding is egregious; for it is by no means only "cruder men" who may be disturbed by the "fear of impotence."

7. Such over-charged epithets suggest that Edward has castration fears and point to an explanation of his passiveness as a lover and husband.

8. This is not to deny that Eliot's insight into neuroses is pretty shallow.

9. Very probably it is the insistence on Christian humility which causes Sir Henry to congratulate Celia when, for

her doubts that her case deserves serious medical attention, he calls her "most uncommon."

10. We knew this long before Freud of course. As Goethe once remarked, "A man does not learn to understand anything unless he loves it."

11. To be sure, I am not suggesting that Eliot's poetry lacks emotion—or more particularly that his religious poetry lacks emotion. These are matters of degree. I am merely pointing to the degree of emphasis upon intellectuality in Eliot's Christianity. It is explicit in his *The Idea of a Christian Society* (London, 1939). Consider this, for instance, on p. 8, *op. cit.:* "We must treat Christianity with a great deal more *intellectual* respect than is our wont; we must treat it as being for the individual primarily a matter of thought and not of feeling."

12. Especially useful on this point is ch. I, "The Individual Explosion," in Grover Smith, Jr., *T. S. Eliot's Poetry and Plays* (University of Chicago Press, 1956).

13. See Leon Edel's interesting sketch in *Literary Biography* (New York, 1959), pp. 70–89.

14. See Gerald Weales, "The Latest Eliot," an essay-review of *The Elder Statesman,* in the *Kenyon Review,* vol. 21 (Summer 1959), pp. 473–478.

The Grotesque-Comic

in the Snopes Trilogy

by LEWIS A. LAWSON

Some readers and critics have had reservations about the success of Faulkner's Snopes trilogy. *The Hamlet,* earliest of the three novels, is accounted the best; *The Town* and *The Mansion* evidence a marked falling-off. Is there any way of explaining this decline except by merely pointing to a failing in craftsmanship, an explanation difficult to accept in the light of the fact that in other works Faulkner was handling much the same material as well as he had ever handled it before? Lewis Lawson has reached the conclusion that the quality of the individual novels might depend on the attitude of the novelist toward his material. With the aid of psychodynamic formulations of the relation of the artist to his material he has pinpointed some of Faulkner's attitudes through analysis of his treatment of the grotesque-comic. It may well be that, in doing so, he has discovered a plausible explanation of Faulkner's general changing attitude toward matters vital to his imaginative life.

Mr. Lawson holds degrees from the East Tennessee State College and a doctorate from the University of Wisconsin. He has published in *College English, Wisconsin Studies in Contemporary Literature, American Imago,* and *Renascence,* and he is coeditor of an anthology of criticism of Flannery O'Connor. The present essay was first published in *Literature and Psychology* (XV, 2, 107–119).

They have been in—alive and have been in motion, I have hated them and laughed at them and been afraid of them for thirty years now.[1]

Early in his career William Faulkner was struck by a vision of the struggle between the old order and the new. And although it took him almost the remainder of his life to write out the vision, his response to a question at the University of Virginia in 1958 indicated that the vision was complete at inception:

Q. You have a new novel coming out soon which is a continuation of *The Hamlet*. Have you had that—did you have that in mind a long time?

A. Yes. I thought of the whole story at once like a bolt of lightning lights up a landscape and you see everything but it takes time to write it, and this story [*The Town*] I had in my mind for about thirty years, and the one which I will do next [*The Mansion*]—it happened at that same moment, thirty years ago when I thought of it, of getting at it.[2]

But even though it struck him with such urgency, the vision was apparently not the inspiration for his earliest writing. Having tried poetry and not succeeded at that, he first turned in fiction to subjects which reflected his interest in contemporary life, for his impression of the meaninglessness of postwar civilization is demonstrated in *Soldiers' Pay* and *Mosquitoes*. These novels, despite their setting, are not essentially Southern, and even though his next book (in order of writing, says Irving Howe[3]), *The Sound and the Fury*, is Southern both in setting and in quality, his focus still seems to be on the meaningless present.

It is only when he turns to the Southern past in *Sartoris* (1929), his third novel in order of publication, that he presents the old order. Then he presents, as nearly as he ever does, Michael Millgate believes, a celebration of the "Southern legend":

The music went on in the dusk softly; the dusk was peopled with ghosts of glamorous and old disastrous things. And if they were just glamorous enough, there was sure to be a Sartoris in them, and then they were sure to be disastrous. Pawns. But the Player, and the game He plays. . . . He must have a name for His pawns, though. But perhaps Sartoris is the game itself—a game out-moded and played with pawns shaped too late and to an old dead pattern, and of which the Player Himself is a little wearied. For there is death in the sound of it, and a glamorous fatality, like silver pennons downrushing at sunset, or a dying fall of horns along the road to Roncevaux.[4]

By the time he wrote *Sartoris* he had, according to his inter-views, also begun to envision the Snopeses. He was, then, during the late Twenties concerned with what life had been, what life had become, and with what he came to consider the force which had soured the old order.

The force is the clan Snopes. There have been many ex-planations of what the Snopeses represent, and perhaps each definition of Snopesism is accurate in its context. One recent explanation will be sufficient to indicate what the family usually represents:

The Snopeses are, in their Southern setting, what a Northerner would probably call "poor white trash," though Faulkner never, to my knowledge, refers to them by that contemptuous phrase. They are, more generally, Faulkner's symbols of our growing cultural mediocrity—the twisted and embittered products of pov-erty, social injustice, contempt, and neglect. They are the fruits of a culture that has largely lost its respect for Faulkner's "eter-nal verities" and that has dedicated itself primarily to the values of the market place—to a cruel catch-as-catch-can economic com-petition in which the sharp bargain, the successful deal barely within the law, the ruthless foreclosure, are not only taken for granted but widely respected, admired, and emulated.[5]

I do not propose to add yet another explanation, nor do I think that Faulkner could have articulated what the Snopeses represented to him when he first conceived them. For my purpose, it will be sufficient to say that to Faulkner they originally represented a threat.

Although they derive originally from Faulkner's short sto-ries and obtrude occasionally in several of his other novels, the Snopeses chiefly inhabit the Snopes Trilogy: *The Hamlet* (1940), *The Town* (1957), and *The Mansion* (1959). Early in the trilogy Faulkner embodied the threat in the figure of Flem Snopes, although Flem is not the first Snopes introduced, nor is *The Hamlet* the first novel in which a Snopes appears. I. O. Snopes had appeared briefly in the Jason section of *The Sound and the Fury,* and Ab Snopes had appeared in *The Unvanquished* as a guerrilla who preyed upon both sides in Mississippi during the last turbulent days of the War Between the States. It is only with *The Hamlet,* however, that the Family Snopes appears, surrounded by a nimbus of mythic, universal evil. In this novel Ab, the progenitor of the Snopeses, comes out of the West, his limping leg and club foot constantly suggesting the connection with the satanic element that he and all of his real descendants possess.[6]

But Ab pales with the introduction of Flem, his son. That Flem was originally conceived as a threatening character is revealed, I believe, by the fact that he comes to us as a villain *manqué,* as a grotesque-comic figure. It is as though Faulkner, even in the moment of personifying that which threatened him, instinctively began an attempt to weaken his adversary by utilizing what investigators later described as the grotesque-comic sublimation. Stated baldly, this theory proposes that the mind will create an image which symbolizes its anxieties, that it then attempts to laugh that image into impotence. Such an action by the mind suggests one of the functions that Wolfgang Kayser assigns to the grotesque in art: "AN ATTEMPT TO INVOKE AND SUBDUE THE DEMONIC ASPECTS OF THE WORLD." [7] The significant aspect of this theory is that of impotence; the threatening figure is harmless in its potential, even though superficially it appears all-powerful. As Annie Reich points out, "the grotesque-comic is characterized by a special form of disguise, that is by particular disfigurement and deformation of the object." [8] Later, perhaps, when Flem had already appeared before him, resplendent and full-blown in his characteristic ugliness, Faulkner could attach more significance to Flem's particular marks of deformity. But Flem's weaknesses must have arisen originally as an unconscious attempt to reduce his power, as Reich contends the mind will do; just as savages, by the use of image magic, caricature representations of their enemies in their preparation for war.

The disfigurement of Flem Snopes is accomplished in several ways, especially through the use of *meiosis:*

The technique of rendering devils flabby is a common literary device which was discussed in rhetorical handbooks under the Greek title, *meiosis,* meaning, literally, "belittling" or "diminution." Diminution may be described briefly as the use of "ugly or homely images" which are intended to diminish the dignity of an object. In a sense, of course, nearly all satire might be included within this broad definition. But a more specific meaning is suggested when we recall Puttenham's description of it as the "disabler," a figure useful to express "derision and for a kind of contempt." Specifically, then, diminution is any kind of speech which tends, either by the force of low or vulgar imagery, or by other suggestion, to depress an object below its usually accepted status. Diminution may be accomplished in a variety of ways. A similarity may be drawn between an object and one which is universally acknowledged to be inferior; the comparison results, of course, in the primary object absorbing the contemptibility of the secondary object. Diminution may also be affected by dwelling upon certain physical characteristics of a person and then, by synechdoche, equating the whole object with that one part. Diminution may be expressed in innumerable other forms; it may appear as direct abuse, irony, litotes, and so on.[9]

Stylistically, Faulkner employs grotesque similes and metaphors to abuse Flem, to suggest that his humanness is tainted and incomplete. When we first meet Flem in *The Hamlet,*[10] he is thus described: "His eyes were the color of stagnant water" (*Hamlet,* 22) and "His face was as blank as a pan of uncooked dough" (*Hamlet,* 23). Such descriptions are unlikely to convince the reader of the essential humanness of the character being described. Later, when Flem accompanies Eula Varner to the train which will take them on their honeymoon to Texas and respectability, he is a "froglike creature which barely reached her shoulder" (*Hamlet,* 149). Even the pronoun "which" lacks the suggestion that Flem is human, not animal, and the reader can only think that the Devil has not only penetrated the Eden of Frenchman's Bend, but also succeeded in taking Eve completely out of the Garden. In *The Town* [11] Faulkner seems to equivocate; Flem appears at the power plant, his eyes "looking like two gobs of cup grease on a hunk of raw dough" (*Town,* 22) but there are no other such images. And, interestingly, there are in *The Mansion* [12] no grotesque descriptive images which would detract from the conception of Flem as a human being, entitled to sympathy and even pity.

Another way in which Flem Snopes is disfigured is the description of his constant chewing, which remains throughout the trilogy his most characteristic habit, so that his face is seen, except for a few significant moments, always contorted into a grimace. Here Faulkner's creative insight was impressive; only recently has an observer written upon the connection between aggression, grimacing, and the comic. As Sidney Tarachow writes, "Certain patients, especially obsessive-compulsives and deeply masochistic ones, express many of their aggressions through facial grimacing. The clown mask may be considered a fixed stylized grimace." [13]

The few times that Flem stops chewing are important. Had the pause occurred only once in the trilogy, it could be interpreted only as a slapstick element utilized, like the dropped jaw, the comic rictus, of Harry Langdon in the movie comedies of the Thirties, to suggest the buffoonery of the character. But its careful repetition gives it more importance. In *The Hamlet* Flem's jaw stops only once, when V. K. Ratliff gets the best of him in the goat deal (*Hamlet,* 85). The jaw ceases again in *The Town* only when Flem fails in the attempt to bribe Gavin Stevens (*Town,* 169). Flem stops chewing three times in *The Mansion,* but one of the times relates to an incident which occurred in *The Town,* where we are told that Flem continues to chew when he is forced to pay for the brass that he had stolen from the town power plant

(*Town*, 22). But in *The Mansion* it is reported that he stops chewing twice when he is confronted with his failure to carry through his plan to steal the brass (*Mansion*, 129). Since the incident marks Flem's first defeat in Jefferson, Faulkner, by the time that he wrote *The Mansion*, must have decided to re-emphasize the significance of the incident by symbolizing Flem's being put on the defensive. In the second instance in *The Mansion* Montgomery Ward Snopes forces Flem to stop chewing, when he demands ten thousand dollars from Flem for arranging that Mink Snopes receive an additional twenty-year term in prison (*Mansion*, 67), but Flem is quickly able to regain the initiative. The last time that Flem stops chewing is at the moment before his murder; when he sees Mink, Flem stops, but—significantly—he resumes his movement before he is shot (*Mansion*, 416).

Fundamentally, the constant chewing makes Flem some kind of monstrous machine, always demanding more, more, until he threatens to consume all of the old order of Yoknapatawpha County. The chewing symbolizes to other characters, V. K. Ratliff and Montgomery Ward Snopes, for example, Flem's ever-increasing penuriousness. Before his success, Flem chews tobacco, but as he becomes wealthy, he changes to chewing gum—a fresh stick every Sunday—and as he becomes rich he can afford to chew only air. The chewing seems to symbolize, also, aggression; each time that Flem stops chewing is the occasion of his failure, when he is forced to be on the defensive. But chewing as aggression in the earlier parts of the trilogy becomes chewing as acceptance of retribution at the very end of Flem's life. Just as Faulkner stylistically ceased to think of Flem as a grotesque in *The Mansion*, so he gives Flem at the very last minute of his life a quality that suggests Flem accepts the rightness of Mink's action. Had Flem been shot before he resumed his chewing, he would have seemed at best pathetic and at worst cowardly or even comical; since he does resume, the result is much different. Faulkner was always too conscientious a craftsman to permit such a misinterpretation through his oversight;

hence the resumption of chewing is deliberate. Flem has somehow gained, perhaps not favor, but certainly stature in his creator's eyes and is rewarded with what amounts to an heroic gesture with which to end his life.[14]

Flem Snopes is deformed in yet another way, and this deformity, impotency, has implications that are fundamental to any consideration of the original conception of Flem. Tarachow has written:

> The essence of the technique of caricature is to enlarge certain selected points in the figure of the body and to call attention . . . to the part of the body to be specifically attacked. Sometimes parts of the body are contracted and even omitted, but generally some part is enlarged. The total result is a comic-grotesque-sadistic effect. The enlargement of a part of the body may be conceived of as a disfigurement, a castration of a kind. . . .[15]

Again, once the character of Flem Snopes was completely visualized, Faulkner was free to utilize the impotency as a device with which he could introduce a thematic point that extends throughout the trilogy: the evil that Flem represents is sterile and self-consuming. But originally Flem was perhaps conceived impotent as an unconscious safeguard against his ultimate triumph. Caricature has always relied upon image magic,[16] and what better way to suggest an enemy's weakness than to question his virility? The original vision of Snopesism may have terrified Faulkner, as he says, so that he used every weapon at his disposal to weaken it. By the time of *The Mansion* he must have felt, however, that he could cope with it; in *The Hamlet* impotency is barely mentioned and seems to be the handicap that Flem must possess before his opponents have an even chance against him. But in *The Mansion* Flem's power no longer inspires much terror, and Faulkner allows Montgomery Ward Snopes to ridicule Flem's impotent condition (*Mansion*, 70), thus arousing in the reader a very slight degree of sympathy for Flem. After all, even Flem compares favorably with a Snopes who determines to rise to the top of his profession, to be *"THE son of a bitch's son of a bitch"* (*Mansion*, 87). Beyond that, Faulkner allows his sometime spokesman, Gavin Stevens, who has appeared in the trilogy to champion opposition to Flem, actually to pity Flem for his impotency (*Mansion*, 430).

Flem is not, of course, the only Snopes who appears in the trilogy; he seems to be a devil surrounded by his imps. Here again Faulkner is working in the tradition of *meiosis*, when he attains the diminution of humans by comparing them with lower animals.[17] Throughout the trilogy the secondary Snopeses frisk along, half-comic and half-terrifying, half-human and half-animal, like the distorted creatures in the paintings of Brueghel the Elder. Faulkner continually associates individual Snopeses with animals: I. O. has a "rodent's face" (*Hamlet*, 163), or is "weasel-faced" (*Town*, 36), and Lump stares "with the lidless intensity of a rat" (*Hamlet*, 329). Collectively, the Snopeses are associated with "colonies of rats and termites" (*Town*, 112) and "an influx of snakes of varmints" (*Town*, 112). The animals that Faulkner utilizes as vehicles for his comparisons are, says Kayser, extremely appropriate:

Certain animals are especially suitable to the grotesque—snakes, owls, toads, spiders—the nocturnal and creeping animals which inhabit realms apart from and inaccessible to man. Partly for the same reason (to which their uncertain origin is added) the same observation applies to vermin.[18]

Faulkner also reveals that he really thinks of the Snopeses as grotesque monsters when he has V. K. Ratliff, who would not be expected to have such knowledge, picture Gavin Stevens as a desert father surrounded by Montgomery Ward Snopes. Flaubert's *La Tentation de Saint Antoine* was one of Faulkner's favorite novels,[19] and his several references to anchorites surrounded by monsters suggests that he knew of the Temptation of Saint Anthony motif that runs through grotesque painting from the Middle Ages to Salvador Dali.

Faulkner really betrays the medieval cast of his mind in imagining the Snopeses when he gives this description of Flem in *The Hamlet:*

—a thick squat soft man of no establishable age between twenty and thirty, with a broad still face containing a tight seam of mouth stained slightly at the corners with tobacco, and eyes the color of stagnant water, and projecting from among the other features in startling and sudden paradox, a tiny predatory nose like the beak of a small hawk. It was as though the original nose had been left off by the original designer or craftsman and the unfinished job taken over by someone of a radically different school or perhaps by some viciously maniacal humorist or perhaps by one who had had only time to clap into the center of the face a frantic and desperate warning (*Hamlet*, 52).

Here Flem is, as a critic has noted, a gargoyle.[20] Faulkner's intention to reduce the threat that Flem, as head of the Snopeses, represents is thus announced early in the trilogy, when Flem's evilness is adulterated by a bit of grotesque humor. And it is in this manner of blunting horror with humor that Faulkner seems to reveal his changing attitude toward Flem Snopes, who begins as a mechanized abstraction of evil and ends as a human being.

Thus a changing attitude toward the personification of the cause of anxiety can be seen in the Snopes Trilogy. At the beginning of *The Hamlet* Snopesism, as represented by Ab and Flem, is apparently a complete threat to the calm, idyllic Yoknapatawpha world. The special menace which they represent is barn-burning, but it remains a vague threat which they use to force their way into the community. Jody Varner, who suffers most from their threat, provides the orchestration which accompanies the successful invasion of the Snopeses: "Hell fire. Hell fire. Hell fire" (*Hamlet*, 21). His helpless cursing seems to identify and emphasize the demonic quality of the Snopes intrusion.

The residents of Frenchman's Bend see nothing funny about the Snopeses at this time; the Snopeses remain intruders, who seem bent upon disturbing the cosmos of Yoknapatawpha with their particularly pertinent aggressiveness. In one of the earliest portrayals of Snopesism, in the short story "Barn Burning," Ab, assuming mythic overtones, tracks horse droppings into the house of Major DeSpain. As Stein has pointed out, this act is symbolic of the corruption of the old order and tradition, but I think that one can go a little further in analyzing this particular act. As elsewhere in Faulkner, the house becomes the structure of Southern society; for example, in the short story "Was," the slaves, that is, the idea of slavery at all costs, live in the plantation house, while the slave owners live out back. In "Barn Burning" Ab is an intruder in the house; by the completion of the trilogy Ab's son, Flem, lives in Major DeSpain's house, but it is a futile kind of living, for Flem can only acquire; he cannot enjoy or enrich his life by living in the house of the aristocracy.

It is thirty years before Faulkner can, as he did at the University of Virginia, counterpose a positive value which is superior to Snopesism:

Q. Sir, you say that you feel that there is hope for the South, yet the Snopeses have taken over Frenchman's Bend, Flem is president of the bank of Jefferson. Are those the men that are going to lead the South out of darkness?

A. They are the men that can cope with the new industrial age, but there will be something left—as this—we mentioned a while ago—of the old cavalier spirit that will appear, that does appear. By cavalier spirit, I mean people who believe in simple honor for the sake of honor, and honesty for the sake of honesty.[21]

The process of changing attitude begins with the introduction of the lesser Snopeses, I. O. and Eck, who appear as clownish figures even at the moment of their arrival in Yoknapatawpha society, when they stupidly try to start a fire in the blacksmith's forge with hog urine (*Hamlet*, 64). The threat of arson by Flem and Ab is effectively negated by the stupidity of I. O. and Eck. Here, as in other places in the trilogy, when the Snopeses seem destined to be victorious, Faulkner steps in with the *deus ex machina* of comedy to

save the residents of Yoknapatawpha County. Perhaps unconsciously Faulkner is beginning to interpose the comic between the threat and his own consciousness of it; this act of
sublimation, says Annie Reich, is the "function of the
comic": "to overcome anxiety while at the same time it is
based on the already mastered anxiety." [22] It should be remembered that Faulkner had already begun mastering his
anxiety by grotesquely deforming Flem, his chief object, in
original conception. After the introduction of the lesser,
comic Snopeses, Flem suffers his first defeat, in the goat deal
with V. K. Ratliff (*Hamlet,* 86), and he loses most of his ability to compel the reader to view him seriously. Thereafter,
the remainder of *The Hamlet* and all of *The Town* are devoted to Flem's outwitting of first the country people and
then the townspeople, in ways traditional to the rogues (such
as Simon Suggs and Sut Lovingood) of Southern folk-humor
of the nineteenth century.[23]

Of course, since the comic, as Ernst Kris writes, holds an
intermediate position between pleasure and the warding off
of emotion, especially fear,[24] there are times in the trilogy, as
in all grotesque humor, when the comic and the terrifying
are mixed. The depicting of Flem as gargoyle reveals Faulkner's ambivalent reaction to him, and such a mixture of response occurs in one of the *raisonneurs* of the trilogy, V. K.
Ratliff, in the tall tale of Byron Snopes's Indian children,
which concludes *The Town.* Here again Faulkner begins the
depiction of the absolute animality of which Snopesism is
capable, but he seems to pull back in horror and to blunt the
threat with comedy. This time, with poetic justice, the threat
is directed against another Snopes: the children try to burn
Doris Snopes at the stake. Ratliff realizes that such an incident provokes dark humor when he says:

What you think you are laughing at is the notion of a big almost
growed man like Doris, playing, until all of a sudden you find
out that what you're laughing at is calling anything playing that
them four things would be interested in (*Town,* 369).

When Faulkner was asked if the story had any other meaning than just being a tall story, he replied, "No. To me it was just funny, funny and a little terrible, too. . . ." [25] Faulkner's comment illustrates Kris's theory that the comic is an interposition, even in language: the French *drôle,* the German *komisch,* and the English *funny* are all "double-edged," in that they partake of both uncanniness and the ludicrous.[26] The incident also illustrates Baudelaire's grotesque laughter, or the "comique absolu," which has an "espèce *une,* et qui veut être saisie par intuition" and which provokes immediate laughter. Baudelaire suggests that laughter elicited by the absolutely comic is spontaneous, but not wholly unconscious of an uncomfortable element, which, if it were possible to understand it, would make the laugher ashamed of himself.[27]

And by and large Faulkner's attitude toward Snopesism in *The Hamlet* and *The Town* is ambivalent; he hates, scorns, and fears it, as he says. But he seems to sense that he can only placate his fear by rendering Snopesism comical. To laugh at anything, as Ludovici shows in *The Secret of Laughter,*[28] is to show "superior adaptation," to show your teeth to it. Old Ab, the man of wrath, and Mink, the murderer, whom V. K. Ratliff calls "the only out-and-out mean Snopes we ever experienced" (*Town,* 79), soon disappear from *The Hamlet.* Flem remains, but the aura of evil that first surrounded him dissipates as he becomes more the clever trickster; his actions are often admired by his dupes, and even Faulkner's model of earthy realism, V. K. Ratliff, falls prey to one of Flem's schemes, the gold-salting of the Old Frenchman place, even though he had earlier imagined Flem capable of terrifying even the Devil with the force of his acquisitiveness. The lesser Snopeses are presented as comedians, or even as objects, in the case of the idiot Ike, worthy of profound sympathy. Faulkner has found the defense against anxiety—comedy.

There is one significant example of the comic as defense in *The Mansion.* Clarence Snopes hopes to receive the nomination for Congress from the Yoknapatawpha district and he appears certain to win it. Suddenly he removes himself

from the race. It seems incredible to anyone who knows anything about some areas of Southern politics that Clarence,
running the usual gallus-snapping, race-baiting, know-noth-
ing campaign, could have been stopped. But he is stopped,
and the method of defeat is comedy. V. K. Ratliff had in-
sured that all the dogs of Beat Two and Frenchman's Bend
used Clarence's pants leg as a relief station as he tried to
make the speech which would secure his nomination. His
backers are so chagrined at the spectacle Clarence presents
that they order him to abandon the race.

The episode is funny and significant. I have been trying to
suggest that Faulkner looked upon the Snopeses both as a
demonic threat and as butts for his derision. In this episode
he utilizes yet another medieval motif; in folklore the Devil
became a clown in time, partly because the tradition arose
that he could be repelled by bodily discharge, as when Mar-
tin Luther was said to have "attacked the devil by expelling
flatus." [29] Such an action is particularly appropriate, for it
would repay the Devil in his own kind, according to those
who speculate that the Greek *diaballein* indicates that the
personification of evil was early conceived of as a "dung-
roller." Twice in the trilogy, here and with the incident of
the hog urine, Faulkner used animal discharge to reduce the
devils-clowns to contempt, just as before he had allowed Ab
to express his contempt for beauty and decency by tracking
horse droppings into the DeSpain mansion.

The final step in Faulkner's changing attitude toward
Snopesism occurs in *The Mansion*. There, despite the fact
that Mink Snopes is to be twice a murderer, Faulkner labors
to give him a system of theology with his presentation of
Mink's thoughts about "Old Moster," and sympathy for
Mink is gained. Diminution is also practiced here, but Mink
is described as a child, not a lower animal. Moreover, Flem,
as I have already suggested, dignifies his life by the way he
takes leave of it, presumably because his ethical system, which
certainly has never previously been mentioned, demands
that he give Mink "lief," the chance to return an injury.

What had begun as a threat ends defeated, but in the process the idea of Snopesism seems to have lost the power to interest and inspire Faulkner. When *The Town* first appeared, Faulkner was asked if he was tired of the Yoknapatawpha chronicle, and he replied, "it's probably not tiredness, it's the fact that you shouldn't put off too long writing something which you think is worth writing. . . ." [30] Here Faulkner was right in his analysis, and perhaps he knew why: during the thirty years of the composition of the Snopes Trilogy the grotesque-comic sublimation had helped him ward off a threat, but in the process it had destroyed his fascination for the subject.

NOTES

1. Frederick L. Gwynn and Joseph L. Blotner, eds. *Faulkner in the University* (Charlottesville, 1959), p. 201. In his excellent *Man in Motion* (Madison, 1961), Warren Beck also discusses the grotesque element in the Snopes Trilogy, but not as a psychological phenomenon.
2. *Ibid.,* p. 90.
3. *William Faulkner* (New York, 1962), p. 33.
4. Quoted by Michael Millgate in *William Faulkner* (New York, 1961), p. 25.
5. Theodore M. Greene, "The Philosophy of Life Implicit in Faulkner's *The Mansion*," *Texas Studies in Language and Literature,* II (Winter 1961), 405.
6. See William Bysshe Stein, "Faulkner's Devil," *Modern Language Notes,* LXXVI (December 1961), 731–732, for further identification of Ab as devil.
7. Wolfgang Kayser, *The Grotesque in Art and Literature,* trans. Ulrich Weisstein (Bloomington, Indiana, 1963), p. 188.
8. "The Structure of the Grotesque-Comic Sublimation," *The Yearbook of Psychoanalysis,* VI (1950), 202.
9. John M. Bullitt, *Jonathan Swift and the Anatomy of Satire* (Cambridge, 1953), pp. 45–46.
10. (New York, 1940). Hereafter, references in the text will be to *Hamlet*.

11. (New York, 1961). Hereafter, references in the text will be to *Town*.

12. (New York, 1959). Hereafter, references in the text will be to *Mansion*.

13. "Circuses and Clowns," *Psychoanalysis and the Social Sciences*, III (1951), 176.

14. See Gordon Bigelow, "Faulkner's Snopes Saga," *English Journal*, XLIX (December 1960), 595–605, who agrees in the main with my interpretation of the conclusion of *The Mansion*.

15. Tarachow, *ibid.*

16. Reich, *ibid.*

17. Bullitt, p. 47.

18. Kayser, p. 182. See also Harry M. Campbell and Ruel E. Foster, *William Faulkner: A Critical Appraisal* (Norman, 1951), pp. 104–105, for the significance of the meaning and sound of Snopes names.

19. Malcolm Cowley, ed. *Writers at Work* (New York, 1960), p. 129.

20. Louise Y. Gossett, "Violence in Recent Southern Fiction," Unpublished doctoral dissertation, Duke University, Durham, 1961, p. 87.

21. Gwynn and Blotner, p. 80.

22. Reich, p. 201.

23. See James L. Roberts, "Snopeslore," *The University of Kansas City Review*, XXVIII (October 1961), 65–71, for a further parallel of the Snopeses and their nineteenth century forebears.

24. *Psychoanalytic Explorations in Art* (New York, 1952), pp. 213–214.

25. Gwynn and Blotner, p. 100.

26. Kris, p. 214.

27. "De L'Essence du Rire et généralement du Comique dans les Arts plastiques," *La Portefeuille*, 1855.

28. (New York, 1933).

29. Tarachow, p. 183.

30. Gwynn and Blotner, p. 107.

"Men of a Smaller Growth":

A Psychological Analysis of Golding's

Lord of the Flies

by CLAIRE ROSENFIELD

Since 1961, when this paper was presented at an annual
meeting of the Discussion Group on Literature and Psychology and published in *Literature and Psychology* (XI, 4,
93–101), it has often been anthologized. It seems to be one
of a very few psychoanalytic studies of a novel which has
come to rival *The Catcher in the Rye* as a subject for
analysis by undergraduates. This is all the more remarkable when it is remembered that Mr. Golding has made no
secret of his indebtedness to Freud's *Totem and Taboo*.
Dr. Rosenfield, though, has finally clinched the indebtedness and its literary implications.

Claire Rosenfield holds an undergraduate degree from
Smith and a doctorate from Radcliffe. She has taught at
Harvard and Texas and is now at Rutgers.

WHEN an author consciously dramatizes Freudian theory
—and dramatizes it successfully—only the imaginative
re-creation of human behavior rather than the sustaining
structure of ideas is apparent. In analyzing William Golding's *Lord of the Flies,* the critic must assume that Golding
knows psychological literature and must then attempt to
show how an author's knowledge of theory can vitalize his
prose and characterization. The plot itself is uncomplicated,
so simple, indeed, that one wonders how it so effortlessly

absorbs the burden of meaning. During some unexplained man-made holocaust a plane, evacuating a group of children, crashes on the shore of a tropical island. All adults are conveniently killed. The narrative follows the children's gradual return to the amorality of childhood, and it is the very nature of that state of non-innocence which makes them small savages. Or we might make the analogy to the childhood of races and compare the child to the primitive. Denied the sustaining and repressing authority of parents, church, and state, they form a new culture the development of which reflects that of the genuine primitive society, evolving its gods and demons (its myths), its rituals and taboos (its social norms). On the level of pure narrative, the action proceeds from the gradual struggle between Ralph and Jack, the two oldest boys, for precedence. Ralph is the natural leader by virtue of his superior height, his superior strength, his superior beauty. His mild expression proclaims him "no devil." He possesses the symbol of authority, the conch, or sea shell, which the children use to assemble their miniature councils. Golding writes, "The being that had blown . . . [the conch] had sat waiting for them on the platform with the delicate thing balanced on his knees, was set apart." Jack, on the other hand, is described in completely antithetical terms; he is distinguished by his ugliness and his red hair, a traditional demonic attribute. He first appears as the leader of a church choir, which "creaturelike" marches in two columns behind him. All members of the choir wear black; "their bodies, from throat to ankle, were hidden by black cloaks." [1] Ralph initially blows the conch to discover how many children have escaped death in the plane crash. As Jack approaches with his choir from the "darkness of the forest," he cannot see Ralph, whose back is to the sun. The former is, symbolically, sun-blinded. These two are very obviously intended to recall God and the Devil, whose confrontation, in the history of Western religions, establishes the moral basis for all actions. But, as Freud reminds us, "metaphysics" becomes "metapsychology";[2] gods and devils are "nothing other than psychological processes projected into the outer world." [3] If Ralph is a pro-

jection of man's good impulses from which we derive the
authority figures—whether god, king, or father—who establish the necessity for our valid ethical and social action, then
Jack becomes an externalization of the evil instinctual forces
of the unconscious. Originally, as in the more primitive religions, gods and devils were one; even Hebraic-Christian
tradition makes Satan a fallen angel.

The temptation is to regard the island on which the children are marooned as a kind of Eden, uncorrupted and Eve-
less. But the actions of the children negate any assumption
about childhood innocence. Even though Golding himself
momentarily becomes a victim of his Western culture and
states that Ralph wept for the "end of innocence," events
have simply supported Freud's conclusions that no child is
innocent. On a third level, Ralph is every man—or every
child—and his body becomes the battleground where reason
and instinct struggle, each to assert itself. For to regard Ralph
and Jack as Good and Evil is to ignore the role of the child
Piggy, who in the child's world of make-believe is the outsider. Piggy's composite description not only manifests his
difference from the other boys; it also reminds the reader of
the stereotype image of the old man who has more-than-
human wisdom: he is fat, inactive because asthmatic, and
generally reveals a disinclination for physical labor. Because
he is extremely near-sighted, he wears thick glasses—a further
mark of his difference. As time passes, the hair of the other
boys grows with abandon. "He was the only boy on the island
whose hair never seemed to grow. The rest were shock-
headed, but Piggy's hair still lay in wisps over his head as
though baldness were his natural state, and this imperfect
covering would soon go, like the velvet on a young stag's
antlers." (81) In these images of age and authority we have a
figure reminiscent of the children's past—the father. Moreover, like the father he counsels common sense; he alone
leavens with a reasonable gravity the constant exuberance of
the others for play or for play at hunting. When they scam-
per off at every vague whim, he scornfully comments, "Like
a pack of kids." Ungrammatically but logically, he tries to

allay the "littleuns" fear of a "beast." " 'Life is scientific, that's what it is. . . . I know there isn't no beast—not with claws and all that, I mean—but I know there isn't no fear, either.' " (105) He has excessive regard for the forms of order: the conch must be held by a child before that child can speak at councils. When the others neglect responsibility, fail to build shelters, swim in the pools or play in the sand or hunt, allow the signal fire on the mountain to go out or to get out of hand and burn up half the island, he seconds Ralph by admonishing the others vigorously and becomes more and more of a spoil-sport who robs play of its illusions, the adult interrupting the game. Ralph alone recognizes his superior intelligence but wavers between what he knows to be wise and the group acceptance his egocentricity demands. Finally, Piggy's role—as man's reasoning faculties and as a father— derives some of its complexity from the fact that the fire which the children foster and guard on the mountain in the hope of communicating with the adult world is lighted with his glasses. In mythology, after all, the theft of fire brought civilization—and, hence, repression—to man. As the new community becomes more and more irrational, its irrationality is marked by Piggy's progressive blindness. An accident following an argument between Ralph and Jack breaks one of the lenses. When the final breach between the two occurs and Piggy supports Ralph, his remaining lens is stolen in a night raid by Jack. This is a parody of the traditional fire theft, which was to provide light and warmth for mankind. After this event Piggy must be led by Ralph. When he is making his final plea for his glasses—reasoned as always—he is struck on the head by a rock and falls. "Piggy fell forty feet and landed on his back on that square, red rock in the sea. His head opened and stuff came out and turned red. Piggy's arms and legs twitched a bit, like a pig's after it has been killed." (223)

The history of the child Piggy on the island dramatizes in terms of the individual the history of the entire group. When they first assemble to investigate their plight, they treat their island isolation as a temporary phenomenon; they want to play games until they are rescued—until their parents reassert the repressive actions of authority. This microcosm of the great world seems to them to be a fairy land.

A kind of glamour spread over them and the scene and they were conscious of the glamour and made happy by it. (33)

The coral was scribbled in the sea as though a giant had bent down to reproduce the shape of the island in a flowing, chalk line but tired before he had finished. (38)

"This is real exploring," said Jack. "I'll bet nobody's been here before." (35)

Echoes and birds flew, white and pink dust floated, the forest further down shook as with the passage of an enraged monster: and then the island was still. (37)

They compare this reality to their reading experiences: it is Treasure Island or Coral Island or like pictures from their travel books. This initial reaction conforms to the pattern of play which Johan Huizinga establishes in *Homo Ludens*.[4] In its early stages their play has no cultural or moral function; it is simply a "stepping out of real life into a temporary sphere of activity."[5] Ironically, the child of *Lord of the Flies* who thinks he is "only pretending" or that this is "only for fun" does not realize that his play is the beginning of the formation of a new society which has regressed to a primitive state, with all its emphasis upon taboo and communal action. What begins by being like other games in having a distinct "locality and duration"[6] apart from ordinary life is—or becomes—reality. The spatial separation necessary for the make-believe of the game is represented first by the island. In this new world the playground is further narrowed: the gatherings of the children are described as a circle at several points, a circle from which Piggy is excluded:

For the moment the boys were a closed circuit of sympathy with Piggy outside. (29)

They became a circle of boys round a camp fire and even Ralph and Piggy were half-drawn in. (92)

Piggy approximates the spoil-sport who "robs the play of its illusion." [7]

The games of the beginning have a double function: they, first of all, reflect the child's attitude toward play as a temporary cessation from the activities imposed by the adult world; but like the games played before the formation of civilization, they anticipate the ritual which reveals a developing society. So the children move from voluntary play to ritual, from "only pretending" to reality, from representation to identification. The older strictures imposed by parents are soon forgotten—but every now and then a momentary remembrance of past prohibitions causes restraint. One older child hides in order to throw stones at a younger one.

Yet there was a space round Henry, perhaps six yards in diameter, into which he dare not throw. Here, invisible yet strong, was the taboo of the old life. Round the squatting child was the protection of parents and school and policemen and the law. (78)

Jack hesitates when, searching for meat, he raises his knife to kill his first pig.

The pause was only long enough for them to understand what an enormity the downward stroke would be. Then the piglet tore loose from the creepers and scurried into the undergrowth. . . .
"Why didn't you—?"
They knew very well why he hadn't: because of the enormity of the knife descending and cutting into living flesh; because of the unbearable blood. (40–41)

The younger children first, then gradually the older ones, like primitives in the childhood of races, begin to people the darkness of night and forest with spirits and demons which had previously appeared only in their dreams or fairy tales. Now there are no comforting mothers to dispel the terrors of the unknown. They externalize these fears into the figure of a "beast." Once the word "beast" is mentioned, the menace of the irrational becomes overt; name and thing become one. At one critical council when the first communal feeling begins to disintegrate, Ralph cries, " 'If only they could send us something grown-up . . . a sign or something.' " (117) And a sign does come from the outside. That night, unknown to the children, a plane is shot down and its pilot parachutes dead to earth and is caught in the rocks on the mountain. It requires no more than the darkness of night together with the shadows of the forest vibrating in the signal fire to distort the hanging corpse with its expanding silk 'chute into a demon that must be appeased. Ironically, the fire of communication does touch this object of the grown-up world only to foster superstition. Security in this new situation can be achieved only by establishing new rules.

During the first days the children, led by Jack, play at hunting. But eventually the circle of the playground extends to the circle of the hunted and squealing pig seeking refuge —and it is significant that the first animal slain for food is a nursing sow—which itself anticipates the circle of consecrated ground where the children perform the new rites of the kill.

The first hunt accomplishes its purpose: the blood of the animals is spilled; the meat, used for food. But because Jack and his choir undertake this hunt, they desert the signal fire, which is dictated by the common-sense desire for rescue, and it goes out and a ship passes the island. Later the children re-enact the killing with one boy, Maurice, assuming the role of the pig running its frenzied circle. The others chant in unison: " 'Kill the pig. Cut her throat. Bash her in.' " At this dramatic representation each child is still aware that this is a display, a performance. He is never "so beside himself that he loses consciousness of ordinary reality." [8] Each time they reenact the same event, however, their behavior becomes more frenzied, more cruel, less like representation than identification. The chant then becomes, " 'Kill the beast. Cut his throat. Spill his blood.' " It is as if the first event, the pig's death, is forgotten in the recesses of time; a new myth defines the primal act. Real pig becomes mythical beast.

Jack's ascendancy over the group begins when the children's fears distort the natural objects around them: twigs become creepers, shadows become demons. I have already discussed the visual imagery suggesting Jack's demonic function. He serves as a physical manifestation of irrational forces. After an indefinite passage of time, he appears almost dehumanized, his "nose only a few inches from the humid earth." He is "dog-like" and proceeds forward "on all fours" "into the semi-darkness of the undergrowth." His cloak and clothing have been shed. Indeed, except for a "pair of tattered shorts held up by his knife-belt, he was naked." His eyes seemed "bolting and nearly mad." He has lost his ability to communicate with Ralph as on the first day. "He tried to convey the compulsion to track down and kill that was swallowing him up." (65) "They walked along, two continents of experience and feeling, unable to communicate." (70) When Jack first explains to Ralph the necessity to disguise himself from the pigs he wants to hunt, he rubs his face with clay and charcoal. At this point he assumes a mask, begins to dance, is finally freed from all the repressions of his past. "He capered towards Bill, and the mask was a thing on its own, behind which Jack hid, liberated from shame and self-consciousness." (80) At the moment of the dance the mask and Jack are one. The first kill, as I have noted, follows the desertion of the signal fire and the passage of a possible rescue ship. Jack is still revelling in the knowledge that he has "outwitted a living thing, imposed their will upon it, taken away its life like a long and satisfying drink." (88) Already he has begun to obliterate the distinctions between animals and men, as do primitives; already he thinks in terms of the metaphor of a ritual drinking of blood, the efficacy of which depended on the drinker's assumption of his victim's strength and spirit. Ralph and Piggy confront him with his defection of duty.

The two boys faced each other. There was the brilliant world of hunting, tactics, fierce exhilaration, skill; and there was the world of longing and baffled common-sense. Jack transferred the knife to his left hand and smudged blood over his forehead as he pushed down the plastered hair. (89)

Jack's unconscious gesture is a parody of the ritual of initiation in which the hunter's face is smeared with the blood of his first kill. In the subsequent struggle one of the lenses of Piggy's spectacles is broken. The dominance of reason is over; the voice of the old world is stilled. The primary images are no longer those of fire and light but those of darkness and blood. The link between Ralph and Jack "had snapped and fastened elsewhere."

The rest of the group, however, shifts its allegiance to Jack because he has given them meat rather than something useless like fire. Gradually, they begin to be described as "shadows" or "masks" or "savages" or "demoniac figures" and, like Jack, "hunt naked save for paint and a belt." Ralph now uses Jack's name with the recognition that "a taboo was evolving around that word too." Name and thing again become one; to use the word is to incite the bearer. But more significant, the taboo, according to Freud, is "a very primitive prohibition imposed from without (by an authority) and directed against the strongest desires of man." [9] In this new society it replaces the authority of the parents. Now every kill becomes a sexual act, is a metaphor for childhood sexuality.

The afternoon wore on, hazy and dreadful with damp heat; the sow staggered her way ahead of them, bleeding and mad, and the hunters followed, wedded to her in lust, excited by the long chase and dropped blood. . . . The sow collapsed under them and they were heavy and fulfilled upon her. (167–168)

Every subsequent "need for ritual" fulfills not only the desire for communication and a substitute security to replace that of civilization, but also the need to liberate both the repressions of the past and those imposed by Ralph. Indeed, the projection of those impulses that they cannot accept in themselves into a beast is the beginning of a new mythology. The earlier dreams and nightmares can now be shared as the former subjectivity could not be.

When the imaginary demons become defined by the rotting corpse and floating 'chute on the mountain which their terror distorts into a beast, Jack wants to track the creature down. After the next kill, the head of the pig is placed upon a stake to placate it. Finally one of the children, Simon, after an epileptic fit, creeps out of the forest at twilight while the others are engaged in enthusiastic dancing following a hunt. Seized by the rapture of reenactment or perhaps terrorized by fear and night into believing that this little creature is a beast, they circle Simon, pounce on him, bite and tear his body to death. He becomes not a substitute for beast but beast itself; representation becomes absolute identification, "the mystic repetition of the initial event." [10] At the moment of Simon's death, nature speaks; a cloud bursts; rain and wind fill the parachute on the hill and the corpse of the pilot falls or is dragged among the screaming boys. Both Simon and the dead man, beast and beast, are washed into the sea and disappear. After this complete resurgence of savagery in accepted ritual, there is only a short interval before Piggy's remaining lens is stolen, he is intentionally killed as an enemy, and Ralph, the human being, becomes hunted like beast or pig.

Simon's mythic and psychological role has earlier been suggested. Undersized, subject to epileptic fits, bright-eyed, and introverted, he constantly creeps away from the others to meditate among the intricate vines of the forest. To him, as to the mystic, superior knowledge is given intuitively which he cannot communicate. When the first report of the beast-pilot reaches camp, Simon, we are told, can picture only "a human at once heroic and sick." During the day preceding his death, he walks vaguely away and stumbles upon the pig's head left in the sand in order to appease the demonic forces they imagine. Shaman-like, he holds a silent colloquy with it, a severed head covered with innumerable flies. It is itself the titled Lord of the Flies, a name applied to the Biblical demon Beelzebub and later used in Goethe's *Faust, Part I,* to describe Mephistopheles. From it he learns that it is the Beast, and the Beast cannot be hunted because it is within. Simon feels the advent of one of his fits and imagines the head expanding, an anticipation or intuition of the discovery of the pilot's corpse. Suddenly Golding employs a startling image, "Simon was inside the mouth. He fell down and lost consciousness." (178) Literally, this image presents the hallucination of a sensitive child about to lose control of his rational faculties. Metaphorically, it suggests the ritual quest in which the hero is swallowed by a serpent or dragon or beast whose belly is the underworld, undergoes a symbolic death in order to gain the elixir to revitalize his stricken society, and returns with his knowledge to the timed world as a redeemer. Psychologically, this narrative pattern is a figure of speech connoting the annihilation of the ego, an internal journey necessary for self-understanding, a return to the timelessness of the unconscious. When Simon wakes, he realizes that he must confront the beast on the mountain because "what else is there to do?" He is relieved of "that dreadful feeling of the pressure of personality" which had oppressed him earlier. When he discovers the corrupted corpse hanging from the rocks, he first frees it in compassion although it is surrounded by flies, and then staggers down unevenly to report to the others. He attempts to assume a communal role whereas formerly his strangeness and nervous seizures isolated him. Redeemer and scapegoat, he becomes the victim of the group he seeks to enlighten. In death—before he is pulled into the sea—the flies which have moved to his head from the bloodstained pig and from the decomposing body of the man are replaced by the phosphorescent creatures of the deep. Halo-like, these "moonbeam-bodied creatures" accompany the seer who has been denied into the formlessness and freedom of the ocean. "Softly, surrounded by a fringe of inquisitive bright creatures, itself a silver shape beneath the steadfast constellation, Simon's dead body moves out toward the open sea." (190)

Piggy's death, soon to follow Simon's, is foreshadowed when the former proclaims at council that there is no beast. " 'What would a beast eat?' " " 'Pig.' " " 'We eat pig,' " he rationally answers. " 'Piggy!' " (104) is the next word. At Piggy's death his body twitches "like a pig's after it has been killed." Not only has his head been smashed, but also the conch, symbol of order, is simultaneously broken. A complex group of metaphors unite to form a total metaphor involving Piggy and the pig, hunted and eaten by the children, and the pig's head which is at once left to appease the beast's hunger and is the beast itself. But the beast is within, and the children are defined by the very objects they seek to destroy.

In these associated images we have the whole idea of a communal and sacrificial feast and a symbolic cannibalism, all of which Freud discussed in *Totem and Taboo*. Here the psychology of the individual contributes the configurations for the development of religion. Indeed, the events of *Lord of the Flies* imaginatively parallel the patterns which Freud detects in primitive mental processes.

Having populated the outside world with demons and spirits which are projections of their instinctual nature, these children—and primitive men—must then unconsciously evolve new forms of worship and laws, which manifest themselves in taboos, the oldest form of social repression. With the exception of the first kill—in which the children still imagine they are playing at hunting—the subsequent deaths assume a ritual form; the pig is eaten communally by all and the head is left for the "beast," whose role consists in sharing the feast. This is much like the "public ceremony" [11] described by Freud in which the sacrifice of an animal provided food for the god and his worshippers. The complex relationships within the novel between the "beast," the pigs which

are sacrificed, the children whose asocial impulses are exter-
nalized in the beast—this has already been discussed. So we
see that, as Freud points out, the "sacrificing community,
its god [the 'beast'], and the sacrificial animal are of the same
blood," [12] members of a clan. The pig, then, may be regarded
as a totem animal, an "ancestor, a tutelary spirit and protector";[13] it is, in any case, a part of every child. The taboo or
prohibition against eating particular parts of the totem animal coincides with the children's failure to eat the head of
the pig. It is that portion which is set aside for the "beast."
Just as Freud describes the primitive feast, so the children's
festive meal is accompanied by a frenzied ritual in which
they temporarily release their forbidden impulses and represent the kill. To consume the pig and to reenact the event is
not only to assert a "common identity" [14] but also to share a
"common responsibility" for the deed. None of the boys is
excluded from the feast. The later ritual, in which Simon, as
a human substitute identified with the totem, is killed, is in
this novel less an unconscious attempt to share the responsibility for the killing of a primal father in prehistoric times,
than it is a social act in which the participants celebrate their
new society by commemorating their severance from the
authority of the civilized state. Because of the juxtaposition
of Piggy and pig, the eating of pig at the communal feast
might be regarded as the symbolic cannibalism by which the
children physically partake of the qualities of the slain and
share responsibility for their crime. (It must be remembered
that, although Piggy on a symbolic level represents the light
of reason and the authority of the father, on the psychological and literal level of the story he shares that bestiality and
irrationality which to Golding dominate all men, even the
most rational or civilized.)

In the final action, Ralph is outlawed by the children and
hunted like an animal. One boy, Roger, sharpens a stick at
both ends so that it will be ready to receive the severed head
of the boy as if he were a pig. Jack keeps his society together

because it, like the brother horde of Robertson Smith [15] and Freud, "is based on complicity in the common crimes." [16] In his flight Ralph, seeing the grinning skull of a pig, thinks of it as a toy and remembers the early days on the island when all were united in play. In the play world, the world of day, he has become a "spoil-sport" like Piggy; in the world based upon primitive rites and taboos, the night world where fears become demons and sleep is like death, he is the heretic or outcast. This final hunt, after the conch is broken, is the pursuit of the figure representing law and order, the king or the god. Finally, Jack, through misuse of the dead Piggy's glasses, accidentally sets the island on fire. A passing cruiser, seeing the fire, lands to find only a dirty group of sobbing little boys. " 'Fun and games,' said the officer. . . . 'What have you been doing? Having a war or something?' " (246–247)

But are all the meanings of the novel as clear as they seem? To restrict it to an imaginative re-creation of Freud's theory that children are little savages, that no child is innocent whatever Christian theology would have us believe, is to limit its significance for the adult world. To say that the "beasts" we fear are within, that man is essentially irrational —or, to place a moral judgment on the irrational, that man is evil—that, again, is too easy. In this forced isolation of a group of children, Golding is making a statement about the world they have left—a world, we are told, "in ruins." According to Huizinga's theory of play, war is a game, a contest for prestige which, like the games of primitives or of classical athletes, may be fatal. It, too, has its rules, although the modern concept of total war tends to obscure both its ritualistic and its ennobling character. It, too, has its spatial and temporal limitations, as the new rash of "limited" wars makes very clear. More than once the children's acts are compared to those of the outside world. When Jack first blackens his face like a savage, he gives his explanation: " 'For hunting. Like in war. You know—dazzle paint. Like things trying to look like something else.' " (79) Appalled by one of the rit-

ual dances, Piggy and Ralph discuss the authority and rationality of the apparently secure world they have left:

"Grown-ups know things," said Piggy. "They ain't afraid of
the dark. They'd meet and have tea and discuss. Then things 'ud
be all right—"
"They wouldn't set fire to the island. Or lose—"
"They'd build a ship—"
The three boys stood in the darkness, striving unsuccessfully
to convey the majesty of adult life.
"They wouldn't quarrel—"
"Or break my specs—"
"Or talk about a beast—"
"If only they could get a message to us," cried Ralph desper-
ately. "If only they could send us something grown-up . . . a
sign or something." (117)

The sign does come that night, unknown to them, in the
form of the parachute and its attached corpse. The pilot is
the analogue in the adult world to the ritual killing of the
child Simon on the island; he, like Simon, is the victim and
scapegoat of his society, which has unleashed its instincts in
war. Both he and Simon are associated by a cluster of visual
images. Both are identified with beasts by the children, who
do see the truth—that all men are bestial—but do not understand it. Both he and Simon attract the flies from the Lord
of the Flies, the pig's head symbolic of the demonic; both he
and Simon are washed away by a cleansing but not reviving
sea. His position on the mountain recalls the Hanged or
Sacrificed god of Frazer; here, however, we have a parody of
fertility. He is dead proof that Piggy's exaggerated respect
for adults is itself irrational. When the officer at the rescue
jokingly says, " 'What have you been doing? Having a war or
something?' " this representative of the grown-up world does
not understand that the games of the children, which result
in two deaths, are a moral commentary upon the primitive
nature of his own culture. The ultimate irrationality is war.
Paradoxically, the children not only return to a primitive

and infantile morality, but they also degenerate into adults. They prove that, indeed, "children are but men of a smaller growth."

NOTES

1. William Golding, *Lord of the Flies* (London, 1958), p. 25. Subsequent references to this work will be noted parenthetically by page numbers in the text.
2. Sigmund Freud, *The Psychopathology of Everyday Life,* as quoted by Ernest Jones, *The Life and Work of Sigmund Freud* (New York, 1957), III, 53.
3. *Ibid.*
4. Johan Huizinga, *Homo Ludens* (Boston, 1955).
5. *Ibid.,* p. 8.
6. *Ibid.,* p. 9.
7. *Ibid.,* p. 7.
8. *Ibid.,* p. 14.
9. Sigmund Freud, "Totem and Taboo," in *The Basic Writings of Sigmund Freud,* trans. A. A. Brill (New York, 1938), p. 834.
10. *Ibid.,* p. 834.
11. There are further affinities to Sartre's *Les Mouches.*
12. *Totem and Taboo,* p. 878.
13. *Ibid.,* p. 808.
14. *Ibid.,* p. 914.
15. William Robertson Smith, *Lectures on the Religion of the Semites.* 3rd ed., with introduction by Stanley A. Cook (New York, 1927).
16. *Totem and Taboo,* p. 916.

In Gertrude's Closet:

Incest-Patterns in Recent Literature

by WILLIAM WASSERSTROM

William Wasserstrom holds an A.B. from Bucknell and an A.M. and Ph.D. from Columbia, where he worked mainly under the direction of Lionel Trilling. As a result of informal studies in psychoanalysis, he undertook to fashion a method of criticism which does not refer to a specific technical apparatus but which enables him, as a matter of course, to trace conscious and unconscious motives in art and culture. Applying this method—which Morris Freedman in a review of Mr. Wasserstrom's *Heiress of the Age.* called a "model of the new anthropology"—to a group of writers who exploit a particular idea or strategy, Mr. Wasserstrom offers what may be described as a social psychology of literature. In addition to several books and anthologies, Mr. Wasserstrom has had essays in *The Prairie Schooner, Literature and Psychology, American Imago, Psychoanalysis,* and *Psychoanalytic Study of Society,* among others. He has taught at Rochester and Swarthmore and is at present with the English department at Syracuse.

The present paper first appeared in *Yale Review* (Winter 1959, 245–265).

WILLIAM PHILLIPS' *Art and Psychoanalysis* opens with Freud's essay on Dostoevsky and ends with Edmund Wilson's on Philoctetes. Everything in the middle, Mr. Phillips implies, is amplification. The unnamed assumption that connects almost all the essays, therefore, is not merely that art blooms out of neurosis but that neurosis is inexpugnably rooted in the Oedipus complex. Saul Rosenzweig's essay on James is designed to demonstrate the aptness of this idea applied to James's life and work; Simon O. Lesser's traces the same influence in Hawthorne's and Anderson's fiction; Phyllis Greenacre's analysis of Swift remarks the "most fascinating problem of Swift's development"—the special "configuration of his Oedipus complex"; Theodor Reik tactfully tells how "The Three Women in a Man's Life" shape motive in all the arts. And the whole attitude is succinct in Henry Lowenfeld's "Psychic Trauma and Productive Experience," where we learn that the artist "constructs his work . . . from unconscious fantasies in which . . . the compelling experience stems from the Oedipus complex."

If the Oedipus situation does indeed occur in one or another of its manifold guises at the center of most great works, it presents us with a number of choices. We can undertake to treat the affair—as Freud and, in quite another way, Edmund Bergler do—as a symptom of the writer's own neurosis. Or we can discover it to be the single dramatic cause— Ernest Jones' procedure—of a complex action. Still another way—its closest parallel is perhaps Erich Fromm's effort to fuse biology and culture—allows us to recognize in the oedipal event a kind of trope with which a novelist portrays his hero's quality and thereby links all other elements in the action of his novel.

The clearest example of this method appears in the classic and in the contemporary European novel of education, where psychology and art, neurosis and form, complex and strategy interact when a young man moves implacably toward an affair with a woman of superior age. In her lustrous presence and as a result of her love, he perceives his own lustre. Madame de Renal in Stendhal's novel, Madame Arnoux in Flaubert's, Madame de Vionnet in James's American version of Continental attitudes, Candida in Shaw's play —these are women whose love empowers their young men to distinguish themselves in this life. Maternalism is present yet inherent, unidentified but enveloping. It does its subtle work within the plot as a whole and is not to be taken as discrete data on the man's inner life or on that of his creator. It is best understood as contrivance—as strategy—and its purpose is to initiate the young men into the duties of adult manhood, to guarantee their moral fitness with this profound attestation of sexual worth. Something of this sort must have been in Freud's mind when early in his career he remarked that a man specially favored by his mother is in fact highly endowed.

The fictional affair, which carries virtually the same burden of meaning, usually signifies the second step in the hero's passage to whatever place his gifts and ambitions are to take him. His first decision had been to leave the place where he had been formed. Having left home and parents, he set off for the great world which, in nineteenth-century romantic fiction, was ready to receive and prize him. Having cut the apron string—having made himself educable—and having learned from a passionately maternal woman the dimensions of his own being, he was next introduced to the very physics, geography, and politics of the world for which this woman is the best of all symbols. But once this information is got, the affair sealed, and no matter how high the cost, he must again cut himself free and move further along the way to power and high station. His aim is not to reshape the world but to exploit it. Sometimes he succeeds, most often he fails. And in the model presented by his failure, we are supposed to comprehend his larger, his tragic success—his rejection of values to which no man of virtue can assent. This is the final stage of his education and of our own: now he is our teacher.

There is nothing especially astute or new in these general remarks which aim merely to set the scene. A few critics—notably Leslie Fiedler and Kenneth Burke—have already remarked on the matter. But Burke's speculations refer less and less to specific texts, and Fiedler is continually forestalled by his own brilliance, by whatever axe he chooses at any moment to grind. And when he writes on this matter, he finds the heft of Dr. Jung's axe peculiarly suited to his grasp.

Unfortunately, the affair cannot be subsumed within what Fiedler calls the Oedipal Archetype: though it suits Freud's it simply does not conform to Jung's requirements. Furthermore, it appears chiefly in novels of education which, in modern letters, must be recognized before they can be understood.

This is indeed the genre which links such disparate works as *Ulysses* and *Doctor Faustus*, *The Castle* and *The Stranger*, *Room at the Top* and *The Counterfeiters*. In these novels the essential rhythms inherent in all stories of education reappear. And the writers continue to re-create the traditional stages in the hero's journey though they alter the order. They see the luminousness of the love that animates its central occasion but invent new modes to portray its intricacy. Often, too, it is clear that a writer's own personal situation supports the act of fiction. Gide and Proust quite deliberately represent in their art the urgencies of their personal lives. Both invest their young men with special powers, represent these as shaped by the impulse to incest, yet allow them to avoid actual profanation.

Gide superimposes a special program and vocabulary on the traditional matter; he engages his heroes in a struggle to find new ways of being, not merely to make their careers by playing the dishonest game according to the old vicious rules. In order to release Bernard and Lafcadio from the dogmas and disciplines of class, he places them outside the ordinary life of society. And he accomplishes this by placing them outside the life of the family which itself serves as the emblem for society at large. Bernard is at bottom no different from Oedipus, in Gide's play, who sees himself "sprung from the unknown" with "nothing on which to base myself, everything to create . . . no one to resemble but myself. . . . It is a call to valor not to know one's parents." The play is tragic: Oedipus is the victim of an illusion and of the gods. But Bernard and Lafcadio are not doomed precisely because they have been freed, by accident of birth, from the task of gaining freedom; from symbolic incest or symbolic patricide.

Released from the corrosions of the life of the body, Bernard learns what love and honor are. He is instructed by a woman whose flesh he avoids but whose spirit he embraces; by Laura, in her turn to be a mother of a bastard, young enough to be desirable but mature and virtuous enough to feel for Bernard little more than a disinterested maternalism. "I used to imagine love as something volcanic," he tells her. "I really thought I should only be able to love in a savage, devastating way. . . . It was you, Laura, who taught me to know myself." Untouched by sin, educated in the purities not the pruriences of love, Bernard alone is able to "clasp in one and the same embrace the laurel and the object of his love." This uniquely endowed young man is the sole source of hope and he returns to society, to his "father's," to the world of custom which through his art he will reshape.

Bernard is the creation of an intelligence at once retrospective and prescient. He is a child of the last century, yet in some ways he serves as a father to all those angry, sad, provincial young men who storm established society in England now. And they in turn represent members of the beat generation everywhere. For if we penetrate the manners and tone, the matter of class and the matter of money, of career and the uses of power today, we realize that the plot is Gide's; the psychology, let us say, Moravia's; the sense of futility, Kafka's; and the mood—outrage with society—not Kerouac's but Fitzgerald's. All these elements transpire when the young men, guided by older women who are deftly and inexhaustibly sensual, discover how love can fire them to incandescence, and then learn in almost the same instant how cold their fire is. These women are midwives of the spirit according to the fashion set by Moravia ten years ago when, in *Two Adolescents,* Luca's nurse, his "second and truer mother," gives him a "second birth" as a result of an "initiation . . . into physical love" which points him toward his final "general love for all things." Moravia joined Plato, Dante, and Freud in a vision of the way a man may rise above whatever scheme of value is ordained by politics and commerce. John Braine and John

Osborne, for example, avoid this moral system even as they adopt a similar psychology. Osborne's hero in *Look Back in Anger,* tutored by Madeline—a "kind of cross between a mother and a Greek courtesan"—must take his place in a society for which this best of conceivable educations has rendered him unfit. Almost precisely because he is a frustrated lover of love he screams his inchoate fury at everyone.

Similarly, in Braine's *Room at the Top,* Joe Lampton's affair with Alice—"Alice, dress me"; "She dressed me with a nurse's efficiency"—teaches him the beauties of love and instills in him a passion for virtue. And this has no value in a sterile and corrupt society. He cannot save his soul by perpetuating the affair with Alice; on the contrary, this decision would stall him in a state of emotional and sexual adolescence. Yet the only ways in which these new manly energies can be used are those created by technology and the welfare state. Ironically, then, Lampton must free himself from this lovely surrogate, must kill her off and move on to take over the duties of an inglorious career. The sundering is psychically necessary but morally absurd, the more painful too because he despises himself for wanting, in Gatsby's fashion, the beautiful and expensive middle-class girls, the sports cars —the sole signs of malehood and success admired in England now—which are got only when you first acquire, at great cost, an adult body and male spirit and then expend both in a waste of shame.

Turning from the least to the most complex adaptations of this plot, its application of the oedipal event, we must say a word about its paradigm—what Joseph Campbell calls monomyth—out of which novels of education materialize. In myth, a hero seems invariably to proceed through three arcane events: separation, initiation, return. Initiation is the stage which Jung sees as part of an archetypal pattern representing man's desire to return to the womb and be reborn free of guilt. What Jung disregards, Freud stresses, and novelists imply, is that initiation involves actual or symbolic incest; the hero's sexual union with the "goddess-mother of the world." In this way, Campbell argues, he is assured that mother nature supports his task, that he is in harmony with the mightiest of powers—that he's plugged in, as Joyce said, to Edenville: omphalos. Mr. Campbell's information runs parallel to that of Lord Raglan, of Gilbert Murray, of Homer W. Smith, and even of Otto Rank. All agree that incest represents an effort of the imagination to conceive the origin and control the rhythms of nature. And Smith remarks that when the people of the East depict the "mother of all living as full of contradictions . . . chaste and lascivious, faithful and treacherous, kind and cruel," they pretty well describe primitive man's sense of his situation. The embrace of the cosmic mother, in Greek myth or Egyptian, in Goethe's imagination or Thomas Wolfe's, is surely a most persistent metaphor portraying our passion for the absolute, our longing to penetrate the center of the mystery of being. There is the heart of the darkness, as Marlow realizes in Conrad's story, and at its core—in the navel of the world—is the magnificent savage prototypical Woman.

These are the longings of the finest persons in the best fiction of our most gifted writers, who not only see in myth the distillation of human experience but also, as Eliot said in 1922, reviewing Stravinsky's *Sacre du Printemps,* find there "that vanished mind of which our mind is a continuation." Thomas Mann, of course, is the most famed adherent of this view and the Joseph stories, his *Doctor Faustus,* present its most elaborate statement. Indeed, his *Faustus* is perhaps the only work in all literature which is designed and plotted to be both archetypal and oedipal. For Mann calculatingly set out to reconcile Jung and Freud, to adapt the most fertile ideas of both men to the native genre, the novel of education, and simultaneously to weave a cogent history of German thought. He saw himself in a tradition begun by Goethe and transmitted by Schopenhauer, Nietzsche, Wagner, and Freud. In *Doctor Faustus,* Goethe's idea was informed with all the learning Mann could command, and the Freudian matter of incest as well as the Jungian matter of race reappear as a synthesis of lawless id and ageless ego; as an "interweaving of inner and outer self," a Wagnerian use of "psychology and myth." "Psychology," in Mann's discourse, refers to the demoniac in which he believed all art is based; and by the demoniac he means "animal . . . naked instinct" as described in Freud's "sexual argument and paradigm"—that is to say, the Oedipus complex. Unfortunately, criticism has lumped together some of Mann's subtlest ideas and tagged these with a familiar phrase—*Das Ewigweibliche.*

In *Doctor Faustus,* Mann does not debate with us or, before our eyes, with himself, the problems involved in reconciling Freud and Jung, oedipal strategy and archetypal pattern. The debate had occurred in the essay on Freud and those on Goethe and Wagner, particularly in "The Sufferings and Greatness of Richard Wagner," where he marveled how Siegfried is born of the "unconscious, of mother-fixation, sexual desire, and fear." For when Siegfried "dreams under the linden tree and the mother-idea flows into the erotic"; when "the erotic mother-complex appears again in *Parsifal*" as Kundry; when in *Tristan,* finally, Wagner realized how he might fuse complex and myth by equating "sexual desire with the . . . world-creating principle" of the artist whose "grueling job" is to create a "world out of nothing"—when Wagner achieved these intuitions, "sex and religion" were so perfectly linked that Mann was certain the composer had achieved "the uttermost limit of knowledge and mastery."

These are some of the opinions, formulated in 1933, which buttressed Mann's own effort to achieve final mastery. Later he was to borrow—from another of his mentors, Dürer—the method which Panofsky says describes the special quality of Dürer's genius, the way he combined the natural and realistic with the grotesque, the phantasmagoric. But though Mann acknowledged his debt to Dürer, he made no mention of a more telling kind of indebtedness to his old friend Hermann Hesse, whose essay, "The Brothers Karamazov—the

Downfall of Europe," appeared in *The Dial* a few months before Mann himself began to write for that journal. Hesse claimed that European culture was being destroyed by the passions of men which for the first time in history were undisciplined by religion. The new psychology shows, Hesse argued, that man is after all an animal whose lusts are not domestic but wild. And when these are unleashed society becomes a wasteland of the passions, a land diseased very much as Oedipus' land was polluted. Hesse saw modern Europe as a place of this kind and he visualized the way out as "a return home to the mothers, a turning back . . . to the source, to the 'Faustischen Müttern.' " The return involves first of all a violation, an oedipal violation indeed, then death and finally rebirth. Only so will the instinctual life of man, which Hesse believed Dostoevsky best understood—"the unconscious [is] . . . the Devil"—be made to serve as the vehicle not of our damnation but of our redemption. Whether or not Mann studied Dostoevsky, he did import Hesse's reading of *The Brothers Karamazov* into *Faustus,* where the dialogue between Leverkühn and the Devil is presented as a conflict between soul and body, consciousness and unconsciousness, ego and id. This scene prepares the way, too, for Mann's portrayal of the way Leverkühn's unconscious life is finally redeemed when the composer becomes, as Hesse argued a modern hero must become, a "sort of combination of Ivan and Alyosha."

These, then, are some of the main sources of Mann's opinion on myth, on art and the continuity and renascence of the race, on sex and its oedipal nature. It was these ideas, which had long stirred his imagination, that were dredged up as he sat composing his master work. It's not necessary to speak of the whole novel, only of the essential quality of Leverkühn's career which begins at the moment when, in the customary way, he departs from home and mother. We trace the beginnings of his official life to this event but we know that his inner life starts to flourish only when his demon is born. And this happens in that instant when desire streams through his being, loosed by the whore of Leipzig: "my sister and sweet bride," "my bed sister." If we violate the chronology of the text—a procedure which Mann himself sanctions—we recall that Mann included in *Doctor Faustus* the legend of Pope Gregory; that he later elaborated its matter in *The Holy Sinner* where whore and wife, sister and mother are one. For what Mann wished to indicate is that naked instinct, the oedipal disease of the flesh, is both the source and object of the spirit's creative thrust. As "substitute gratification," it reappears in Leverkühn's unnatural desire to know the whole mystery of being and to portray its ironies in a dissonant music which, paradoxically, mocks the forces that make life a sneer on the face of a faceless cosmos.

But Freud alone is not enough, for Freud did not love philosophy, Mann noted in the essay, "Freud and the Future," and Jung does. Jung applies "analytical evidence" which shows how art and myth destroy time and space and help to link man to his origins, to the "folk," the "mythical collective." In *Faustus,* Freud and Jung are linked when Leverkühn's mother arrives at the Schweigestills, and departs taking her mad, "lost and erring son back to childhood." We know at last the whole range of implications contained in what Mann called the "per du," the breakthrough of Leverkühn's music to society at large and, simultaneously, the breakthrough of the German spirit to the whole community of men. It is an atonal music which, like Wagner's, leads a "Kundryish double life" idolized by "initiate and suffering and supersensitive souls"; loved by ordinary people who respond as if it were a "Sunday afternoon symphony." Thus Leverkühn's music bridges the gulf between what Mann called high art and what he called accessible art and recapitulates Goethe's achievement, his way of joining the "ego and the outer world." Furthermore, at the time his mother arrives, his music no longer portrays stark nonchromatic irony; instead it exploits a far richer figure, one that subsumes not dissonance alone but consonance too. "At the end of this work of endless lamentation," Leverkühn breaks through his own five-note system and gives us "the high G of a cello," a "hope beyond hopelessness" which, like Queequeg's lantern —"symbol of a man without faith, hopelessly holding up hope in the midst of despair," Melville said—"abides as a light in the dark." Unlike Melville, however, Mann blended metaphysics and psychology. And we learn that Leverkühn was worthy of final redemption because as a man and as a composer he drew double sustenance—from "the breast of the woman he called Mütter and Du," from that of Frau Schweigestill whom he called "Mütter and Sie."

In the womb of "the mothers," Leverkühn had first come into being, had discovered his genius, had been reborn; there he returned, in madness, once his music had established his own claims to immortality by singing of the endlessness of the human spirit. Introducing that special amalgam of sex and religion stressed in Wagner's music drama, Mann traced the roots of art to an ineradicable, savage, instinctive, incestuous desire within man's devilish unconscious. Then, placing Leverkühn under Frau Schweigestill's wing, he showed how desire can be purified and transformed into a perfect mathematics of music which, rooted in human history and in mother earth, portrays to anyone who will listen the deathlessness of disinterested love. Passionate and dying animals we are; nevertheless, Mann said, the rhythm of our unconscious lives is composed of those unending tones which all myths record and which all great tragic art so lovingly celebrates.

In modern letters, the only work even more ambitious than Mann's is Joyce's. And Joyce, of course, denied psychoanalytic or Jungian influence or even interest; once he outgrew Ibsen he recognized only one teacher, Dujardin. Nevertheless, Joyce was better informed in these matters than he liked to admit. In his usual way, too, he sought out not the obvious but the recondite, not Freud but Otto Rank with whom he seems to share some special attitudes on language, myth, art, and artists. It is likely that he came on these speculations in Rank's first monographs, published during 1907 and 1908. For Joyce dated the manuscript of *Ulysses* 1914–1921, but we know that he spent eight years thinking about the work and another eight writing it. By 1913, Richard Ellmann says, he had worked out the theory of *Hamlet* he was to incorporate into the fiction. There is good reason to think, therefore, that Joyce also incorporated Rank's argument on the way all artist-heroes hope to recreate the world within themselves. Like primitive men, they seem to believe there is a magic in words which allows them to give miraculous birth to new forms. And Rank traced this attitude, as he was to trace everything, to the biological process by which men are born. "The lower mouth of the woman which makes man materially," he wrote, an artist unconsciously identifies with the upper mouth of man.

Rank's thought is striking enough but by no means unusual in a time when all members of the avant garde turned inward, hoping to find there what previous generations had gone without. In some ways, he was simply a man of that generation speaking in his own fashion on common matters. The interest of his remarks is special only because Joyce may have found his ideas peculiarly suited to define Stephen's situation and effort. "In the virgin womb of the imagination," Daedalus says in the *Portrait,* "the word was made flesh." Socrates, he answered Eglinton in *Ulysses,* "from his mother learned how to bring thoughts into the world." This is the burden of Joyce's own effort, surely, in the lying-in hospital where literary style gestates and is born during the three-day delivery of Mrs. Purefoy's son. It is there, too, that Rank's whole theoretical system is compressed yet evident—including even the idea of birth trauma. "Got a pectoral trauma," Stephen says. "Digs up near the Mater. . . . Stand and deliver. Password."

Joyce's phrase, "Digs up near the Mater," reminds us that Stephen-Telemachus-Hamlet-Daedalus is our twentieth-century apogee of all the young men from the provinces who are introduced to their own malehood as a result of a liaison with motherly women. Mater is not Mrs. Daedalus—her word is *Repent*—but Molly whose word is *Yes*. "In woman's womb the word is made flesh but in the spirit of the maker all flesh that passes becomes the word that shall not pass away." And Molly's own highest destiny will be achieved once she helps Stephen to fulfill his vocation, to speak the word that will not pass away.

Stephen cannot feel himself a man, cannot take up his "digs" with Molly, until he overcomes remorse for having severed the umbilicus binding him to Mother Church and Grandmother Eire—the "corpse-chewer" and "the old sow that eats her own farrow." Plagued by conscience and sterilized by guilt, believing that he not cancer killed his mother, not her flesh but her spirit, he arrives in night-town. And in that desperate, frenzied moment when he pleads with his mother's spirit to give him the word which will allow his own *logos* to form, help him to overcome the "pectoral trauma" and deliver, transmute "the daily bread of experience into the radiant body of everliving life"—in that instant he is told again, Repent. This is the teaching of an exhausted whoredom and Stephen has no choice but to destroy his mother, the whore of Christ. Brandishing the ashplant, he "kills" her and now is ready to turn to the whore of Babylon, Molly, Gea-Tellus herself, steep himself in her rhythms, her flesh, her nature.

It is at this point, too, that he and Bloom finally confront each other. Joyce had long since prepared us for their meeting, their kinship, and had supplied many subtle conjunctions of motive and of mood. But the most apt, the most tellingly Joycean touch occurs when a little later on Bloom, showing Stephen pictures of his family, offers Molly to him. In this even we recognize how Stephen's anticipatory dream, very early in the fiction when a man had offered him creamfruit melons, is fulfilled. And it comes when, for the first time, Stephen is accessible to Molly's effect, is ready to take up his digs with the only woman who, to echo Yeats's line, can be the singing master of his soul. Bloom is qualified to make the offer because he has moved beyond either envy or the ordinary wants of paternality and passion, and has become, like Joyce's image of Shakespeare, an "androgynous angel." This man no longer hopes for issue in the body of a living son because he himself embodies the very spirit itself of fatherhood. Offering Molly to Stephen is the best conceivable expression of this spirit. And in consequence, their affair will be a consummation of the sort required by nature, by myth, and by the novel of education, and yet will involve no unnatural lusting after forbidden fruit. No sin is involved; no guilt; neither patricide nor matricide. No scruple is evoked because not even a shred of oedipal taint remains. Because they are not rivals, they can share both a common body and a single, unsullied spirit. As a result, Bloom and Stephen will become consubstantial, equal in power hence of the same flesh. Thus Joyce's use of the oedipal strategy is not strange and private but familiar and public—even in the outermost reaches of peculiarity. For his final intention, what he called metempsychosis, would be realized when the father and the mother and the son are one.

Like Joyce, Kafka realized that the life of heroism bloomed only when somehow a severing of the self is accomplished. Unlike Joyce, he believed that any reenactment—conscious or unconscious—of the rituals of rebirth drew on what were, in his view, the vilest forms of passion and turned the best of men into patricidal beasts. His heroes refuse the gambit not because they don't want to be reborn or free but because they reject the moral situation which rebirth and freedom force on them. Kafka, therefore, adapted the novel of education to suit the requirements of his exquisite morality. He dismembered the body of his work, then reconstituted its parts in a new organism shaped entirely in his own imagination and modeled on laws which he himself alone ordained.

His motive is not, however, much more abstruse than that of the current English writers who curse court, castle, and counting house for consuming the best human energies:

"There's nothing left," Osborne says, "but to let yourself be butchered by the women." This is exactly what K. and Joseph K., those hunger artists in the craft of denial, refuse to allow. Unlike, say, Joe Lampton, Joseph K. turns his back on passion—on the act of vermin love—and on the book of civil law: pornography. He turns his back on both the ordinary demands of the body and the extraordinary wants of the soul, for when he rejects Leni, the nurse-mother-courtesan to whom arrested men are especially attractive, we realize too that he will refuse to enter the door opened for him by the priest in the cathedral. Because he is not a commercial traveler he will not allow himself to be turned into a Block— "it's actually me who is thus addressing Medusa," Kafka wrote to Milena—even if this refusal means that he will never enter man's estate. He will not allow himself to be butchered, either by women or by God. And when Kafka denied the Talmudic definition of manhood—a man without a wife is not a human being—simultaneously he rejected the solace of faith. Both denial and rejection, during that episode in the cathedral, must surely be rooted in the Bar Mitzvah ceremony when the boy, that dauntless and innocent traveler from the country, arrives and hopes to enter the Ark itself. It is an occasion that perfectly interlaces matter and mind: it implies sexual self-assertion at the precise instant that it requires absolute self-abnegation. And this was a Kierkegaardian pairing of modes which epitomizes the very absurdity Kafka admired but could not swallow. The law, like Kierkegaard's Absolute, dictates that a man is admirable only when he commits the most despicable acts. The most bestial of all, within the nature of man and sanctioned by the Law, commands him to commit all the crimes of passion—incest and matricide and patricide—before he can fulfill his destiny, please himself, and placate God.

All this, in Kafka's two important novels, is portrayed by plot and endorsed by imagery which in turn expands a metaphor lifted from the remarks that open *Fear and Trembling*. "When the child must be weaned, the mother blackens her breast, it would indeed be a shame that the breast should look delicious when the child must not have it." Leverkühn never was weaned, we know, and as a result flourished. But Joseph K.'s situation, the sign of his state of arrest as well as his later difficulties—all this is linked to the odd fact that his breakfast has failed to appear. The scene is a kind of paraphrase of Kafka's favorite text: Frau Grubach, his landlady whose apron string he eyes obsessively, and the maid, Anna, have hidden their breasts. Indeed, each of the women in both novels is associated, directly or indirectly, with the service or provision of food and drink—a fact that signifies Kafka's opinion of a woman's essential quality and not of her occupation or rank. The conceit is at the heart of the Priest's remarks, too, when he accuses Joseph K. of casting about too much for outside help, especially from women. That is, he implies that Joseph K. is unweaned or improperly weaned. For "when the child must be weaned," Kierkegaard continued, "the mother has stronger food in readiness." Although Kierkegaard spoke of the life of the spirit, Kafka—literalist of the imagination—applied this metaphor to the life of the body. And in his fiction stronger food includes the sustenance of passion which imagery portrays as a "struggle of vermin," a combat where each sucks the other's blood: Frieda and K. "like dogs . . . tore at each other's body." Kafka's task, then, at the moment when Joseph K. awakes, is to create a novel of education in which the hero *refuses* a "mother's" embrace—turns from the stronger food—yet forges a way of heroism which discredits passion but does not demean man. His aim in general is to create martyr-heroes who are spokesmen of the ineffable and creators of the uncreatable; hunger-artists for whom acceptance of no food at all is the proper mode of self-weaning. He himself, we know, was a vegetarian—wouldn't even eat fish—and his heroes are men whose genius is stoked by a metabolism that creates energy far greater than that generated by the fusions of sex.

In the beginning of *The Castle,* however, K. is bemused.

Longing to overcome helplessness, to achieve status as defined in the Talmud, hoping to storm the great world—the Castle itself—he decides "to cast his anchor in some mothersoil" and he selects Klamm's mistress Frieda. "It was the nearness of Klamm that had made [Frieda] . . . so irrationally seductive." He chooses Frieda and not Amalia who is, like him, a pariah in this closed community. And we realize that she is not to his taste precisely because loving her would accomplish nothing in the furtherance of his plan to achieve phallic manhood and public recognition in this village where love is not incidental to the larger matter of politics but is its very center. He had "never yet . . . seen vocation and life so interlaced as here," K. remarks, thinking how Klamm's power over his services is far outdone by "the very real power that Klamm possessed in [his] . . . bedroom." How beauti-fully it fits Kafka's own sense of outraged helplessness—this conviction that all women are the property of the Absolute, of the Count, of Klamm, of the Examining Magistrate or the Judge: of Father. "From your armchair you ruled the world," he wrote to his father. And he allowed us only this view of Klamm too, "at a desk in the middle of the room in a comfortable armchair." When late in the novel he finally realizes that "with Frieda's love . . . he was still not conquering Klamm," he changes his plans but he does not change his opinion. He never modifies his belief that sexual and social power are got only when the absurd and disgusting oedipal drama is ritualistically performed.

These themes coalesce and the images recur during the final moments of the fiction when Frieda decides to leave him and to take in his place Jeremiah, his assistant. K. and Frieda quarrel and she blames him for cruelty, neglect, saying that Jeremiah had long wanted her, had lain in watch for her, but "that was only a game, like the play of a hungry dog who nevertheless would not dare leap on the table." None of K.'s arguments convince her, not even his most penetrating, his contention that Jeremiah doesn't love her and merely hopes "to insinuate himself in your bedroom and feel himself for once a little Klamm." But she's preoccupied with her new pleasure. Gently, and with "loving cajolements"—"he's shivering, he's hardly had any food"—she ushers her perfect son-lover-patient back to bed, murmuring that her duty is to nurse him till he's well.

K.'s education is incomplete and he achieves no victory in Kafka's unfinished novel, no pyrrhic triumph comparable to that in *The Trial*, where Joseph K. walks "with the knowledge of death walking on one side of me, And the thought of death close-walking on the other side of me, And I in the middle with companions, and as holding the hands of companions." These are of course Whitman's lines. It may be sheer coincidence that we recall "When Lilacs Last in the Dooryard Bloom'd" when, at the end of Kafka's novel, we observe Joseph K.'s sense of his splendor as he moved toward his doom. Having cut the string he is no longer "arrested." And having refused the sustenance of Leni's breast, having turned from the comforts offered at the breast of mother church, he is freer than anyone. He is now his own wife, his own Isaac, his own Abraham, his own God, dying by virtue of the absurd: death itself visualized in Kierkegaard's fashion as a knife. "The martyrs do not underestimate the body," he wrote elsewhere; "they cause it to be elevated on the cross." His education completed, his heroic task accomplished, he dies hoping that he has purified his flesh enough to transform the act of dying into an indestructible monument to man's perpetual martyrdom.

Kafka did in fact shape a more substantial monument than he knew. It is a double-edged blade that kills Joseph K., cuts him down, builds him up, and points toward his unswerving love, so Camus believes, for what crushes us and "gives birth to hope in a world without issue." Indeed, Joseph K.'s performance provides the model for what Camus calls the rebellion of the absurd hero who, like his predecessors in this genre, completes his education, penetrates the Orphic mystery and is transformed; he becomes a master over rather than the victim of the forces that destroy him. Although *The Stranger* is by no means either the best of novels or the most polished statement of Camus' views, it raises all the issues with which we are preoccupied—the question of motive and form in art; the tortuous effort either to maintain and rephrase Christian thought or to formulate a new ontology outside Christianity—and subdues these concerns within the familiar genre and its enclosing drama. "In every rebellion," Camus said in *The Rebel*, "is to be found the metaphysical demand for unity, the impossibility of capturing it, and the construction of a substitute universe. Rebellion . . . is a fabricator of universes. This also defines art." It is a remark that summarizes all the issues raised in modern letters. But it is best applied to *The Stranger*, where Camus shows that a rebel-hero whose impulse to stand firm despite his fate, to feel at home in a cosmos that provides only the most temporary of shelters—that this man is sustained by a particular metaphysics and impelled by a peculiar psychology. Blending naturalistic philosophy and psychoanalytic theory, Camus composes a fiction of rebellion and simultaneously distinguishes between neurosis and art, between Oedipus complex and oedipal strategy. For the rebel-hero-artist who chooses to carry his own rock to the top of his own hill is not a neurotic casting about for "substitute gratification." Rather, he recreates the world in his image and in his idiom in order to say why the fate of man is a condition of the nature of man and of being.

Read as a study of alienation, *The Stranger* seems to present fairly dull, repetitive casebook material on schizophrenia—on the way desolating illness occurs when values are dissolved. Read as a tragedy written by a star pupil of Sartre's, it seems almost a textbook example of existentialism. Meursault is a man with an insatiable passion for the absolute who refuses to say what he does not know, refuses to pretend to feel what he cannot feel. He is a rebel but his rebellion is incoherent and inchoate in a society where "any man who doesn't weep at his mother's funeral runs the risk of being condemned to death." In a society committed to illusion, he is an outcast. And the most pervasive illusion of all is belief in God, the hope that men are not alone in the universe; faith in a place beyond the grave. Only when you overcome illusion do you overcome alienation from the sources of the self; only when you overcome alienation can you rebel against society. Rebelling against society you overcome the fear of dying. Overcoming this—existential anxiety, as Tillich calls it—you are emptied of hope: hope of love, of justice, of salvation. Embracing despair, you achieve the final stages of rebellion and you are free—free to perceive how the universe of the human spirit is indestructible despite the absurd destructiveness of the universe.

All this is familiar enough. But it is unnecessarily crude and it overlooks, for example, what the French critic Roland Barthes calls "the theme of the sun which . . . is . . . developed mysteriously, with the obsessive urgency of a leitmotif." Neither M. Barthes nor any American critic has realized that this imagery is not an adjunct of structure but its core. In *The Rebel* Camus remarked that current American fiction is superficial because it rejects "the search for a fundamental psychological motive that could explain and recapitulate the behavior of a character." In *The Stranger,* which is made so as to sustain such a search, imagery of heat, light and fire define Meursault's impulse and its psychological ground quite as Sophocles in *Oedipus Rex* relied on this same imagery to portray similar motives. For *The Stranger* is not simply a tragedy in the existentialist manner. Steeped in the imagery, sharing some of the purpose of Sophocles' play, it fuses myth and the novel of education, adds Kafka to Sophocles and Freud to Kafka, in order to underpin the metaphysics of rebellion with a proper psychology of rebellion.

Referring to other matters, Kenneth Burke has formulated a way of accounting for the method Camus exploits and which works "regardless of any neurotic motives." When you find an abstraction, he says, reduce it: "reduce the idea of 'god' to the idea of 'parenthood,' then reduce the idea of 'parenthood' to terms of sexual imagery." This is a natural process of imagination and a resource of language which Burke has a name for—the personalizing of abstractions—and it identifies unconscious motives in any given text. In *The Stranger* we have a perfect illustration of Burke's idea. The imagery of fire, borrowed from Sophocles, is sexual indeed. Erich Fromm and others have noted that "fire is a frequent symbol of God [and] . . . often a symbol of love and of sexual passion." Freud was more precise: he said that the symbol represents incestuous wishes.

What the imagery defines, then, is a conflict within Meursault and a paradox in Camus' moral imagination. Both conflict and paradox involve mother, passion, death, freedom. "What is the god singing in his profound Delphi of Gold and Shadow?" the Chorus asks in *Oedipus Rex*. And Meursault, Camus once remarked, who is at first a man "in love with the sun that casts no shadows," does not realize until the end that "there is no sun without shadow and it is necessary to know the night." The origins of realization occur during that terrible moment on the beach, facing the Arab's knife, when Meursault feels "a fiery gust" as if "the sky cracked in two . . . and a great sheet of flame poured down through the rift." "The cymbals of the sun [were] clashing on my skull . . . and gouging into my eyeballs." It is the "same sort of heat as at my mother's funeral" and causes the same disagreeable sensations. We know that heat at the funeral and on the beach, the sun in Thebes and in Algiers, are linked when Meursault remarks how Perez, his mother's former lover, "had a slight limp." For at the funeral and on the beach Meursault finds himself not in Thebes itself, which Sophocles called "the sunwhipped City," but in a Thebes of the spirit of which he must be purged. Only when this son purges himself of the oedipal passion that heats him—the passion embodied in the heat of the sun and in the fire glinting from the Arab's knife—will he be able to move on. Unremittingly, then, he takes "that step, just one step forward" which causes the Arab's reaction and his own. It is indeed absurd that the stupid business involving a gamin and a pimp should provide the occasion for this profound event, but absurdity is of course to the point. And absurd or not he must take that step else he is doomed: he will never know what love and freedom are—both the sun and the shadow— and therefore will never make his peace with the awful amoral fact of death.

All this is crucial to the paradox in which plot denies what imagery confirms. For Camus shows how the earliest form of human engagement—of a boy to his mother—underlies a man's sense of enslavement by all the abstract furies that plague him. Meursault must murder his mother before his rebellion is complete, before he can feel truly free. That is why he comes to feel guilty of matricide even though it was the Arab he had killed. Now it is clear why the novel opened on Meursault's visit to his mother: her death had not released him to assume his duties because it had made absolutely no mark on his emotions. Things are as they had always been. Only when, like Dedalus, somehow he can actively kill her and not passively accept her death can he be truly free to accomplish his task. In his case, what must be overcome is the sense of alienation and the frozen terror. Not until Meursault has committed murder—much as Paul Morel in Lawrence's novel lovingly kills his Gertrude—and accepted his guilt will he be reborn, "ready to start life all over again," even at the instant of death. Till then he is a stranger to himself and to being itself, ill-equipped to assume the duties of the absurd hero.

What Camus believes is that the condition of human freedom is acquired only when we engage in the absurd murder of those we loved first in order that we may learn how to love ourselves or anyone else. For human existence is not only metaphysically absurd but also it is psychologically absurd. It invariably involves murder. Whether or not this is planned or incidental is irrelevant: it is inevitable. "I am free, Electra," Orestes says the instant after he kills Clytemnestra in Sartre's *The Flies*. "Freedom has crashed down on me like a thunderbolt."

Sophocles condemned Oedipus for trying to outwit his fate, for tempting and outraging God's holy law and for holding no immortal power in awe. But Camus and Sartre commend their heroes for precisely this kind of disregard. They believe that the passion which stirs the body is inextricable from the passion that stirs the spirit. And because the oedipal passion is the most powerful, it most accurately portrays the absurd hero's special virtue, the cogency of his dilemma, the condition of his victory. At the center of our physical universe, they say, is a metaphysical absurdity; at the center of metaphysical absurdity is moral absurdity; and at the center of moral absurdity is psychological absurdity. Once we accept the absurdity of necessary murder as the prime fact of life, only then can we destroy without hate, can we rebel without guilt, can we love without illusion, can we die without terror. "The Oedipus of Sophocles," Camus wrote in *The Myth of Sisyphus,* "like the Kirilov of Dostoevsky . . . declares the formula of the absurd hero. Ancient wisdom unites with modern heroism."

Motive and plot, imagery and paradox, myth and the novel of education blend when the light and fire of the sun gouge into Meursault's eyeballs and strike him blind. Beyond cosmic darkness he sees that he must destroy the tie that binds him to his mother and therefore to life, the tie which till then he had disclaimed. Murder is Camus' figure of speech, his metaphor for what was once called shriving the soul of evil in order to free the soul to love God. Oedipus had hoped "from blasphemy [to] stand apart," had failed and in consequence "the crackling blast of heaven Blows on his head and on his desperate heart." Meursault must be wholly blasphemous else his life will simply attenuate and end. An atheist, Camus substitutes for the old metaphor another more suited to his own persuasion. And Meursault, like Christ, rejects his mother so that he can finally become what Camus believes is "the only Christ of which we are worthy."

Whether or not we agree with Mr. Phillips' bias in *Art and*

Psychoanalysis on the ineradicable ties between art and Oedipus complex, we can say that the oedipal event appears in fiction when a writer creates a character who must first be a man before he can become a hero. Whenever the time is out of joint and a man undertakes to set things right; whenever a hero aspires to storm the absolute, defeat death, scorn the gods, re-create the world's body—literature and myth claim that this most esteemed of men can do his job only when he gains power through incest or its surrogate. And until he meets a woman who can perform this service, he is unable to release precisely those energies which alone can serve him in the execution of his duties. Only then is he able to strike for freedom, won as a result of one or another kind of parricide. However diverse the achievement of each unique modern artist, therefore, each comes to maturity in certain recognizable ways. And each finds that the genre of education, which engages our instinctive as well as our public lives, presents the best and most orderly vision of human nature and human purpose that remains today.

The same theme and genre occur in American writing, too, of which I have said barely a word. But in our society sex has been long considered a matter apart from the main business of life. In American letters, absolute knowledge results not when the body and its passions are exalted but when the body is purged of its passion. From Dimmesdale and Deerslayer to Jake Barnes and Sam Fathers, passion is derogated and purity is prized: pure manly power is best got in the wilderness. When traces of the traditional matter do appear—in *Pierre* or *Light in August*—these signify sterility not fecundity, a corrosion of virtue not the ground of honor. Let us put this down not to pettiness in our society or naïveté in our letters but to the discipline imposed by the national legends we inherit and to the centuries of English Christian thought which help to give these legends their tone. And if we really want to locate the fiction which most closely parallels the European, we must substitute heroine for hero and return to the nineteenth century. It is this genre that molds the host of novels which try to define the quality and portray the destiny of American women. And it is full blown in *The Golden Bowl.*

In a way quite different from our own, however, European writing is haunted by Sophocles' figure. Its heroes set off on a journey that leads either to self-betrayal or self-fulfillment, death or rebirth. A man's success hinges on whether or not he is, as Burke wrote in 1939 as if with one eye back on *Ulysses* and one eye forward to *The Stranger,* "completely reborn." And rebirth requires "a killing of the old self," a "snapping of the total ancestral line," traced not through the father but through "the mater" who is after all "semper certa" in our universe of fathomless motion. Indeed, Burke predicted that fiction would present this "terrible emancipatory crime" as "symbolizations of matricide." It is startling to see how accurate many of Burke's speculations have turned out to be. But even more striking is the way Oedipus' restless spirit moves from cellarage to battlements throughout the drama of our lives and literature, and finally joins Dedalus and Meursault, Leverkühn, Ghost and Hamlet—in Gertrude's closet.

Author and Title Index

All references refer to the text; the notes are not indexed, except where the reference in the notes constitutes additional material. Headnotes have not been indexed. Entries marked with an asterisk (*) refer to essays in this collection. Works of literature or nonpsychological criticism are indexed under the name of the author.

ABRAHAM, Karl, "Zwei Beiträge zur Symbolforschung," 67

Adler, Alfred, 39, 191n, 241n

Aeschylus, *Eumenides*, 13

"Alcestis and *The Cocktail Party*" (Heilman, R. B.), 241n

Alexander, Franz, 115, 130n; *Fundamentals of Psychoanalysis*, 129n; "The Need for Punishment and the Death Instinct," 129n

Allen, Donald, 45

"Amazons in Ancient Greece, The" (Engle, B. S.), 73

Anderson, Sherwood, 276

Apuleius, 82; The Psyche story, 87, 92n

Archetypal Patterns in Poetry (Bodkin, M.), 34n

Aristotle, 2

Armed Vision, The (Hyman, S. E.), 34n

Armstrong, Edwin A., *Shakespeare's Imagination*, 30, 32

Arnold, Matthew, 2

"Art and Neurosis" (Trilling, L.), 6

Art and Psychoanalysis (Phillips, W., ed.), 3, 275, 297-98

Art of Loving, The (Fromm, E.), 241n

Artist and Psycho-Analysis, The (Fry, R.), 153

Astralmythen der Hebräer, Babylonier und Aegypten (Stucken, E.), 80

Autobiographical Study, An (Freud, S.), 152, 154, 161

BACHOFEN, Johann Jacob, *Mutterrecht und Urreligion*, 75

Bacon, Francis, 162, 164

Baker, Richard, *The Drood Murder Case*, 130n

Barthes, Roland, 294

Basler, Roy, on Tennyson's *Maud*, 32; *Sex, Symbolism and Psychology in Literature*, 36n

Baudelaire, Charles, 96; "De l'Essence du Rire et généralement du comique dans les arts plastiques," 255

Baudouin, Charles, 27; *Psychoanalysis and Aesthetics*, 35n

Beck, Warren, *Man in Motion*, 257n

Bergler, Edmund, 27, 38, 276

Beyond the Pleasure Principle (Freud, S.), 153, 154

Bigelow, Gordon, "Faulkner's Snopes Saga," 258n

Blotner, Joseph L., *see* Frederick J. Gwynn

Blüher, Hans, 173

Bodkin, Maud, 2, 13, 31, 32; *Archetypal Patterns in Poetry*, 34n

Bonaparte, Marie, on Poe, 29; Freud's preface thereto, 166